IN THE WAKE OF THE BALKAN MYTH

Also by David A. Norris

TEACH YOURSELF SERBO–CROAT

THE NOVELS OF MILOŠ CRNJANSKI: An Approach through Time

In the Wake of
the Balkan Myth

Questions of Identity and Modernity

David A. Norris
Senior Lecturer
Department of Slavonic Studies
University of Nottingham

First published in Great Britain 1999 by
MACMILLAN PRESS LTD
Houndmills, Basingstoke, Hampshire RG21 6XS and London
Companies and representatives throughout the world

A catalogue record for this book is available from the British Library.

ISBN 0–333–75168–X

First published in the United States of America 1999 by
ST. MARTIN'S PRESS, INC.,
Scholarly and Reference Division,
175 Fifth Avenue, New York, N.Y. 10010

ISBN 0–312–22175–4

Library of Congress Cataloging-in-Publication Data
Norris, David A.
In the wake of the Balkan myth : questions of identity and
modernity / David A. Norris.
    p. cm.
Includes bibliographical references and index.
ISBN 0–312–22175–4 (cloth)
1. National characteristics, Balkan—Historiography.   2. Balkan
Peninsula—History—19th century—Historiography.   3. Balkan
Peninsula—History—20th century—Historiography.   4. Yugoslav
literature—20th century—History and criticism.   5. Yugoslav War,
1991–1995—Literature and the war.   I. Title.
DR24.5.N67   1999
949.6'0072—dc21   99–11217
                                                                                    CIP

This book is printed on paper suitable for recycling and made from fully managed and
sustained forest sources.

10   9   8   7   6   5   4   3   2   1
08   07   06   05   04   03   02   01   00   99

Printed and bound in Great Britain by
Antony Rowe Ltd, Chippenham, Wiltshire

Contents

v

Contents

List of Maps and Plates

Preface

A great deal of attention has been paid to the Balkans and specifically to the areas affected by the Yugoslav wars of the 1990s. Much of the analysis has concerned the history, politics and sociology of the region in an attempt to elucidate and explain how a country could disappear and produce the bloodiest conflict in Europe since the Second World War. This book takes a sidelong look at the region from a different perspective. The different historical experiences of the Balkans, particularly the many centuries of Ottoman occupation, have produced fears and anxieties which are specific to the region by their extremity but not unknown elsewhere. These underlying cultural differences are inscribed in fictional narratives by writers and film-makers from the region. The narratives play out and expose these fears and anxieties over a broad range of themes and symbolic representations. In this book, I focus on issues concerning identity in terms of Balkan and non-Balkan cultures, and continue by examining questions of modernity and the ever-present dread of primitivism which is highlighted in certain types of narratives.

I begin by following the emergence and development of the term 'Balkan' itself, along with the culturally charged cognate terms of 'Balkanize' and 'Balkanization'. It soon becomes apparent that the geographic referent in this case is much smaller than Europe's south-eastern peninsula. In Chapter 2 I examine textual representations by British travel-writers, journalists, poets and others who have written about the region. There is a consistent pattern of recording certain types of portraits and reflections which tend to show the peoples of the Balkans as noble savages. Such signs are never far removed from the related signs of barbaric primitivism and severely limit the scope for cultural dialogue. In Chapter 3, having looked at the Balkans from outside, we turn to look at the issue of negative imagery from the perspective of Balkan authors. The views expressed abroad are internalized and expressed in narratives about the clash of two worlds where cultural differences and prejudices are highlighted. There are four novels by three different authors discussed in this context who variously present the problem of a minor culture facing a special form of cultural colonialism.

The subject matter for Chapter 4 begins from the premise that negative imagery produced in the West denies Balkan identities access to the European sphere of modernity. The quintessential image of modernity is the city and many aspects of English and Western literature in general have been closely linked to urban environments. However, urbanization in the Balkans with its history of sudden discontinuities has produced a more extreme representation of city life. In Chapter 5 I examine a number of novels and stories which show images from an Ottoman urban environment and from the metropolitan life of Belgrade. Much of the literature is burdened by the city as an expression of civilization which is under constant threat from more primitive forces outside. The threat is translated into moments of great crisis when all that is valued is lost and destroyed. In the last chapter, the moment of crisis under examination concerns responses to the recent conflicts in former Yugoslavia in literature and on film. Some writers try to make sense out of events by trying to connect them with others in the past, while others focus on incomprehension and the unreality of the war. They represent the most extreme narratives trying to give form to a critical moment and as such rework issues addressed earlier in relation to questions of identity and modernity in the Balkans. The structure of the book begins and ends with the wars in former Yugoslavia, and therefore sources for detailed analysis are taken from that region. This area, as discussed in Chapter 1, is at the heart of what constitutes the cultural sign of the Balkans.

I owe the initiative for this book to my wife, Vladislava Ribnikar, when she remarked one day, 'Why don't you write a book about foreigners' views on the Balkans?' As is often the case with such research, the focus of the finished product has shifted and falls more on Balkan responses to those views. I am grateful for her help at each stage of the enterprise. She has read and commented on various versions of the manuscript as I worked it through from a few rough ideas into a more coherent whole. My students of Balkan cultural studies, literature and history have been another important source of encouragement, debating ideas and discussing material which I introduced into our classes both with me and one another. They would ask the kind of awkward questions which made me discard some claims and clarify others. I also wish to extend my thanks to Dr E. D. Goy and Mr Dušan Puvačić who read the final manuscript and made valuable comments on matters both of style and substance. I have used published translations of the texts in English where they exist. Other translations are my own. Of course, I am entirely responsible for any errors or inaccuracies in the book.

David A. Norris

Acknowledgements

I am grateful to the publishing house Prosveta for permission to use the photographs found at the end of Chapter 4. They originally appeared in Milanka Todić's book on the history of Serbian photography, *Istorija srpske fotografije (1839–1940)*, published by Prosveta and the Museum of Applied Art in Belgrade, 1993. I also wish to extend my thanks to the National Museum in Belgrade for their permission to reproduce the portrait of Prince Miloš of Serbia on the book cover.

Pronunciation Guide

It is standard practice to use the original spelling of place names and other proper nouns in reference to the areas of the Balkans covered by Serbia, Croatia, Bosnia and Montenegro. The language spoken there was, until recently, considered to be one linguistic entity with the hybrid title of Serbo-Croat. After the wars in the region which occurred in the first half of the 1990s and the consequent desire of the warring parties to see themselves and to persuade others that they are different cultural units and independent political states it has become commonplace to recognize Serbian, Croatian and Bosnian as separate languages. Whichever practice is accepted the rules for pronunciation are the same and spelling is by and large phonetic. Most letters of the alphabet(s) can be recognized from English. The ones to watch for are:

c   always pronounced like **ts** in *cats*
č   like the **ch** in *church*
ć   similar to **č** but softer like the **t** in *tune*
dž like the **j** in *judge*
dj similar to **dž** but softer like the **d** in *dew*
h   always pronounced in the throat as **ch** in Scottish *loch*
j   always pronounced as **y** in *yes*
r   is always trilled as common in languages such as Spanish (not in the throat as in French).
š   like the **sh** in *show*
ž   like the **s** in *pleasure*

Vowel sounds are pure and tend to be short, eg **a** is pronounced more as in northern English *bath*.

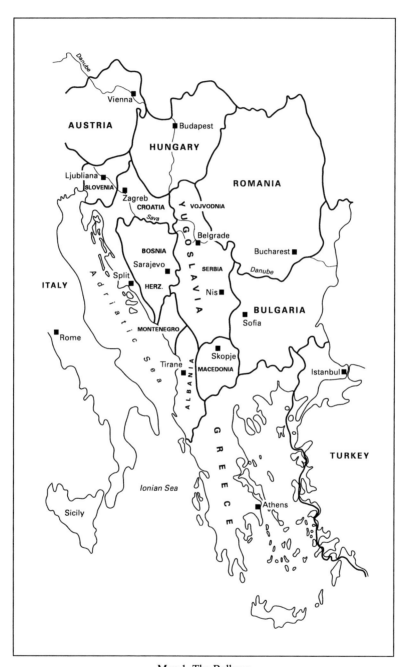

Map 1. The Balkans

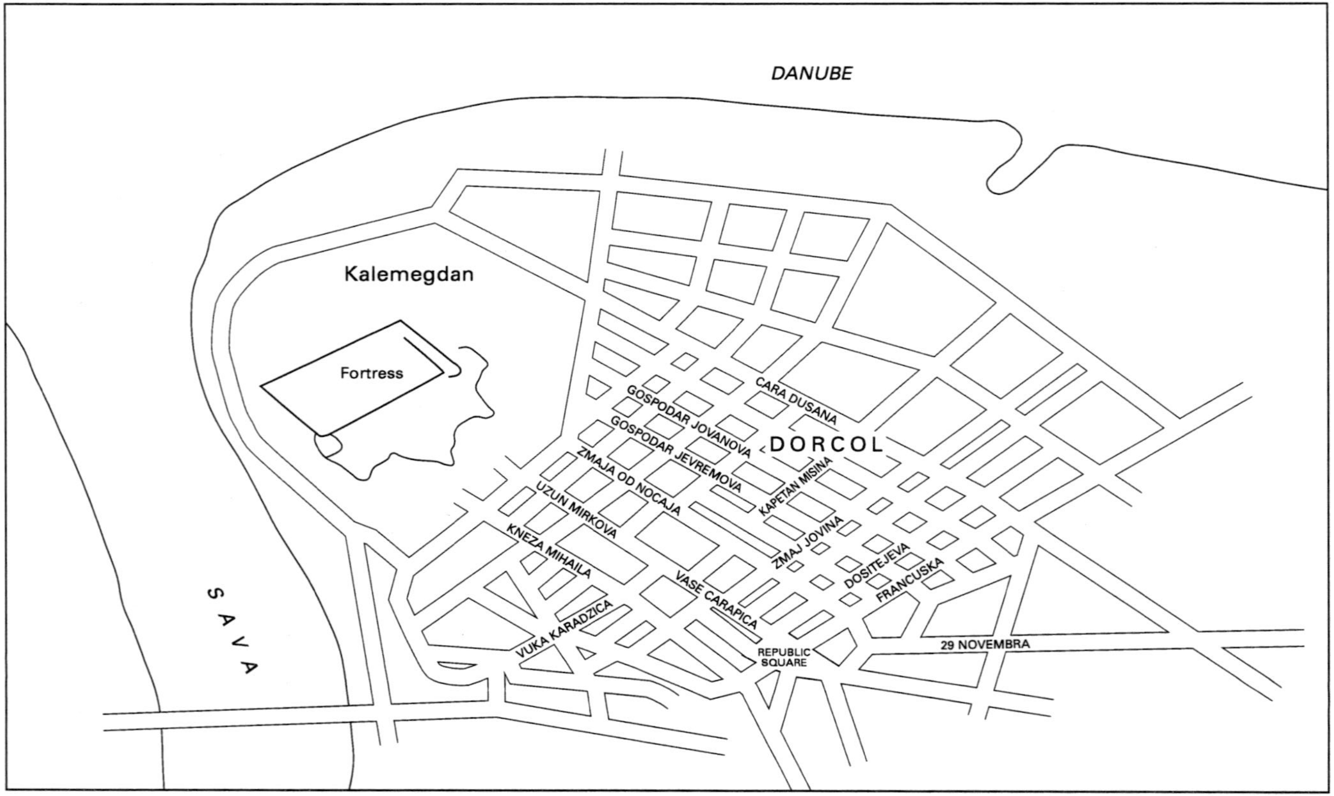

Map 2. The Centre of Modern Belgrade

1 Constructing the Balkans

A VERY BALKAN TALE

The eyes of the world's media were very firmly focused on the Balkans during the Yugoslav civil wars between 1991 and 1995. Armed conflict first began in Slovenia when the Yugoslav People's Army, as it was then called, was sent to recapture the border posts taken over by Slovenia's territorials. That was at the end of June 1991. Then, the fighting spread to other regions, firstly to Croatia and later to Bosnia in April 1992. The world was shocked at the brutality shown to civilian populations and the ferocity of the destructive forces which spread throughout the region. Many diplomatic attempts were made to try and get the different factions to sit down and agree a peace plan. All such attempts failed because the leaders on all sides were prepared to lie about their intentions in order to influence the international community to see the justice of their side of the story. Sanctions were deployed against Serbia and Montenegro, known as the Federal Republic of Yugoslavia from April 1992, for its part in fermenting conflict amongst the Serbian, Croatian and Moslem communities living in other republics of former Yugoslavia. Many angry and concerned citizens around the world urged their political leaders to become involved and help to stop the bloodshed of innocent people. Governments were reluctant to consign large numbers of armed forces to a war which could last for years. The experience of Vietnam in particular was not forgotten in America's White House. Different countries took different sides in the war as it continued in Bosnia; Russia supporting the Serbs and NATO the Moslems and Croats. In fact, the Bosnian war became a factor in other states' foreign policy as they jockeyed for position with one another in other parts of the globe. Various issues were raised; not just the traditional enmity between Russia and America, but also the question of Turkey's future influence in the Balkans and Black Sea area and the whole question of the power or powerlessness of Islamic states. The hostilities were finally brought to a standstill by outside intervention. There have been many pages written about the course of events and the political background. Numerous documentary films have been produced to

1

explain the reasons for what happened. In the minds of many people who devoted much time to trying to understand what was happening, there seemed to hover a suspicion that we are dealing after all with the Balkans and what else can we expect. The region and its people are dangerous. This *a priori* cultural context provided an interpretative framework in which events were received abroad. Hence, this is a book about the Balkan myth, its development and its implications for how the cultures of that region understand themselves and are understood abroad.

I shall begin in an anecdotal fashion to expand on the problem which seems to me to be of critical significance here. During the war in Bosnia I had a telephone call from the editor of a TV arts programme. She was putting together an item on Yugoslavia's only Nobel prizewinner for literature, Ivo Andrić. Some new translations of his work had recently appeared and given that he was born in Bosnia there was a wider interest in his literary output than would usually have been expected. Yugoslav literature and other aspects of cultural life received scant attention abroad before the war and can be expected to sink back to the same level of obscurity once the successor states achieve a *modus vivendi*. As our discussion was coming to a close she asked me what I knew of another Bosnian author who was about to appear in English translation; the writer Meša Selimović and his novel *Derviš i smrt*.[1] I explained briefly the action of the story. It is set in an unspecified historical period, perhaps the seventeenth or eighteenth century, in an unspecified small Bosnian town. The main character and narrator is Ahmed Nurudin, head of the Moslem *tekke* in town. His brother has been arrested by the local authorities but no-one knows why he has been taken into custody and kept in prison. Nurudin feels a duty to use his position in order to help his brother, but he is also reluctant to become involved since some powerful local notables are at work who will not allow their authority to be questioned. Making cautious enquiries, he discovers that his brother has already been murdered in his prison cell. Nurudin is a weak, vain and ambitious man. He is a danger to all who cross his path, whether friend or enemy. He is prepared to denounce anyone in such circumstances and to manipulate the political situation in pursuit of revenge and his private goals. He initiates a chain of events which leads to a local rebellion and the downfall of those responsible for his brother's death. He then assumes power. Nurudin is a conspirator who takes advantage of the confusion, violence and chaos brought by the uprising which he himself sets off. At the end of the novel, we find him writing his own last words, waiting to be arrested himself. Circumstance and chance are the only agents governing both human behaviour and historical fate.

My account of the book was too tempting for the editor to resist commenting that it all sounded 'a very Balkan tale'. Given what was happening in Bosnia at the time her remark appears reasonable. The novel is full of political intrigue, arbitrary justice, murder and prison. The Bosnian landscape is described as a dangerous place where life is open to manipulation by a few individuals whose influence expands ever outward until they too are forced to face defeat. The story seemed to correspond to a series of events then unfolding in Bosnia when warring factions faced one another and news reporters made frequent references to the actions of local warlords. Yet, at the same time, I could not help but feel that the correspondence between the fictional world of Selimović's novel and the reaction of the editor was just all too convenient. Is it possible that it was too easy to make the connection? After all, the plot is as much Shakespearean as Bosnian. Does Hamlet not have the problem of taking revenge or Macbeth face the issue of assuming power and then losing everything? At such a basic level of plot these and many other literary works develop themes which might be considered archetypal. The editor's connection between fiction and reality was immediate and spontaneous. This spontaneity rather than being simply the product of a quick and lively mind was also guided by the Balkan myth which is made up of both belligerence and deceit, a potion of hostility and intrigue, which will inevitably lead to images of victims and aggressors. This mythic structure was very much at work during the years of the Yugoslav civil wars, seemingly justified by events but also active as an interpretative framework. Such myths do not reflect historical and geographic realities, rather they construct our visions of those realities. This chapter concerns the provenance and history of the development which has given rise to this extreme pole of negation contained within the Balkans.

I intend to trace the development of the term as a geographic reference and how it came into West European usage. From its initial appearance as a geographic referent, the name of the peninsula quickly acquires very firm cultural connotations, leading to the coinage of cognate forms such as 'Balkanize' and 'Balkanization'. We find some early examples which refer to the ambivalent nature of this region in Western imagination, but the real deepening of the term's semantic complexity opened with Romanticism when the West first came face to face with modern Serbian and Greek cultures. From the end of the nineteenth century for various political and geostrategic reasons the Serbian area of the Balkan Peninsula has attracted much greater interest. The writings of journalists, travellers and poets are witness to the development of an image of a noble Serbian savage which has not been lost in the twentieth century but has indeed become more complex. The sign systems applied by the media in their coverage of the civil wars in former Yugoslavia can be seen as the culmination of a semiotic development in relation to Balkan and Serbian culture which stretches back over 150 years. By examining how this cultural cartography has developed in English we can trace how the demands of political economy can shape a semiological process. In other words, we can examine the ideology which functions alongside the creation of myths in the international symbolic order. In its semiotic terms we can see how elements of signification keep returning, combining in new associations, but are open only to a defined set of meanings which form the basis of the myth itself.

FROM A GEOGRAPHIC TERM TO A CULTURAL SIGN

Europe has three great peninsulas which jut out from the main continental landmass into the Mediterranean Sea. Looking from west to east they are the Iberian, the Appenine and the Balkan Peninsulas. The southern tip of the Iberian Peninsula marks the entrance into the Mediterranean and the south-western corner of Europe, facing outward into the Atlantic. The Balkans mark the south-eastern corner and the land passage from Europe to Asia. It is a land mass surrounded by the Adriatic, Aegean and Black Seas, comprising a mixture of ethnic, linguistic and religious groups. On the one hand, from an early period the area could be regarded as a region of division where the Eastern Orthodox Church and the Catholic Church confronted each other after the Great Schism of 1054 when the Christian world was decisively divided between Orthodox and Catholic spheres. The Greeks, Bulgarians and Serbs in the southern, eastern and central Balkans followed the Orthodox rite, while the Croats and Slovenes in the western and northern areas remained with Rome. On the other hand, this act did not

lead immediately to the creation of two worlds separated by different religious cultures. European identity was still based on the idea
of being a Christian world, while elsewhere other places were defined by their non-Christianity. More powerful events were to happen
which would create the structure of Otherness by which the West
has come to define the Balkans.

The more significant events began with the spread of the Ottoman Empire into the Balkans and the fall of Constantinople in
1453. Consequently, the region sprang to the notice of the West
when, as described by Kiril Petkov, 'The horrors of the fall of
Constantinople became a commonplace.'[2] Later, the Pope sought
the help of Henry VII to join 'a decisive action against the Ottomans' which the King declined in a letter of 12 January 1494.[3] Gerard
Delanty, in his book *Inventing Europe: Idea, Identity, Reality*, regards the loss of Constantinople as 'one of the really decisive events
in the formation of European modernity'.[4] Furthermore, he goes
on to affirm that 'the sixteenth century resistance to the Turks'
was essential for the foundation of European identity.[5] Within 100
years of the fall of Constantinople the Ottoman Empire included
the whole of the Balkan Peninsula and beyond, having pushed
northwards and taken Buda in 1541. The collapse of Constantinople and the arrival of the Turks caused a major shift in the way
Europeans imagined their continent. There was now a new border
dividing the Christian from the non-Christian world. Furthermore,
on the other side of that border there existed a large and powerful
military threat which was to maintain its presence in the Balkans
for almost 500 years. The Balkans have variously been described
as the place where East meets West, not belonging fully to either
world. It is Eurasia, the ambivalent lands between what is properly
East and what is properly West, a bastard borderland. Delanty's
description of the region as 'a zone of transition between two civi-
lisations' is characteristic of the view that the Balkans can only be
identified in relation to its geostrategic position by which, it could
be said, 'The Balkans and the Adriatic Sea constituted western
Europe's last line of defence against the Muslim East.'[6] It is this
geographical position which marks the beginning of the narrative
which produces images of extreme negativity.

Despite initial fear at the thought of the Infidel being so close,
trade began to expand between London and the Adriatic ports.
The Turks were content to leave these ports as free areas so long
as they continued to pay them an annual tribute. The merchants

of Dubrovnik and other city states acted as go-betweens, importing from the West and selling spices and the more exotic produce from the interior of the Ottoman Empire. Some of these men became wealthy traders and opened up branches of their business in the port of London in order to expand their commerce with western and northern Europe. There were, however, few Westerners who ventured further than the Adriatic coast into the Balkan interior. Of those who did, they tended to prefer the occupying Turks to the indigenous populations for a number of reasons. British foreign policy had little interest in military or political involvement in this part of the world until well into the nineteenth century. Consequently, it was possible for British travellers to establish a *modus vivendi* with the authorities there who acted as their hosts and were men of power and influence in the world; while the local Christian population was excluded from public life, colonized and downtrodden. It was known that a substantial number of the Christian population had converted to Islam and 'became part of the Ottoman military and governmental system'.[7] This absorption of a portion of the population proved Ottoman imperial success. Thus, aristocratic British travellers felt that their meetings with the Turks were like the coming together of two imperialistic nations able to appreciate their mutual successes. So, a kind of mutual backslapping between fellow-conquerors 'was common to British travel literature and later to western journalistic accounts: while such works often manifest a tension between empathy for the Ottoman rulers and opposition to Islam, the former usually predominates'.[8]

One of the important tasks for colonizing powers is to map and name their new territories. To name gives ownership a deeper representation, since putting the shape of the land into one's own phonological and morphological structures and making it into a proper noun allows the colony to be appropriated more fully. It has been given an accent which belongs purely to the colonizer and not to the colonized. It has been given form to appear in legal documents, in military documents, to be idealised in poetry or ridiculed in satire. Ottoman cartographers were no exception and, like their Western counterparts, they worked on their lands in southeastern Europe. They referred to their provinces as 'Rumelia':

The term 'Rumelia' originated with the Byzantines, who called themselves 'romaioi' and their lands 'Romania'. In the Islamic world, the Byzantines were called 'Rum' and the lands of the

Eastern Roman Empire 'Bilad-i Rum', 'Memleket al-rum' (Land of Romei). Thus, the Ottoman Turks took the term 'Rumelia' from the Byzantine 'Romei'.[9]

The Ottoman terminology reflected the Byzantine world which they had destroyed. The assumption of title to the land by reference to prior rulers and inhabitants aims to enforce present legality by assuming a prior one. For example, the names of many British colonies were anglicized forms of native terms, such as Canada taken from an American Indian word. However, such attempts usually lead to a distortion of what the original term means or refers to. The Ottoman term implied a greater respect for Byzantine authority than was deserved by the actual political and territorial power which it possessed at the time of the Ottoman colonization of the region. The new cartographers erased the majority Slav inhabitants from the map, a practice which the Ottoman government continued by using the term 'Rum', cognate with 'Rumelia', to refer to the Christian population of the Empire, whether Orthodox or otherwise. In the same sense, Ottoman practice continued to keep alive the memory of classical antiquity in the region, that this land was the centre of the Eastern Roman Empire where the Emperor Constantine founded a new seat of authority on the site of the Greek settlement of Byzantium, on the bridgehead between two continents. Ottoman cartographers also used the term Balkan. The word is Turkish in origin and means 'a chain of mountains', usually wooded. It was used to refer specifically to a chain of mountains in what is now northern Bulgaria and called the Stara Planina range.

The Balkans were cut off from many of the mainstream intellectual and cultural trends which are generally regarded as characteristic of Europe. The Renaissance was echoed only in the city states of the Adriatic. Traders there had very strong commercial ties with the Italian ports of the region and studied at Italian universities. It was only natural that influences in art and literature would seep across the sea to Dalmatia where the first modern literary idiom in the Balkans was produced. The Enlightenment was hardly heard of at all, with one or two notable exceptions on the northern fringes of the peninsula. It is this lack which became of crucial importance to the formation of the idea of the Balkans since, as Delanty describes, 'The idea of Europe became increasingly focused on the idea of progress, which became synonymous with European modernity. This was above all an achievement of the Enlightenment.'[10]

However, the West viewed the Turkish territories in the region with a certain blend of mistaken identity: 'For people who were imbued by humanistic ideas, these countries were veiled in mystery and were adorned in the imagination with the beauty of Antiquity and the attractiveness of Eastern exotics.'[11]

Interest in the peninsula began and grew with the West's territorial expansion. Frequent wars between the Hapsburg or Russian and Ottoman Empires often resulted in some minor border changes during the eighteenth century, but nothing crucially changed:

> In 1717 Prince Eugene took Belgrade in the fog, a triumph publicized all over Europe. This was the redemption of a fortress of the Orient, a city where six months before Lady Mary Wortley Montagu studied Arabic poetry. It mattered little that Austria would have to surrender Belgrade again in 1739, for as in the case of Azov, likewise back and forth, the idea of Eastern Europe thrived upon this very uncertainty.[12]

The Balkans, like Azov, then, was a point of transition where Europe met the Orient, and the whole of Eastern Europe was implicated in this idea of frontier land. In fact, we do not have to go so far as the records of British or other Western visitors to find evidence of the low esteem in which the indigenous population was held. James Porter, British Ambassador to the Porte, returned to England overland in 1762, travelling through the Balkan Peninsula. One of his party was a Jesuit priest called Bošković, from Dalmatia, educated in Italy, and 'an eminent scientific geographer'.[13] His world was moulded entirely by the West. He intended to make numerous observations but was not able to carry many instruments with him. However, he did leave behind notes of the geography, ethnography, linguistic and social information about the territories through which they travelled, principally modern Bulgaria. He was in the peculiar position of being able to communicate with the inhabitants, himself speaking a South Slav dialect close enough to the dialects which he came across to enable communication, but beyond which he could find no common ground in culture and outlook. They remained, for him, virtual savages with no understanding of the modern world living on the borders of European civilization. Thus, the construction of the Balkans as a suspicious territory is intensified.

In Western Europe this region was known by various names which, like the Ottoman terms, reflect the presence of classical antiquity. On the one hand, it was called the Greek or Hellenic Peninsula to echo the achievements of Greek civilization. On the other hand, it was called the Roman or Illyrian Peninsula by those who respected more the legacy of imperial Rome; Illyricum being the name of the Roman province in the central-western area of southeastern Europe. As a reflection of contemporary political realities the term Turkey-in-Europe also came into circulation. At the beginning of the nineteenth century, with changes in geographical science, Western geographers turned to favour the application of topographical features to the naming of the land and, as yet another example of outsiders applying wrongly an indigenous geographic term, took the Turkish word Balkan and gave it a much broader territorial referent, to mean the whole of the great south-eastern peninsula. Their mistake partly rested on a misunderstanding. Although very active in mapping Europe during the eighteenth century, taking advantage of the advances in instruments introduced during the Enlightenment period, Western cartographers remained relatively ignorant about the Ottoman provinces. They lay outside the old idea of an European identity established around Christianity because of the Islamic faith of the dominant governing class, and outside the new ideas of a progressive identity based around the ideas of the Enlightenment which had failed to spread south of the river systems of the Lower Danube and Sava which mark the northern limit of the peninsula. Geographical knowledge of the region was largely drawn from the maps of Ptolemy produced in Classical times but rediscovered 'in the West by means of manuscripts imported at the beginning of the fifteenth century from the expiring Byzantine empire'.[14] These maps show a long mountain range dissecting the peninsula from the northern edge of the Black Sea to the southern reaches of the Adriatic Sea, referred to as the Catena Mundi. There is no such mountain range, but it was assumed that the Balkan range named by Ottoman cartographers constituted the eastern reaches of this much larger chain. The mistake is even more understandable when we take into account that the Turks also used *balkan* as a generic term for all mountains. Western cartographers must have become convinced that whatever *balkan* means, it must be the dominant topographical feature south of the Danube. Unfortunately for them, the topographical feature which can be best described as dissecting the peninsula is the valley system provided by the Morava and Vardar rivers running north to south. Jovan Cvijić, one of the best-known Serbian geographers from the beginning of this century, wrote a monumental work on the Balkan Peninsula covering many different anthropological, geological and cultural features. His remark on the naming process focuses on the fact that the region is unable to escape its colonial past: 'The two mistakes, from which stem the establishment of the name, trace their origin from Classical antiquity and Turkish times. These errors connect us with the significant and stormy history of the peninsula; they lend a special interest to its name.'[15]

According to *The Oxford English Dictionary* the earliest reference to the term Balkan is 1835 with mention of the 'Balkan mountains'.[16] However, in English as in other languages it soon becomes a much broader geographical territory. In an encyclopaedia entry of 1891 the Balkan Peninsula is described as the land mass which divides the Adriatic from the Aegean Sea with its northern border following the line of the Lower Danube and Sava Rivers. The entry continues to state that Greece is 'not regarded as being covered by the term'. The provinces which the term covers are 'Bulgaria, Eastern Roumelia, Bosnia, Herzegovina, Novi-Bazar, Servia, Montenegro, together with the purely Turkish provinces of Adrianople, Salonika, Kossovo, Scutari, and Janina'.[17] The description adds a large element of confusion to the term it intends to describe, namely the Balkan Peninsula, since it has now removed its southern half and most of its western coastline on the Adriatic. In effect, all geographic sense is now lost and another agenda is being prioritized. The 12 provinces listed here more accurately lie between the Adriatic and Black Seas. They contain the Slavonic Orthodox and Islamic populations of the region. The term has become a reference for the more extreme sense of Otherness to the West.

Further steps to isolate the Balkans and increase the sense of Otherness or borderland about the Balkans were taken with the adoption of the forms 'Balkanize' and 'Balkanization'. 'Balkanize', according to *The Oxford English Dictionary*, is a verb which means 'to divide (a region) into a number of smaller and often mutually hostile units, as was done in the Balkan Peninsula in the late 19th and early 20th centuries'. The first recorded use of the term was after the First World War in 1920, but it has remained in British political vocabulary ever since. So pervasive has the level of connotation of political instability, fragmentation and aggression become that *The Oxford English Dictionary* now defines Balkan geographic space with a specific metaphoric addition as 'pertaining to the peninsula bounded by the Adriatic, Aegean, and Black Seas or to the countries or peoples of this region; *spec.* with allusion to the relations (often characterized by threatening hostilities) of the Balkan states to each other or to the rest of Europe'.[18] These semantic developments are fraught with contradictions in relation to actual historical events. The 12 provinces listed in the encyclopaedia were, by the end of the First World War, consolidated into the four states of Albania, Greece, Bulgaria and the Kingdom of Serbs Croats and Slovenes. Far from being a period of fragmentation, the historian Barbara Jelavich comments on the First World War as 'an event that was to complete the unification of the Balkan states'.[19] Since then, as earlier, the region has witnessed wars and periods of peace, alliances of Balkan states against each other and alliances aimed at economic and political co-operation, examples of the Balkan countries acting in concert to further joint interests. The Balkan myth produces images which do not correspond to the historical events to which they are supposed to refer.

The source of the Balkan myth lies in the West. The peninsula represented the last opportunity for colonial expansion in Europe. As the Ottoman Empire declined through the nineteenth century, the Hapsburgs and Romanovs became rivals to fill the power vacuum. Other Great Powers also found their interests affected in one way or another, for example Britain was concerned about naval supremacy in the Eastern Mediterranean and what would happen if the Russian navy could use the Black Sea as a safe haven from which to extend its military power. The build-up of the arms race and the instability of the alliance systems during the first decade of this century give the context to the increase in tensions around Europe and the assassination of the Archduke Franz Ferdinand on 28 June 1914 in Sarajevo. The assassination by a Bosnian Serb, Gavrilo Princip, was an act against Hapsburg colonial rule in Bosnia. However, the event offered a solution and explanation for the huge destructive forces seen in the war which followed and which, co-incidentally, precipitated the end of the continental colonial system which had formerly kept Eastern Europe under alien imperial rule. The myth of 'Balkanization' is a product of the West's fears of the cultural Other. It is an extension of its colonial discourse. It compacts a culturally varied territory into a threatening unity which both justifies Great Power colonialism in Europe and releases it of the responsibility for the origins of the First World War. As a cultural sign what came to be recognized as the Balkans has two functions. Firstly, it indicates a borderland of transitions from Europe into Asia, the site of Eurasia. Its mixture of Orthodox and Moslem populations defines it as Other in relation to the West, backward in economic, cultural and political terms. Secondly, the denial of history and removal of all logic to the organization of geographical space transforms the peninsula into a cultural isthmus which unites the West with the Classical sources of its own origins in Greece.

A number of similarities can be noted between this development of Balkan as a cultural sign and what has become known as Orientalism. The idea of Orientalism has become widespread particularly through the work of Edward Said. He maintains that certain patterns of representations about the East, here usually referring to the Arab-Islamic world, have developed in the West which portray the East as naturally inferior. The supposed inferiority stems from fear and anxiety brought about by contact with the alienating sense of Otherness which Western cultures felt on contact with the East and is also based on an attraction for the exotic which is felt to be taboo or repugnant. Orientalism is a discursive practice described by Said thus:

> When it came to what lay beyond metropolitan Europe, the arts and the disciplines of representation – on the one hand, fiction, history and travel writing, painting; on the other, sociology, administrative or bureaucratic writing, philology, racial theory – depended on the powers of Europe to bring the non-European world into representations, the better to be able to see it, to master it, and, above all, to hold it.[20]

By 'metropolitan Europe' Said specifically means the West, a qualification which he adds elsewhere.[21] The qualification is more accurate since the West has noted the sense of the exotic in the Balkans, created it as a cultural sign which means hostility, and experienced it for much of recent history as a colonized territory, like much of the Orient. The idea of the Balkan sign can be substituted in many of Said's formulations concerning Orientalism and the Orient since it too 'has helped to define Europe (or the West) as its contrasting image, idea, personality, experience. Yet none of this Orient is merely imaginative. The Orient is an integral part of European *material* civilization and culture.'[22] In other words, the Balkans may be regarded geographically as European territory, but it has been written out as a part of European culture. It is the empty side of European consciousness of itself, determined by lack and ambiguity. And yet, it functions to reinforce the West as 'self-confidently "progressive", "modern" and "rational"'.[23] The West is a full signifier, replete with positive meaning which has created and requires its cultural Other, the Balkans.

There is another important way in which the Balkan myth overlaps with Said's views on Orientalism. Said's idea of Orientalism as a discursive practice is backed up by the West's political, economic and military superiority which imposes a global, institutionalized infrastructure. As Said points out in relation to the Orient: 'No Arab or Islamic scholar can afford to ignore what goes on in scholarly journals, institutes and universities in the United States and Europe; the converse is not true.'[24] Likewise, the countries of the Balkans cannot ignore the outside world. The sanctions on trade, transport, educational and sporting links which cut Serbia and Montenegro off from the outside world greatly damaged the lives of ordinary citizens by contributing to food shortages, job losses and rampant inflation, although the policy produced no ripples beyond the immediately neighbouring countries in the region. It is possible, which is not to say that it is advisable, to imagine the languages of those small nations all but disappearing from Western universities. They already exist only on the periphery of university curricula unless funded by *émigré* communities as in, say, Australia. However, to paraphrase Said, 'the converse is not true' in that it is impossible to imagine the study of English, French or German reduced to the same level in those countries which are less powerful. Therefore, we can see the difficulty experienced in the Balkans in denying the negative images which circulate about them. European identity as inherently Western requires that the sign of fullness be reinforced by Balkan inferiority. The peoples of the region have to accept their position otherwise to deny the negative image strikes at the heart of the meaning of European civilization. They become complicit in their inferiority. The creation of the Balkan myth is another form of cultural colonialism similar to Orientalism 'because the Orient was weaker than the West, which elided the Orient's difference with its weakness'.[25]

A particular consequence of this elision of weakness with difference has been the development of an 'orientalist framework' for an internal Balkan myth.[26] During the Yugoslav civil wars Slovenia and Croatia made huge propaganda ploys to present themselves as not Balkan but truly European by history, by their affiliation to the Catholic rather than Orthodox church, by being an essentially pluralist society with the same democratic traditions as elsewhere in Central Europe. They presented the Serbs, on the other hand, as semi-Asiatic, inclined towards despotic forms of government, and excluded from European traditions since '"Europe" does not include the Orthodox church, "byzantine" culture or the Balkans'.[27] This is actually another example of the domino effect throughout Eastern Europe since the fall of the Berlin Wall when each state in turn has tried to shift the frontier of where Eastern Europe begins to their border, leaving themselves associated with the West, and their neighbours still outside in the cold of non-European identity. Culturally and politically, the history of Slovenia for most of this century has been focused in a southern direction by its inclusion in Yugoslavia from 1918 to 1992. Geographically speaking, the River Sava, one of the acknowledged markers of the northern limit of the Balkans, flows by the northern edge of Slovenia's capital city Ljubljana. However, there exists a Slovenian mental map of former Yugoslavia in which they were in the north, and everyone else in the south, in the Balkans. A British journalist, Mark Thompson, recalls being seen off at Ljubljana railway station by a friend when he set off from the Slovene capital to visit Subotica in Serbia. His friend wished him 'a good stay in the south'.[28] Thompson had to remind him that Subotica is geographically to the north of Ljubljana. The Balkans have been consistently written out of the symbolic geography of the continent. The cultural cartography of the peninsula has been drained of all European formulations which relate to identity and modernity. For this reason, and given that the same process is still continuing, this book has been written in order to explore the means by which this process has been implemented from the West, and the sorts of effects it has produced in the Balkans themselves.

2 Textual Representations

ESTABLISHING AMBIGUITIES

The image of the Balkans as a space which is different and alien if not actually threatening has persisted in many varied types of textual representations found in English and other Western languages.[1] It is significant that the region was becoming known at the same time that it was conquered by the Islamic Ottoman Empire with armies from the East, roughly around the same time that other non-European forces such as the Moors in Spain and the Mongols in Russia were being driven out. This fact alone is the most important to understanding what has been described as 'a trend towards the "orientalization" of south-eastern Europe and the Balkans'.[2] We can trace this development from 'the middle of the sixteenth century when the first book in English on the Ottoman Empire appeared'.[3] Since 'orientalization' is given in quotation marks it is to be assumed that the word is not meant literally. Rather, it suggests an exotic even menacing form of Otherness. Shakespeare's *Twelfth Night*, written around 1600, provides us with an early example of such a description. The play is set in Illyria, the name by which the Dalmatian coast was known in Elizabethan times when the Adriatic formed Christian Europe's border with the Ottoman Empire.

Twelfth Night opens in the court of Orsino, the Duke of Illyria. The heroine, Viola, is sailing down the coast with her brother when a violent storm wrecks their ship and she is thrown onto the shore. She has heard of Illyria and of the Duke but she knows very little about the place. It is a mystery to her. She believes that her twin brother, Sebastian, is dead and resolves to stay until her situation and future become more certain and so asks the captain who has rescued her to present her as a eunuch at the court of Orsino. She plays the role of a young man who acts as a go-between for the Duke delivering messages to the countess Olivia whom he loves. Olivia does not return his love, but does fall in love with Viola playing the part of a handsome boy. Meanwhile, Viola falls in love with Orsino. Her brother is not dead but has been cast onto a different part of the coast. He believes that Viola died in the storm. Antonio has been saved from the shipwreck alongside Sebastian.

The two of them resolve to go to the nearby city, although Antonio is wary as he had once fought against the Duke's navy and his face is known to the Duke's men. However, he accompanies Sebastian out of friendship pointing out to him that the country is dangerous for those who do not know it: 'Being skilless in these parts; which to a stranger,/ Unguided and unfriended, often prove, / Rough and unhospitable.'[4] Wandering around town Antonio sees Viola dressed as a man and mistakes her for her twin-brother. Viola, naturally, knows nothing about him and in the ensuing confusion Antonio is arrested by the city authorities. Still unaware of Viola's real identity he thinks that his friend has betrayed him. There are further complications to this plot and other sub-plots which tend to point in these same directions. The city, its society and the events in the work are characterized by mystery, intrigue, play with sexual identities, confusion about identities, arbitrary justice and violence. Shakespeare's Illyria is a threatening place.

It is known that Shakespeare was not at his best when it came to geography: for example, he once gave Bohemia a coastline in *The Winter's Tale*. His Venice, Naples, Malta and Cyprus were not real geographical places. However, as I have discussed, cultural cartography is a strong motivating factor and what is relevant for Shakespeare's choice of Illyria is the level of connotation. English sailors were acquainted with both the Italian and Dalmatian coasts of the Adriatic Sea. Merchants from the Illyrian ports established trading posts in London in Elizabethan times. These ports were independent city states with majority populations of Slav speakers, but with strong religious, cultural and economic links with Italy. They represented a typically Mediterranean culture, easily recognizable and accessible to merchants and travellers from Shakespeare's England. On arriving in the town Sebastian asks Antonio, 'I pray you, let us satisfy our eyes/ With the memorials and things of fame/ That do renown this city.'[5] However, to the foreigner, any architectural pleasures afforded by Dalmatian cities such as Dubrovnik, Zadar or Split were mixed with the knowledge of the very close proximity of the Turks. Given the fear with which Christian Europe regarded the growing power of this Islamic Empire, the connotations of opulence and latent hostility in Shakespeare's Illyria correspond to the changing shape of the European imagination of his day. The connotations of Illyria reveal an ambiguous approach in which there is a mixture of the Italian Renaissance and an unexplained, underlying violence. The incongruity of this link and of the ambiguity expressed in *Twelfth Night* reveals the feeling of danger surrounding Europe's new eastern frontier.

Knowledge about the interior of the Balkans was much more limited than knowledge about Dalmatian Illyria, to which foreigners had easier access, although awareness of the peninsula slowly spread over the next two centuries. The Turks' attempts to push further into Europe and capture Vienna were not fully resolved until the Treaty of Karlovci in 1699, when the defeated Ottomans made territorial concessions to the Austrians which more or less made the border between these two competing imperial powers the river systems of the Sava and the lower reaches of the Danube. Thus, the northern extent of the Balkan Peninsula was Europe's frontier with Islam and the region was to become more central to the foreign policy of the European continental powers. Territory around the border region changed hands from time to time. Meanwhile, many Slavs from the south, mainly Serbs, migrated north into the Hapsburg Empire in order to escape the Ottoman threats to the local populations. Later, during the Napoleonic Wars, the French occupied the Dalmatian coast and united it with Slovenia to form the Illyrian Provinces. With Napoleon's defeat this territory passed into Austrian hands. The border areas around the peninsula were in a constant state of flux as different powers fought for possession of them. This instability only served to increase Western anxieties about the dangers of the region.

More travellers were making journeys further into the Balkan interior and leaving behind descriptions of their experiences. One such was an Italian by the name of Alberto Fortis who went into the Dalmatian hinterland and wrote a book, *Travels into Dalmatia* (1774), about the people who lived there and their wild habits. While life for the Balkan peasant may not have differed much from his counterpart in Western Europe for many past centuries, changes were beginning to take place at the end of the eighteenth century in land tenure, agricultural innovations, new technological developments, spread of urbanization and new forms of social experience which were passing by the Balkans. Byron's involvement in the Greek wars of independence and his death there in 1824 was a factor in stimulating the spread of a certain European sentiment about the Balkan region. His experience in the region has been described as being lived out with all the Romantic intensity of his own writings:

Byron, having a heart as heroic as his imagination, threw name, fortune, life itself into the cause of Greece. He equipped a ship, paid troops, gave subsidies to the treasury of the insurrection, shut himself up in the most dangerous city, took part in battle, and was ready to die for the glorious past and the doubtful future of a people which had been unacquainted even with his name.[6]

The impressions circulated abroad tended towards stories both about fascinating individuals, now trying to free themselves from Turkish rule, and also about primitive peoples.

In his book, *Travels into Dalmatia*, Fortis also included mention of the folk customs of the area and he wrote down some examples of local folk songs. This event was the beginning of the modern imagining of the Balkan cultural space. European Romanticism encouraged a thirst for the contradictory mixture of the exotic and the authentic which created urgent demands. The demand for the exotic can be seen in the early vogue for Oriental tales invented by Western authors to respond to new literary tastes stimulated by the opening up of Asia. The authentic was the search for national roots stimulated by such philosophers as Johann Gottfried Herder in, for example, his 1772 'Essay on the Origin of Language'. The study of language and cultural forms was at the same time a search for the legitimation of the national community as an organic unity. The search for cultural forms to fill this gap focused firstly on the oral folk traditions on the Celtic and Scandinavian fringes of Europe. Folk poetry and oral ballads were considered to represent an original picture of the soul of the nation. They were thought of as the oldest surviving projections of a communal spirit lost to modern man. It was then discovered that such songs and a whole oral culture had survived as a living tradition in the Balkans far longer than in the West. The stagnation caused by centuries of occupation by the Turks who gave no value to the Christian culture of the local population had created an environment which stunted the development of written culture. Thus, Romanticism, with its twin obsessions for national poetry and for the exoticism of the East, established our modern sense of the Balkan cultural space. Herder included translations of Fortis's songs in his collection of national poetry from 1778–79. The centre was looking to the geographic periphery to recapture an essential idea of authenticity.

English literature of roughly this period provides ample evidence of contemporary enthusiasm for folk cultures from Europe's outlying regions. Sir Walter Scott translated some Serbian folk songs into English from the German translations. Furthermore, in his novel *Waverley*, published in 1814, he writes about an English officer who becomes involved with the Scottish Highlanders during the rebellion of 1745 and who comes to appreciate features of their traditional culture which is about to be lost forever with their military defeat. At one point his eponymous hero is in conversation with Flora, a Highland chief's sister, who remarks to him:

> 'The recitation', she said, 'of poems, recording the feats of heroes, the complaints of lovers, and the wars of contending tribes, forms the chief amusement of a winter fire-side in the Highlands. Some of these are said to be very ancient, and if they are ever translated into any of the languages of civilized Europe, cannot fail to produce a deep and general sensation.'[7]

These sentiments reveal a great deal about contemporary attitudes and the attraction which oral cultures held for Scott. Such ancient poems are an 'amusement' to the Celtic Highlander, while in the modern world they 'produce a deep and general sensation'. The French author Prosper Mérimée 'was responsible for the hoax known as *La Guzla*, a work that appeared in France during the 1830s, purporting to be "Illyrian folk poetry"'.[8] Mérimée took his title from the traditional one-stringed instrument called a 'gusle' which was used to accompany the singing of traditional folk ballads by the South Slavs. The world was easily fooled and the poet Alexander Pushkin, 'convinced the poems were of Serb origin, translated them into Russian'.[9] It seems an understatement to remark that, 'The Romantic Movement was marked by concern with the distant past and with folk culture.'[10] Many contemporary visions of our world were in the process of creation, and the Romantic Movement contributed by inventing an idea of the cultural forms most appropriate to the preservation of the distant past. And 'civilized Europe' was soon to receive someone who would help promote and spread knowledge about such folk songs, one of the key figures in Serbian culture of the nineteenth century, Vuk Stefanović Karadžić.

Vuk Stefanović Karadžić was born in Tržić in 1787, a small Serbian town near the border with Bosnia, and his remarkable life ended in Vienna in 1864. His career began with the First Serbian Uprising in 1804. The Serbian leader Kara Djordje, his name meaning Black George in English, attacked the occupying Turkish forces. The rebellion began as an expression of the huge discontent against the local Pasha and his harsh regime rather than as a revolution against Ottoman rule, although it soon became a fight for national liberation. The Serbs were successful and Belgrade with its strong fortress of Kalemegdan at the confluence of the Sava and Danube rivers was taken from the Turks at the end of November 1806. Karadžić was one of the few Serbs of his day who could read and write and as such was necessary to the embryonic Serbian government. The temporary Ottoman weakness was caused by problems elsewhere in the Empire, but once these were resolved the Sultan was able to turn all his efforts against the Serbs and to retake the territory in 1813. Most of the leadership fled over the Danube into Austria, including Karadžić. Arriving in Vienna he met the Slovene Janez Kopitar who encouraged him in a new enterprise.

Most of the Slavonic nations of Eastern Europe generally were in a similar position. For centuries they had been subjugated by other stronger states. The Poles, having lost their independence only at the end of the eighteenth century, and the Russians, who were an imperial power themselves, were in a different position. However, the Czechs, Slovaks, Croats and Slovenes under the Austrians, and the Serbs, Macedonians and Bulgarians under the Turks had the status of colonized peoples. The language of government, commerce and law was the language of the oppressor nation forming a master discourse under which they were forced to live. Their own languages were excluded from public life and were for personal use only. They were the tongues of a largely uneducated, rural, peasant population. There was a need to codify the modern spoken forms and to adapt a suitable orthography. For example, when writing their own language the Croats would use German, Italian or Hungarian spelling rules depending on which part of Croatian territory they lived. The Serbs were in a worse position, since the only institution which had kept alive a written form of the language was the church. The liturgical language had come under the influence of the Russian liturgical language and developed into a hybrid called Slaveno-serbski. This hybrid was different from the vernacular in vocabulary and syntax, and in effect had to be learnt as a foreign language. Its alphabet was not even suitable for the vernacular, as it contained letters for some sounds which did not exist in normal speech, and did not have the letters for some sounds which did exist. Kopitar encouraged Karadžić to develop a new orthography dedicated to vernacular Serbian and to codify its grammar. Karadžić took to the tasks with enthusiasm and, despite much opposition from the Serbian Orthodox Church, he completed them. Opposition arose as a matter of principle, in that the language reforms were taken as an attack on the liturgical language and the standing of the church as a social institution, and also on issues of detail. For example, Karadžić worked on adapting the Cyrillic alphabet for use with modern spoken forms based on a phonetic approach. His maxim was 'Write as you speak'. However, he proposed to introduce the letter 'j' into his new alphabet to represent the sound of 'y' as in English 'yes'. Church leaders criticized Karadžić for subversion at this point, claiming that he intended to introduce a letter which traditionally was not used in the Cyrillic alphabets of the Orthodox Church. It was a part of the Western, Latinate tradition and was, therefore, a Roman Catholic letter. However, these reforms were not his only work in his lifelong career. He translated the New Testament into his modern form and encouraged new poets to use his reformed alphabet and write in the vernacular rather than use the sonorous but elitist liturgical language. In addition, he wrote on the anthropology and the folk customs of the Serbs and, above all, he collected and published many of the folk songs which were acquiring fame abroad. It was this aspect of his work which evoked most interest in the countries of 'civilized Europe'.

Karadžić worked initially from memory, writing out songs which he knew, and later travelled to listen to them being sung in villages in Serbia and Bosnia, noting down what he heard. His work soon attracted the attention of Jakob Grimm who, in 1823, wrote a review of Karadžić's third volume of national songs in which he states that he 'wants to report without delay on an undertaking begun without any noise (that is the way in which good and fruitful things usually begin), which will in time make the whole of educated Europe take notice and as a start will inevitably have beneficial effects for the editor's native land'.[11] Grimm's 'educated Europe' was obviously feeling that 'deep and general sensation' about which Scott's character comments. However, the 'beneficial effects for the editor's native land' were not all that they turned out to be. A number of other effects can be traced back to the attentions from abroad and Karadžić's work. First, the collection and publication of the songs signalled the end of the oral tradition as it had existed. Oral traditions wither in the face of written forms; they have no sense of permanency and transmission is based purely on personal contact. All European cultures have gone through this process but in the nineteenth century they were attracted to Serbian culture as if to a museum of preserved artefacts. Furthermore, they were generally interested only in the epic ballads telling the stories about 'the feats of heroes', to return again to Scott's novel, and tended to ignore all other aspects which included story-telling, riddles, lyrical songs, and a whole infrastructure of features which exposed a much greater variety of patterns, forms and themes than were contained within the single genre. The West simplified and impoverished the totality of those oral traditions. Western imagination was captured not by Balkan traditions in their Balkan context but by those traditions interpreted according to the demands of European Romanticism. The image of the Balkans created in the West has nothing to do with the world in which the people of the Balkans actually lived.

This important juncture for the recognition of Balkan identity opens up the first and most important misunderstanding between the Balkans and the West. Western images were established on an identity of the Balkans as Other and alien to the modern world. It was a distant and exotic world on the borders of the Orient. However, the West was offering cultural recognition to that world, offering it a place in the European family of cultures, while keeping it as a separate space which was not and would not in the future be fully integrated. However, it was an offer which was impossible to refuse. From a Balkan point of view it was the first and perhaps last chance for recognition which would bestow legitimacy and inscribe their small cultures which had been isolated from Europe for so long into larger cultural frameworks. It is here the misrecognition arises. As Todorova points out, the nations of the peninsula did not regard themselves as at all Oriental: 'Balkan self-identities constructed during the nineteenth and twentieth centuries were invariably opposed to "oriental others": geographical neighbours, e.g. the Ottoman Empire and Turkey, as well as regions within the area itself and portions of one's own historical past (usually the Ottoman period and the Ottoman legacy).'[12] Thus, their entry into Europe was conditioned by a set of expectations which did not correspond to Balkan expectations. Such recognition from outside was not divorced from the older idea of the Balkans as a potentially hostile space, in fact it promoted the idea. Although redolent here with positive markers, such songs and the culture associated with them were not part of Scott's 'civilized Europe' or Grimm's 'educated Europe' and could always be reinvented to produce alternative, negative imagery.

THE NOBLE SAVAGE

The Russian philosopher of language Mikhail Bakhtin has become a byword for the concept of dialogics in study in the humanities. His conceptual system has often been regarded as erratic since he tends to use one term with one meaning in one position, then to use it with an apparently different meaning elsewhere. We ought to regard his work, in fact, as being a developing project in which he continually takes further earlier conclusions, thinks through them again from a slightly different perspective in order to cast further light on the possibilities of his ideas. He may not be a systematic thinker in that respect, but he is a highly stimulating one. He developed an idea which for him linked the defining characteristics of the novel to that of social organization at large. Although the focus of his own work remained largely on the novel he discussed the wider social implications too. For him, the novel is the generic form which comes closest to reflecting the state of language in society. He sees language as a field of ideological struggles in which different voices participate, a world-in-words which is termed heteroglossia. In this world different languages, each representing a particular point of view on the world, come into contact with one another, colliding and constantly transforming themselves and one another. There are numerous ways in which utterances influence one another. Given that they are never totally distinct from surrounding heteroglossia, neither are their meanings ever entirely distinct and singular. Rather, meanings are formed in contact with other utterances, such that each utterance is already half someone else's. One utterance by its action on another is said to re-accentuate a meaning, adding something of itself. Having received this rejoinder, the first utterance then appropriates this re-accentuation, making it its own, thus sending out a succession of rejoinders as the re-accentuated words are accepted into a total semantic field of that word which includes all previous intonations and utterances too. Even a rejection of the intentions of others constitutes contact with and rubbing up against alien meanings and influences.

As each utterance, made of language, represents a point of view on the world, it follows that such points of view cannot be separated from their articulation and the genre which governs their limits and boundaries. In their continual transformation, these boundaries are never frozen. They constantly position themselves and are positioned according to the complex interchange of rejoinders and counter-rejoinders. The central idea of a dialogue of voices representing social classes, individual professions, gender positions, the oppressed and the oppressor is shaped as they rub up against one another. They appropriate the words of others, and in so doing realize themselves in the worlds of others. Individuals come to consciousness of themselves only in the cracks between the different languages in which they participate. There are those powers which try to contain and control this overflow of voices. Such dominant discourses, representing totalitarian outlooks, are termed monoglossic. They tend towards suppressing other voices, leaving only their own voice, but can never succeed for ever. Realization of the self, therefore, demands some participation in a dialogue to achieve recognition in the eyes of another. Bakhtin remarks on the possibilities for dialogue in the field of international relations in a short article for *Novy Mir*:

> In the realm of culture, outsidedness is a most powerful factor in understanding. It is only in the eyes of *another* culture that foreign culture reveals itself fully and profoundly (but not maximally fully, because there will be cultures that see and understand more). A meaning only reveals its depths once it has encountered and come into contact with another, foreign meaning: they engage in a kind of dialogue, which surmounts the closedness and one-sidedness of these particular meanings, these cultures. We raise new questions for a foreign culture, ones that it did not raise itself; we seek answers to our own questions in it; and the foreign culture responds to us by revealing to us its new aspects and new semantic depths.[13]

Two factors are immediately striking from this quotation. The first is Bakhtin's faith that this dialogue is generated by a degree of democratic and egalitarian tolerance, stirred by a natural curiosity about others. The second is that the dialogue is mutually beneficial. Perhaps mutual benefit would be the automatic result from a dialogue in which the parties concerned share equally in the boundaries of speech and the definition of genres. However, this is not usually the case. Such factors have to be determined by negotiation in which not all parties are equal. Balkan entry into the international symbolic dialogue of cultures was conditioned and qualified from the beginning.

Romanticism was the beginning of a process in the nineteenth century which encouraged the development of the Balkan myth and gave it the form of textual representation. The dialogue was now open, but it was to continue to hark back to its roots in the Romantic period. British attention was once more directed to the situation in the Balkans as it became an object of international notice. With the decline of Ottoman power, Austria and Russia were eagerly waiting to assume the position of the dominant power in the region. The British public was ready to receive more information about this little known area and in the 1840s two articles appeared with accounts of two separate journeys taken into Montenegro. The coast of Montenegro with the port of Kotor was in Austrian hands. The small state behind the coast rose steeply into the mountains and it was there that the Montenegrins had managed to keep their independence alive. They were the only Balkan people to preserve some autonomy from one or other of the powerful empires interested in controlling the peninsula. Over the years they developed a form of government in which the Bishop, or Vladika, of Montenegro assumed temporal as well as spiritual power. That being said, the country was divided into a clan system and each family jealously guarded its independence so there was little in the way of central government. The line of succession of the Prince-Bishops passed from uncle to nephew; as in the Orthodox Church, while parish priests may marry, the so-called Black Clergy may not. In 1831 Petar Petrović Njegoš, a highly energetic and far-minded man, became Vladika.

One of the earliest references to Montenegro comes from a visit made by an English couple in 1843. The centrepiece of the author's interest was the visit which they made to Njegoš at his military emplacement overlooking a Turkish fortress at Lake Scutari. The fact that he sat and had lunch with an English lady while under fire from the Turks was an impression which was not lost on Njegoš. He did not fail to recount the incident to another party of visitors from England two years later. The observations recorded from the visit of 1843 include many similarities with later accounts. The article opens with the point that we, and the author of the text, know little about this region: 'Few nations of Europe have been less known than the Montenigrians [*sic*], and the name even of their country is seldom found on maps.'[14] Admission of such general ignorance continues into the beginning of the twentieth century, when another traveller makes his preparations to journey from London to Cetinje and recalls being asked by curious friends, 'whether Cettigne was not the capital of Bulgaria, and whether the Montenegrins were not blacks'.[15] As was common at the time, the author uses the Italian spelling for the name of the Montenegrin capital. Such lack of knowledge, however, has never prevented certain writers from making absurd generalizations and forming conclusions based on very flimsy evidence. They are unable to see what is really taking place and, thus, describe events which tax the imagination of the reader as if reading a fictional text. Indeed, in this instance we can see how literature and narrative fiction are discourses which generally urge visitors abroad to formulate opinions about foreign cultures, and it would appear that Scott's novel *Waverley* functions as a kind of archetext for these early visitors to Montenegro.

The author of the text who visited Njegoš in 1843 describes how he and his wife travelled from Kotor to Cetinje where, he comments, 'few remained that night in Cettigna but ancient men'.[16] The Vladika was away at the siege which the English couple were thirsting to witness. References to the military nature of Montenegrin culture are frequent in all these works. That evening they were entertained at dinner and we read how the visitors 'heard of wars and of rumours of wars; listened to heroic ballads, chanted by a warrior, and accompanied by a species of one-stringed fiddle'.[17] The description seems simple enough, except that from other comments in the text it is clear that there is a language barrier which is only overcome occasionally and with great difficulty. Despite this, there is no doubt that the ballads are 'heroic'. I suggest that there is something in the expression here which is a return to traditional Highland entertainments, and that 'civilized Europe' was predisposed to ballads about 'the feats of heroes' whatever their real subject matter.

There is further evidence of the influence of Scott's novel as a constructive principle on the British imagining of Montenegro in the second account from 1845. This journal concerns a group of naval officers whose ship anchored in Kotor and who wished to visit Njegoš in Cetinje. Upon first meeting him the author records that although he might have expected a certain 'savageness of manner', in fact he discovers that 'the Vladika is decidedly one of nature's gentlemen'.[18] They too are entertained in the evening, and the author notes that 'the whole thing put one in mind of Donald Bean Lean's cavern'.[19] Donald Bean Lean is the Highland chieftain invented by Sir Walter Scott for his novel *Waverley*. In these circumstances it appears that Bakhtin's notion of international dialogue in which cultures open up to each other is very optimistic given that the English visitors can only see Montenegro through the prism of a fictional world invented some decades before.

Another similarity between Scott's world of Scottish heroes and that of the Montenegrins is war against a much larger enemy. In the Highlands of Scotland this was a war against the English, while for Montenegro it was a war against the Turks. Hostilities in Scotland were long over, but the same epithets of independent spirit and of a natural innocence which Scott applied in his novel can be found again in the texts about Montenegro. During the campaigns against the Turks in 1877 a British journalist visited Cetinje. He was present when news of a Montenegrin victory reached the capital and recorded the following events:

> The scene that followed almost baffles description. The people surged along the street, firing, shouting, singing, leaping with joy. It is an enthusiasm, an ecstasy, unintelligible, impossible in a civilised country – hardly to be expressed in civilised terms. Yes, these are children! – children in their primitive simplicity, in the whole poetry of their being; children in their speech, their politics, their warfare; and this is the wild, self-abandoned delight of children.[20]

The journalist's text describes the Montenegrins not yet formed for 'civilized Europe' but who are the living embodiments of the national ballads, heroic epic figures themselves. He emphasizes an innocence in their child-like behaviour and primitive simplicity which is a step projecting them along a path to their reincarnation as noble savages. The stress on innocence is essential to the ambivalence of the whole description since it is this aspect which neutralizes the otherwise barbaric sign of the primitive savage, investing them with a spiritual depth lost in other societies. In this way, 'civilized Europe' can satisfy its own desire for release from constraint and share for a moment in this ecstasy, as Hayden White comments on this particular aspect of Victorian society:

> In the Victorian imagination primitive peoples were viewed with that mixture of fascination and loathing that Conrad examines in *Heart of Darkness* – as examples of what Western man might have been at one time and what he might become once more if he failed to cultivate the virtues that had allowed him to escape from nature.[21]

At issue is not the correctness or otherwise of English interpretations of Montenegrin society since all transcultural mediation is

going to result in some degree of distortion. More important is the
resulting imbalance in the dialogue through which cultures come
into being. English discourse on the subject indicates the growth
of a new kind of cultural colonialism by which as Europe's small
nations emerged in the nineteenth century the shape of their presence was being constructed to maintain their inferior position,
specifically here as children with no right to exercise their own
voice and refusing them the right to real recognition.

During the same year that the journalist visited Cetinje, Tennyson
celebrated the Montenegrin victories with the poem 'Montenegro'
in which he eulogizes them for their wild and defiant independence against much superior numbers. The poem closes as follows:

> O smallest among peoples! rough rock-throne
> Of Freedom! warriors beating back the swarm
> Of Turkish Islam for five hundred years,
> Great Tsernogora! never since thine own
> Black ridges drew the cloud and brake the storm
> Has breathed a race of mightier mountaineers.[22]

'Tsernogora' is a rough transliteration of the indigenous name of
the country 'Crna Gora' which translates into the Italian form
'Montenegro' or 'Black Mountain'. Tennyson's tone not only echoes
the sentiments first excited by the translations of the epic poems
into English, but also many of the sentiments and expressions found
in Sir Walter Scott's novel *Waverley* in connection with the Highlanders. Tennyson's poem opens with reference to the eagle: 'They
rose to where their sovran eagle sails'. Such references to the eagle
are quintessential comments on a Romantic vision which associates
together images of mountains, nature and freedom. In the novel
Waverley, the eponymous hero is keen to visit the people of the
Highlands and is guided there by a Highlander. On their journey
the guide points out the sight of an eagle flying above with a comment that there are 'no such birds as that in England'.[23] The terms
in which Tennyson praises the Montenegrins as 'Chaste, frugal,
savage, armed by day and night' also echo Waverley's impressions
of the integrity and capacities of the Highlanders. Both for the
journalist and for Tennyson we can isolate an agenda from earlier
times on which they could call for expressing this primitiveness,
neutralize it, yet also maintain an ambiguity of potential danger
should these children ever reach adolescence or these mountain
men come down from their heights. These texts represent typical

examples of the dialogue as it developed during the nineteenth century between British and Balkan cultures. In critical times the image of the Balkans has always been drawn to correspond to the objectives of outside interests. In Europe a new kind of colonialism began to make itself felt, one which might actually support the rights of small nations to their independence while still denying them entry into the great dialogue, refusing them the right of real recognition; a profound form of cultural imperialism.

Ambivalence towards the image of Balkan culture and society can be clearly seen in a comparison of two books both published in 1907, *Through Savage Europe* written by a journalist Harry De Windt and *An Observer in the Near East* penned by the writer and traveller William Le Queux but published anonymously. The two authors undertook very similar journeys, beginning from Kotor, climbing to Cetinje, through Dalmatia and Bosnia before entering Serbia and continuing into Bulgaria. They interviewed and talked to similar kinds of people and witnessed similar kinds of events. However, nowhere would it be possible to find two such opposing interpretations of everything which they saw. Harry De Windt was a supporter of Austrian rule in Bosnia and their territorial aspirations there. He regarded everything in connection with the Slav populations to be at fault. He justifies the title of his travels because 'the term accurately describes the wild and lawless countries between the Adriatic and Black Seas'.[24] His description of 'wild' is not the 'self-abandoned delight of children' but a much darker barbarism. By contrast, the anonymous author of the other book is opposed to Austrian rule in the Balkans remarking of the political situation: 'All through the Balkan peninsula the weak are to-day being crushed by the strong. The Austrian eagle has over-shadowed and grasped Bosnia, she has her talons in Servia, and is casting covetous glances upon gallant little Montenegro.'[25] Once he reaches Belgrade he concludes that negative reporting about the Serbs in the British press is the influence of an Austrian propaganda machine established to spread 'false news, being supposed to emanate from reliable sources in Belgrade'.[26] In actual fact the two authors are motivated not by concern for the situation in the Balkans itself but by the policies of different factions amongst the Great Powers towards the Balkan states in the event of war.

Harry De Windt's descriptions of Cetinje are a complete inversion of the discourse about the noble savage such that he appears to take the same sentences full of admiring tones and simply replace any positive marker with its opposite. So, speaking of how he always tries to imagine what a new place which he is about to visit is like, he says that he 'had pictured Cettigne as a fiercely guarded stronghold, buried in the heart of mountains – a town of frowning arches and dark, precipitous streets, swarming with armed men and bristling with fortifications'. These lines seem to have been inspired by the description written by the visiting journalist in 1877. However, De Windt finds the reality to be very different: 'Cettigne stands on a dreary plain ... There is no visible sign here of the war-like spirit which has made this little country famous throughout Europe. From a distance the capital resembles a straggling French village.'[27] His stay is a burden to the traveller who can find little to do in his spare time. Any compliment concerning the place always seems to be accompanied by some peculiar qualification such that, for example, the Grand Hotel in Cetinje has very good food but De Windt adds that 'this is chiefly owing to the fact that a few years ago members of the diplomatic corps resided in the hotel'.[28] Cetinje, of course, being the capital of an independent country, was home to embassies and their staff from other countries. Only foreigners can bring civilization to the Balkans in De Windt's view. The Montenegrins have been stripped of their innocence.

De Windt's narrative is full of negative generalizations, such as: 'There is a dull, drab look about most Servian towns, which seems out of place in a country so nearly adjoining the bright and gorgeous East.'[29] His words even deny the Balkans their exoticism, the brightness of the Orient. There is nothing there which could attract the foreigner. He exploits the Balkan myth to the degree that this territory of transitional space between West and East is reduced to nothingness. It has no existence and is drained of all colour and life. By contrast, De Windt finds plenty to praise in his journey through Bosnia, although what he finds positive has nothing to do with the local population. He notes the following changes which have occurred since Austria took over administration of Bosnia in 1878:

> We in England can form no conception of the marvellous transformation effected here by Austria in that short space of time, nor even faintly realise the almost magical rapidity with which the recently barbaric provinces of Herzegovina and Bosnia have been converted into growing centres of commerce and civilisation. While travelling from Ragusa to the Servian frontier, I met,

in every town or village, with some fresh and wonderful proof that the Austrians (generally regarded as a stay-at-home nation) are really the finest (and quickest) colonisers in the world.[30]

This highly favourable comment is an unusual remark for De Windt, but it does lend an insight into what he finds favourable – and it is very little to do with the Balkans. This period of history in Europe was, not unlike today, a confusing time of changing alliances: Germany and Austria on one side, France and Russia with Britain on the other. The Balkans were one of the most sensitive questions in Europe because of Ottoman weakness. In 1903 a palace *coup d'état* in Belgrade had replaced the pro-Austrian King Aleksandar Obrenović by his pro-Russian dynastic rival Petar Karadjordjević. Austria imposed sanctions against Serbia in 1906, refusing to allow the transport of Serbian goods across its territory to the West. Two years later Austria annexed Bosnia and thus created conditions in which Serbs living in Bosnia would plan the assassination of the Archduke.

The author of *An Observer in the Near East* returns to a language inspired by the legacy of Scott's discourse on the Scottish Highlanders but which has by 1907 been successfully transferred to Montenegro. For him Cetinje is certainly not like a 'French village'. He says that the long main street 'reminds one of a small country town in England'. It is 'a little city in the sky', while Montenegro itself is described as 'perhaps the most interesting country in all the Balkans'.[31] So, from the beginning the author admits a strikingly different set of impressions from visiting the same place in the same year as De Windt. But, even in this book, the author's praise and positive attitude is underlined by a certain ambiguity which reveals his reserve for the possibility of finding real barbarism. While the Montenegrin military cult is viewed with admiration it is simultaneously kept at arms length:

> Here, in Cetinje, in the heart of these wild, desolate fastnesses, one seems so far removed from European influence, and yet how great a part has this rocky, impregnable country, with its fierce soldier-inhabitants, played in the politics of Eastern Europe, and how great a part it is still destined to play in the near future![32]

The distance is maintained by employing the Romantic vocabulary of an age long past, by signalling movement away from European culture and by placing Montenegrin concerns within a specific geopolitical framework over which the Great Powers were in struggle.

The Balkan myth furnishes ideas of Balkan primitivism, of peoples who ought to be colonized and have their affairs run by foreigners, or who embody a defiant, independent spirit to resist such outside interference. The latter view is the consequence of the same dialogue. The same signifiers refer to both images but are attributed with different values; the noble savage and the primitive barbarian are never far apart. The twentieth century has seen extreme examples of both the negative and positive poles of this sign.

TWENTIETH-CENTURY REPRESENTATIONS

The Balkan myth and the accompanying images of the Serbs have a limited range of signifiers which have proved to be remarkably productive especially in times of war. The First World War saw the beginning of a cycle of textual representations in the twentieth century which clearly rework images present from the days of European Romanticism. John Reed, an American journalist who is best known for his eyewitness account of the Russian Revolution, *Ten Days that Shook the World* (1926), reported from the Serbian army camped around Niš after the Austrians had taken Belgrade in 1915. He was impressed by the efforts that the Serbian army and government had taken against the much superior numbers of the Hapsburg army and in spite of the famine and disease which gripped the country as a consequence of the war. Travelling in the territory still occupied by the Serbs, he describes at one point a representative from the Press Bureau attached to military headquarters at Kragujevac in the following terms:

> [He] was saturated with European culture, European smartness, cynicism, modernism; yet scratch the surface and you found the Serb; the strong, virile stock of a young race not far removed from the half savagery of a mountain peasantry, intensely patriotic and intensely independent.[33]

The surprising factor in this description is the way in which it so closely echoes the expressions of both the journalist and Tennyson from forty years previously. The Serbian officer is firstly described as 'European' in terms of both appearance and attitude towards the world. However, what lies beneath this veneer of civilization is far more important. The reality of the figure of the Serb is associated with youthfulness, independence and an ambiguous 'half savagery'. The peasant origin of the man is inevitably linked to a mountain home. By Reed's day, this particular attribute has become a necessary epithet in descriptions of Serbs. Judging from the journalist's articles and the places he visited from Niš to Belgrade, he himself hardly saw any mountains during his stay. The real mountains of Serbia are further to the east and south of the areas from which Reed wrote his articles. Another necessary addition which Reed included in his dispatches from Serbia was a translation of part of a ballad in the folk epic style with the title 'The Bombardment of Belgrade'.[34] Reed repeatedly harks back to images and signs of Serbian culture and identity from previous representations.

The First World War continues to provide numerous examples of Serbian cultural identity which echo earlier texts. There were many British men and women serving with the Serbian army as medical corps or working in Serbia for the Red Cross. They left behind many descriptions of varied types, memoirs, journalistic essays, private letters which attest to the perseverance of the limited range of sources for evoking Serbian identity and praising those elements which are most useful in time of war. Another example of the necessity for some 'savagery' in times of war comes in a book by Jan Gordon published in 1916 with the title *A Balkan Freebooter: being the true exploits of the Serbian outlaw and comitaj Petko Moritch, told by him to the author and set into English.* It contains an extraordinary account of an honest man who is wrongfully arrested and finds that despite all his efforts to the contrary he is forced into a life of crime. However, as a criminal he maintains a strict code of honour, helping those who help him and punishing those who would do him harm. The narrative at one point digresses to another character who is sitting in a Belgrade prison with Moritch:

> At this time in Belgrade gaol was a strange and interesting character named Dimitrie Phillipovitch, in whom one may find concentrated much of the Serbian spirit of those times, the fearlessness and hate, and pitilessness culminating in a contempt for human life, which in pre-war days would have been incredible to most of us, but to which now many are inured.[35]

The narrative at this point is not the first-person narration of Moritch, but is a comment made by an outside voice. Gordon himself is commenting on the character of Phillipovitch and those qualities which in peacetime would not be so attractive but which are now those very attributes deemed necessary by the war. An air of positive militarism is attributed to Serbian culture and traditions. This image of positive militarism was reinforced during the war by many acts showing respect for certain aspects of Serbia culture. In 1916 a committee was established in Britain to promote the celebration of the anniversary of the Battle of Kosovo, the famous battle of 28 June 1389 from which the Serbs traditionally trace their defeat by the Turks. Pictures of Prince Lazar who led the Serbian side were distributed, while the epic ballad about the battle was translated and information was distributed to British schools to help them mark the event.[36] It was also during the war that the name of the country was changed from Servia to Serbia to remove connotations of 'servility'. This change was brought about by a concerted effort of the British press: 'Sometime between August, 1914, and April, 1915, the name of the country was quietly "raised" by the newspapers to *Serbia*.'[37]

Further evidence of the power of language and other forms of representation in creating as much as reflecting views of historic realities in relation to Serbia of this period continues to appear after the war with great persistence on the side of positive militarism. Sometime after the First World War in an encyclopaedia titled *The Book of Knowledge: A Pictorial Encyclopaedia for Readers of all Ages* there is a section on military uniforms. The first picture of the section 'Soldiers of Many Lands' is of a Montenegrin sentry,[38] while the entry on Montenegro refers to its 'rich literature of patriotic songs and ballads'.[39] Historians frequently express themselves in similar tones. In a standard history of the region Montenegro is described as an 'Homeric society of mountain chieftains'.[40] In his book *A Short History of the Yugoslav Peoples* Fred Singleton describes the Serbian army's struggle against the far superior numbers of the Hapsburg army at the end of 1915 as a feat of 'desperate heroism'.[41] As the Balkan myth underpins the development of the theme of the noble savage in British representations of Serbian cultural identity, so those images result in recurring messages of positive militarism. A return to similar sentiments is expressed during the Second World War when, despite there being a unified state of Serbs, Croats and Slovenes for the preceding 20 years, the evocation of distinctly Serbian traditions runs apace, invariably illustrated as examples of positive values.

In 1942 W. A. Morison published translations of some Serbian epic ballads with a lengthy introduction by him, returning to the cultural form for which Serbian culture found its first recognition beyond its own borders. He observes that the ballads are not historically accurate, and yet is still able to make the remark that 'they do give a fascinating picture of the history of the Serbs from the twelfth century on'.[42] For Morison this 'fascinating picture' is more real and has more substance than historical accuracy, and he links the image of struggle contained in the poems by analogy to the contemporary situation in Europe. However, Morison's analogy appears understated in comparison with the remarks made by Rebecca West in her book *Black Lamb and Grey Falcon*. The book is her travelogue around Yugoslavia in 1937, but was not published until the war years. In the epilogue to her two-volume account she turns to the theme of Serbian heroism, and the tragedy of Kosovo, thinking of the danger Britain also faced during the Battle of Britain as she writes, 'The difference between Kossovo in 1389 and England in 1939 lay in time and place and not in the events experienced, which resembled each other even in details of which we of the later catastrophe think as peculiar to our nightmare.'[43] She extends the metaphor, and likens the story of the fall of the Serbian Empire as narrated in the epic poem on that subject to Chamberlain surrendering Czechoslovakia in Munich. Both Morison and West follow a semiotic path which began some 120 years before them, relying on a set of limited signs to produce a message which stands in very constricted historical horizons.

The dominant motifs of the noble savage and positive militarism were images which began with Romanticism's valorization of the Serbian epic and eventually came to dominate Serbs' image of themselves. Lena Jovičić was a writer of mixed parentage, having a Serbian father and a Scottish mother. She divided her time between Britain and Belgrade. With her background she was in an unique position to know both worlds. Her first book, *Pages from Here and There in Serbia*, was published in 1926. It was written in English and published in Belgrade with the intention of trying to extend knowledge about Serbia abroad. Her next book came two years later and was published in England. It was simply called *Yugoslavia*, and was one of a series of books aimed at British children to inform them about other countries. When describing Belgrade she discusses the problem which others describe as the 'Orientalism' of the Balkans in a way which reveals her internalized 'foreign' point of view: 'East meets West in a curious jumble, and in view of such extremes and contrasts you cannot but feel that there is a gap somewhere. The connecting link between one and the other is missing, and so you constantly find that you suddenly drop into the gap.'[44] Jovičić acknowledges that there is something 'missing', characterizing indigenous culture by a sense of absence and lack. When she talks about Montenegro the influence of earlier English texts is again evident in her own words: 'this race of bold mountaineers has a strain of naive simplicity in its blood, and even the fiercest warriors are not far removed from the child'.[45] There has been little development of that image over the decades, such recognition does not guarantee access to a voice to negotiate one's own path.

These images were open to reinvention and manipulation for a war effort during two world wars. However, there is always in such cases an uneasy suspicion concerning the other aspect of the West's imagination of savagery, in the shape of barbarism and chaos. This is not to say that violence and aggression have not taken place, but the explanatory frameworks at some point always seem to imply the truth of Balkan mythology. The myth fulfils the simple strategy of crystallizing complex issues into readily transmissible formulae. The truth in many instances is that what really happens there is of less importance than the broader strategic interests of larger nations. Therefore, with no control over their representations abroad, what is at stake in Balkan historical realities is oblivion and disappearance. Small cultures have a vulnerable existence, dependent on and yet resistant to the foreign gaze, positioned always on the periphery. The power of the myths continues today, revealing its origins in the past and inserting signs as appropriate.

Much reporting of the Yugoslav civil wars in the British media has been characterized by the persistence of the West's Balkan mythology. It is enough for a journalist to use the term 'Balkan' in order to prepare the ground for the introduction of an apocalyptic tone, an unstoppable violence which threatens the future in vague terms. The *Guardian* journalist Ian Traynor has a typical article of this kind. The very title evokes a satanic and primordial imagery: 'Threat of wider Balkan inferno haunts West'. The bulk of the article, however, offers an insightful analysis into the negotiating positions between the Serbs, Croats and Moslems at that stage in the war. He carefully weighs the different interests of each side and considers the political checks and balances which face Presidents Milošević of Serbia, Tudjman of Croatia and Izetbegović of Bosnia-Hercegovina. Then, he closes his article with reference to the all-encompassing 'Balkans':

The signs are that, without international mediation, the main Balkan players are moving towards a complex set of deals and accommodations. But an awful lot can easily go wrong. All sides are riven by power struggles. The scope for sabotage is immense, ushering in a bigger war and consigning the West's strategy of containment to the heap of failed policies on the Balkans.[46]

The structure of his article concludes on a note which evokes a number of elements repeated, in various ways, in the past. Wars are concluded with complex negotiations which by their nature are delicate and may produce unforeseen results. But in this case there is an accumulating hierarchy of signs which threaten danger surrounded by a context in which the West has responsibility as for children, now dangerous children. Then, carefully ranged one after the other, we have 'main Balkan players', 'power struggles', 'sabotage', 'bigger war'. Traynor creates a picture of chieftains pursuing private goals, surrounded by others following their own, different agendas, in a fragmented and destabilizing world which threatens Western ideals of harmony and peace. Just a glance at other titles and subtitles in the press confirms the instant appeal of the term 'Balkan': 'Ambiguity rules in Balkan tangle',[47] 'Rifts widen over crisis in Balkans'[48] – i.e. the crisis is causing further problems for the international community unable to agree a policy, 'Ghost of Vietnam haunts Clinton Balkan policy'[49] – i.e. mention of Balkans implies a threat to stability outside its own territory. The production of a Balkan semantics is based on a narrow range of persistent images, reinvented as appropriate in each historical moment.

The power of the same sign system, now invested with opposing negative values, continues in relation to the image of the Serbs. Men in uniforms, often bearded, seen playing musical instruments, singing and drinking have become commonplace in the media. They hark back to imagery of the folk epics, sometimes even commenting directly on the recent reinvention of selected aspects of the oral tradition witnessed during the conflict. One picture in particular shows how a 'mud-covered Bosnian Serb soldier takes part in a camouflage training exercise'.[50] The picture is published with no article for further explanation. The soldier is naked to the waist, his torso smeared with mud, a knife between his teeth and wearing a Rambo-style headband with his back against a tree trunk, trying to melt into the undergrowth. The closeness to 'nature' now takes on an altogether more sinister appearance than the 'innocence' of children unspoilt by civilization. These Serbs are, as before but in a different context, described as 'mountain men', their naturalness taking them close to animal savagery as they 'move in packs'.[51] Serbian soldiers 'grunt and bark orders'.[52] Otherwise, they are 'those redneck country boys up in the hills, [who] want to erase this city. Its subtleties are too complex for them to resolve.'[53] The Bosnian war nearly became an archetypal battle between civilization and non-civilization, between mountain and city, in which one headline reads 'Sarajevo repels the mountain menace', relying on a sign system in relation to the Balkans and the Serbs which has been periodically reinvented over the last 170 years, since the Romantics first turned their attention to the folk epics.[54]

So far in this chapter I have argued that the basis of a militaristic, peasant Balkans is a Western invention derived from Romantic aesthetics which privileged the national authenticity discovered in folk epics. Transferred to the British imagination, these terms tend to have maintained a positive value. The focus of this debate is not the extent to which these images are true reflections of historical realities, but how they have been made available as part of wider strategies to order and prioritize interpretations of events in the Balkans. The journalist Mark Thompson admits his fascination for many of the 'larger-than-life types' about whom he writes in the years leading up to the Yugoslav wars, commenting, 'Heroic and epic culture still gravitates around such personalities, for better or worse.'[55] However, the question is, whose discourse creates this 'heroic and epic culture'? Other small cultures in the world, those which we might view as more colonial societies in a classical sense, established a culture of resistance to the foreign voice with the aim 'to reclaim, rename and reinhabit the land'.[56] However, the peoples of the Balkans, and of Eastern Europe in general, have not been in a position to reclaim a history for themselves and a voice of their own: the Balkans was even named after a misrecognition which has persisted to today. In conclusion, I intend to look at a text written by a former resident of former Yugoslavia, the Croatian author Dubravka Ugrešić, who reflects on the extent of dialogue between the West and her home.

THE ANXIETY EFFECT

Dubravka Ugrešić from early days was out of favour with the new nationalist government elected in Croatia in 1990 with Franjo

Tudjman as President of state. Opposing the movement towards nationalist policies and then taking a determined stand against the war, she was attacked publicly in a campaign organized from the centre of power against all rivals. Such officially orchestrated operations were a common feature of the governments of all the successor states which appeared on the territory of the former Yugoslavia. Consequently, Ugrešić left Croatia in September 1991 for Amsterdam from where she left for Wesleyan University in Middletown, Connecticut, to teach for six months from January 1992. She has subsequently resigned her post at the research institute where she worked in Zagreb, and has since lived in virtual exile. At home, before the civil war in Croatia, she was better known as a writer of wry, humorous fiction, most of which has been translated into English. Author of numerous short stories, she has also published two novels, translated into English as *Steffie Speck* and *Fording the Stream of Consciousness*.[57] The characteristics of her prose are a large number of intertextual references which often link her fictional worlds with those of other authors and question the status of the literary text. In *Steffie Speck*, for example, she gives her heroine the task of getting a man in her life, often writing in the style of stories in popular women's magazines, but also adding references to Madame Bovary and to Snow White. She sets the text out like a sewing pattern, advising readers when they may cut the passage or perform other operations. The narrator provides a choice of endings as advised by her mother, friends and others. More recently, Ugrešić has changed the subject matter and style of her writing.

During her stay in Middletown, America, for those six months Ugrešić wrote a series of newspaper articles published in Amsterdam. She then collected them together and they were published in English translation as *Have a Nice Day: From the Balkan War to the American Dream*. She originally thought of her book as 'My American Dictionary'.[58] Each chapter is a word which presents a typical American object or concept such as 'The Organizer', 'Jogging', 'Harassment' or 'Coca-Cola'. She holds each word up for inspection, worries at it, examines its connotations, opens up its semantic reaches, and then brings it into contact with events at home. She explains that she considered it her 'dictionary' because her whole world was changing. Everything which had been there for 50 years was disappearing and everything had to be changed. Croatia certainly was not alone in this process. The end of Yugoslavia brought immediate changes to many areas of life. Ugrešić comments, 'Good or bad, right or wrong, that was the age in which we had lived: those were the letters we had learned, those were the books we had read, the objects we had possessed, the films we had watched, the streets we had walked' (p. 15). She describes it as a denial of all that had ever been, and challenging the concept of what reality they were living in. In fact, she says how when typing out her manuscript for publication as a book she 'mistakenly typed **f** instead of **d**, and my dictionary became a fictionary' (p. 17). The mistake was, she felt, an appropriate one since *'reality no longer existed'* (p. 17). All the articles taken together present a study of one individual's world crumbling away, but because it no longer exists she needs another world which does exist to act as a prism through which she might be able to catch glimpses of that other world. So, this is the reality of the Balkan war looked at through the American dream.

Ugrešić makes frequent reference to differences between East and West, in fact using American society as the epitome of all that which is Other to her East European and her Balkan world. In order to give some order to her world she draws up two lists of words as pairs of opposites one with the heading Western Europe, the other Eastern Europe (see p. 22):

Western Europe	Eastern Europe
right	left
organized	disorganized
democracy	democratic symbols as a substitute for democracy
civilized	primitive
legitimate	illegitimate
rational consciousness	mythic consciousness
facing the future	a necrophiliac preoccupation with the past
predictability	unpredictability
an orderly system of criteria and values	absence of system
individual consciousness	collective consciousness
citizen	nationality

Ugrešić's lists contain a synopsis of the Enlightenment project which apportioned positive values to the West and negative values to the East. She seems to continue playing the game of ordering reality according to the two types of Europeanicity. One is replete and the other is characterized by absence, but both are identified by their relationship to each other. For herself, as the book unfolds, she comes to prefer a no-man's-land somewhere between these two extremes. As she travels home to Zagreb, full of anxiety for the future, but not keeping her American dream with her as a comfort, on the flight she appears to forget all about New York, bagels, life on the campus of Wesleyan University. Instead, when she is in transit at Amsterdam Airport she regards her moving from one plane to the next, bound for Zagreb, as 'a route of inner freedom' (p. 225). She finds a security in being in the transitional space, left alone to be whosoever *she* chooses to be, without the pressures of external definition, living 'under the artificial airport lights like a postmodern exhibit, in a transitional phase, in an ideal shelter, in limbo, in an emotionally aseptic space' (pp. 225-6).

This journey goes through various stages as the author negotiates her way through the signs of East and West, keeping a critical distance from the centres of both worlds. At an early stage she contemplates the lack of knowledge with which foreigners used to treat her '*Yugoslovakia*' (p. 28). She recalls that her country was often talked about as 'the fear of civilized Europe' (p. 28). It is not possible for Ugrešić to avoid the same phrases and rhetoric developed in the West about her homeland over the past century and an half. So, she refuses to admit to being Serb or Croat and is identified as one of those people 'with "those little guys" above the letters of my surname' (p. 29). The 'little guys' are the diacritic marks above consonants as in Ugrešić. This form of identify satisfies her, anything to keep a distance from the reality of 'this cruelty, this senseless destruction' which the war has brought (p. 32).

At home there is a war, death and destruction on a large scale. Everything which had once been valued from Titoist days is turned about face and is now assigned a negative value:

> Just as every tragedy recurs as farce, so all the former Yugo-symbols have been transformed into their opposite: Tito's baton (the symbol of brotherhood and unity) has become a fratricidal stick, a gun, a knife, with which the male representatives of the former Yugo-peoples are annihilating each other. The towns and villages through which the baton-relay passed are today being demolished like towers of cards: in almost the same order, from north to south. (p. 173)

The baton described above was relayed from place to place until its final destination where it was ceremoniously presented to President

Tito as part of the celebration of the Day of Youth. Ugrešić's reflections maintain that the outer signs and symbols have not changed. Entry into the Yugoslav wars and the collapse of the country was gained by simply shrugging the shoulders and turning sideways at first, then turning upside down. One of the symbols which stays in her memory of multinational Yugoslavia is the ring dance or *kolo*:

> The kolo was danced by representatives of the nations and nationalities of Yugoslavia dressed in their national costumes. They all danced all the different dances from all the different regions, in harmony: they tripped, jigged, stamped, twirled, bopped as appropriate. That ring dance, the symbolic crown of Yugoslavia, comprehensible to all literate and illiterate Yugoslavs alike, has today become its opposite, a lethal noose. (p. 172)

This is a world which is being destroyed, and in such a world as order collapses and undergoes a painful transformation into a world yet to be determined, so the semiotic processes which represented that old world collapse, become distorted, merge into new meanings, and are seen 'in a new arrangement' (p. 173). What the author has to say about her own country in its extreme crisis could be said for Eastern Europe as a whole. The Communist system, however obtrusive in people's lives and totalitarian in its monopoly of power, had granted some kind of order and security of basic needs. Now, its disappearance has brought chaos while privatization policies introduce opportunities for some and personal disaster for others as factories have to scale down or close and nationalized property reverts to previous owners. In the realms of health and education what was always available and free, in short supply and technologically not very advanced, may be now more difficult to obtain and then only at a price. Ugrešić thinks on this collapsing world, her world, while living in the brash and confident American dream. Here, reality consists of museums dedicated to Coca-Cola, watching television, health addiction. This is a contrasting world which keeps throwing new light on the painful collapse of home, while the painful collapse of home sometimes throws new light onto the artificiality and smug comfort of the American dream. Ugrešić's book is about these 'parallel worlds' brought together by disaster (p. 13).

Ugrešić's refusal to comply to the stereotype arises from the very fact that she sees the falsity of the East–West division. There are differences, but also crossovers and complex exchanges. The reality of war in the Balkans reinforces the validity of the Balkan myth as an absolute truth. Thinking on the reporting about the war, she notes how the images invoked of refugees and of desperation 'absolutely coincide with the Balkan stereotype'. However, she also points out that there is a clear level of civilization there but 'no one asks how it is that many of these desperate people have a decent command of the English language'. In fact, the truth of Balkan reality is that it is soaked with imagery from the American myth. She gives examples such as a knife being called a 'rambo' in slang, soldiers wearing headbands 'like Sylvester Stallone', referring to the town of Knin as 'Knin Peaks', and Serbian paramilitaries in Croatia as 'Kninjas', cartoon character soldiers wield knives and wear 'Reeboks'. While she watches Sarajevo being bombed on American television, her mother in Zagreb is watching 'Santa Barbara' (pp. 110–11). America functions as a synecdoche for the West described in Ugrešić's earlier placed list of differences between East and West.

Ugrešić's list at first seems to present two contrasting sign systems; one values civilization, good government, order and progress, while the other summarizes a rural barbarism where tractors have yet to take the place of ox-carts. It is an invention of the West's imagination and one which structures our imaginative response to all other events there. It is a refinement of the monolithic image of Eastern Europe which persists no matter how many times it is pointed out that 'the determination of many in the West to view the area as a cultural and political monolith was the product of a misapprehension'.[59] Yet, we can still read comments which essentialize the region as a whole: 'Autocracy, absolutism, centralization, divine sanction – such are the terms that historically and consistently describe the political culture of East European civilization for well over a thousand years.'[60] Another example offers a description of the oppressive nature of collective consciousness there, the poor economic performance and bureaucratic rigidity; it concludes, 'If one regards Soviet Communism as a disease, then it seems that Eastern Europe may have had a pre-disposition to the infection.'[61] Ugrešić's lists are not discreet, but together form the two parts of a single sign, the fear of Western civilization at the possibility of its own destruction with an implosion of its values. She, on the other hand, focuses on the complex exchange between the two sides of this sign. People see the Balkan myth reflected in the war they see on their television screens, but the myth functions as an interpretive framework against which those images are given meanings. In more ways than one, Ugrešić makes a strong point when commenting: 'Balkan reality, then, does not identify with the Balkan myth but, once again, with the American one' (p. 111).

Ugrešić is concerned at the spaces open to her for negotiation. She is unable to accept the label of an East European writer and cross over into the American mainstream literary world as such, into the space awarded to this category. From the perspective of the American book market, East European literature is published and read not for its aesthetic qualities but for ideological reasons. It provides stories about the politics of the individual against the state. It would probably be possible to take up this one problem fruitfully; how does the largest book market in the world assign value to writers from different parts of the globe? Ugrešić, and other East European writers, have had no input into the creation of their zone in American culture. With no input into the definition of that space, she rejects it as she rejected the pressures in Croatia to lend her public support to the national cause, to manipulate her place as a writer and public figure for the regime. The zone of the East European writer in America appears too uncomfortably close to the prescribed zone of the writer in Croatian society for which she had left her country. However, the demand of the American book market to package the product in a way which gives maximum benefit to marketing is a very different demand from that made on writers in Eastern Europe. The two dialogues internally conducted instil in Ugrešić a frightening similarity but they begin from and conclude with very different intentions. However, in considering an inter-cultural leap into the Western book market Ugrešić comes up against this barrier.

The American dialogue is controlled by the demands of the American market for books by writers from Eastern Europe. The stereotypes precede the writers themselves. Ugrešić records a conversation with an American journalist who asks her, 'What do you think about communism?' Trying to steer the conversation back to what she considers her professional role to be, Ugrešić responds, 'We're talking about literature.' The rejoinder comes, 'Let's leave boring questions about literature to Western writers. As an East European writer and intellectual you surely have far more interesting things to talk about than literature' (p. 139). Ugrešić is not allowed to influence the boundaries of the dialogue, her zone is defined for her. Dialogue is used to confirm the images which are already fixed in the West about Eastern Europe. These models of international symbolic orders and intercultural dialogues are models of recognition. Entry into those spheres is achieved through recognition by the outsider, the foreigner. A culture has to establish its presence to enter the international market place of representations where cultural forms are the currency and cultural identity the banking system. Control of the market confers power over the exchange and reception of cultural images. Such control is exercised by the West, by the world's larger cultures. The smaller cultures of Eastern Europe have an investment in establishing their presence, but no control over its shape.

Concern over the production of representations has been one of the major issues in many recent discussions on the problems of minorities and marginalized groups. At the beginning of his essay 'The Politics of Recognition' Charles Taylor summarizes the problem thus:

> The thesis is that our identity is partly shaped by recognition or its absence, often by the *mis*recognition of others, and so a person or group of people can suffer real damage, real distortion, if the people or society around them mirror back to them a confining or demeaning or contemptible picture of themselves. Nonrecognition or misrecognition can inflict harm, can be a form of oppression, imprisoning someone in a false, distorted, and reduced mode of being.[62]

To a large degree, Taylor's argument follows a Bakhtinian model in that identities are formed 'always in dialogue with, sometimes in struggle against, the things our significant others want to see in us'.[63] These remarks correspond to a vision of Europe composed of two signifying parts, Western and Eastern Europe invented together 'as complementary concepts, defining each other by opposition and adjacency' in which Eastern Europe signifies absence and Western Europe is an overburdened sign equivalent to Europeanicity.[64] Ugrešić's experiences from America reflect the dialogue and struggle of Eastern Europe and particularly the Balkans with their 'significant others'. Even before her, another cosmopolitan-minded writer from the region of former Yugoslavia commented on the problems of nonrecognition and misrecognition in a similar vein on the types of images in circulation of 'those – what-do-you-call-'em – srbo-krkrs'.[65]

3 The Balkans Talk Back

THE DRAMA OF HUMAN MISUNDERSTANDING?

In all the world's literatures we find examples of novels about foreigners and foreign lands. Characters travel abroad and there the process begins, acted out in countless narratives in which our fascination for the alien Other is revealed; whether that fascination consists of fear, loathing, or a secret desire to possess the Other. Fascination is the peculiar mixture of feelings involving both dread and obsessive need which constructs our sense of the exotic. It is when, as Bakhtin puts it, culture reveals itself 'in the eyes of *another* culture'.[1] In English literature the novels of Conrad and Forster, amongst others, provide examples of such narratives. They are examples of the novels of Empire in which British soldiers, traders, administrators, adventurers go to the colonies to perform their duties. This subject in literature has been described as the international theme and at least one Serbian critic has written extensively on it in relation to both English and Serbian literatures. In the course of his work on this problem, Svetozar Koljević at one point describes the action of such stories being motivated by 'the drama of human misunderstandings owing to different horizons of cultural expectations'.[2] However, there appears behind the term 'drama' to lurk an inspired neutrality in that there is a suggestion of clash, of the possibility for Bakhtinian dialogue, and also of a generic working out of a problem. Positionality is a great factor in determining the ways in which the dialogue between two different cultures may be played out and an international theme be motivated. Most work in this area has been concerned with either the novels of Empire or images about minority groups such as blacks in America. Balkan literatures present us with a different set of issues with regard to such representations because of the construction of the Balkan myth abroad and its acceptance at home.

Others who have written more markedly than Koljević about the representations of foreigners or of minority groups in major literatures include Edward Said. He characterizes the limitations of these representations as those 'that follow upon disregarding, essentializing, denuding the humanity of another culture, people or geographical region'.[3] The following example of such an image is taken from Conrad's *Heart of Darkness*. Marlow is telling his story about sailing up the African river when he sees a woman by the bank. He describes her thus:

> She walked with measured steps, draped in striped and fringed clothes, treading the earth proudly, with a slight jingle and flash of barbarous ornaments. She carried her head high; her hair was done in the shape of a helmet; she had brass leggings to the knees, brass wire gauntlets to the elbow, a crimson spot on her tawny cheek, innumerable necklaces of glass beads on her neck; bizarre things, charms, gifts of witch-men, that hung about her, glittered and trembled at every step. She must have had the value of several elephant tusks upon her. She was savage and superb, wild-eyed and magnificent; there was something ominous and stately in her deliberate progress. And in the hush that had fallen suddenly upon the whole sorrowful land, the immense wilderness, the colossal body of the fecund and mysterious life seemed to look at her, pensive, as though it had been looking at the image of its own tenebrous and passionate soul.[4]

The passage is an apt illustration of a dehumanised image in that it is not a description of the African woman walking by the river but an evocation of Marlow's colonial outlook. It conveys the impression of ambiguity, of attraction and at the same time repulsion, of being savage and superb, straying between exotic and erotic formulations. Said comments on the work of such authors that they 'do not merely reproduce the outlying territories: they work them out, or animate them'.[5] In the passage above Marlow imagines an African totality from the perspective of an English ivory trader. The woman comes to represent his state of mind and is denied any voice, any participation in dialogue. These works are an implicit part of the structures of colonialism since they 'developed and accentuated the essentialist positions in European culture proclaiming that Europeans should rule, non-Europeans be ruled'.[6]

The representation of the possibilities for dialogue between different cultures found in narrative fiction is the issue of the relationship between major and minor cultures. Some cultures are in a position to make demeaning images of others, and to transfer those images to the other culture. The space for dialogue in these circumstances is narrowed. Even in those narratives in which a more sympathetic creation of the colonized subject is expressed, such as in E. M.

Forster's *A Passage to India*, the dominant voice is that of colonial administration, while others from the British community who are not so arrogant like the teacher Fielding exist to provide a positive role model for Indians. Mrs Moore, the name of the kindly English lady in Forster's novel, becomes a cry for help for all those who feel oppressed. There are few circumstances in which there are equal voices in dialogue, raising new questions for ourselves, and this positionality is typical of the representation of foreign characters in major, Western, literatures:

> All cultures tend to make representations of foreign cultures the better to master or in some way to control them. Yet not all cultures make representations of foreign cultures *and* in fact master or control them. This is the distinction, I believe, of modern Western cultures.[7]

The inclusion of foreign characters in minority literatures, bringing in an outsider who represents the voice of a dominant culture, forces the issue of dialogue, or lack of it, to the front.

Authors from the Balkans confront the negative imagery which circulates about their cultures particularly when incorporating dominant outsiders in their narratives. I shall focus on four novels by different authors each of whom animates the relationship between domestic and foreign culture variously. The earliest novel is *Seobe* (*Migrations*, 1929) by Miloš Crnjanski, then *Travnička hronika* (*The Days of the Consuls*, 1945) by Ivo Andrić, and finally two works by Slobodan Selenić: *Prijatelji* (*The Friends*, 1980) and *Očevi i oci* (*Fathers and Forefathers*, 1985). The first two have been translated into English, and some extracts from *Fathers and Forefathers* are also available in translation. These authors and their works span the twentieth century, covering a wide range of styles, while the stories are set in different historical periods and geographic regions. The action of Crnjanski's novel occurs outside the Balkans with a regiment of Serbs going abroad to fight on behalf of the Austrians against the French in the middle of the eighteenth century. Andrić's novel involves the arrival of a French Consul in the Bosnian town of Travnik during the Napoleonic period. The first novel by Selenić is set in Belgrade and is included as an interesting example of an internal cultural division between a sophisticated Belgrade citizen and an Albanian peasant who comes to Belgrade at the end of the Second World War. We have seen in the previous chapter ways in which the Balkan myth has been productive in the region itself. The final example is a more classical illustration of major and minor cultures in contact. It involves Stevan Medaković and his English wife, Elizabeth, who comes to live with her husband in Belgrade toward the end of the 1920s. The precise relationships between characters and what brings them together is treated variously. But in all of them the essential problem remains how to understand another culture, how to represent it in terms of narrative fiction when the outside culture regards itself and is regarded internally as dominant.

MILOŠ CRNJANSKI: THE POETICS OF EXILE

Miloš Crnjanski was born in 1893 in the town of Čongrad situated some forty miles due north of the point where the present-day borders of Romania, Hungary and Serbia intersect. He was born and brought up in the Hapsburg Empire, in the towns of southern Hungary, in which there lived a substantial Serbian population. When the First World War broke out he was a student in Vienna, from where he was conscripted into the Austrian army and sent to the front. His active soldiering did not last long since he was diagnosed as having tuberculosis in 1915 and spent most of the war on non-military duties. He began writing poems with a distinct anti-war tone in 1917, publishing them in a well-known literary journal in Zagreb called *Savremenik* (*The Contemporary*). With the formation of the Kingdom of Serbs Croats and Slovenes, as the united Yugoslav state was first proclaimed, at the end of 1918, Crnjanski soon went to Belgrade. He became immediately involved with a group of avant-garde artists, writers and musicians who used to meet regularly in the café of one of the city's fashionable hotels, the Hotel Moskva. He quickly acquired a reputation as a keen polemicist, involved in all the literary debates of his day. This Modernist generation of writers and artists was a bohemian group engaged in radical experiments with the form and content of their art, similar in outlook and temperament to their contemporaries elsewhere in Europe and North America.

During the 1930s Crnjanski's literary work continued with numerous lyrical travelogues, but no new major novels or poetry. It was not, however, this area of his life which was to prove crucial to what was going to happen later. Finding it impossible to live from writing alone he began a career with the Royal Yugoslav Diplomatic Service. As press attaché at the Embassies in Berlin and Rome, he did not disguise a certain admiration for some aspects of the regimes of Hitler and Mussolini. Back in Belgrade he began to publish a journal mainly devoted to cultural issues, but definitely right-wing in its political orientation. He supported the dictatorship of the Karadjordjević monarchy through these years. His previous involvement in literary debates became more politicized and he was openly critical of many public figures who were inclined towards communism. This activity helped to bring these people to the attention of the German authorities when they occupied the country during the Second World War. In 1941 Yugoslavia was put under enormous pressure to sign a pact with Hitler to allow the passage of German troops across its territory. These troops were intended to help Italy's campaign in Greece. The pact was signed but was immediately followed by a *coup d'état* in which the army brought down the government and renounced the agreement. Shortly after, on 6 April 1941, Hitler bombed Belgrade and Yugoslavia was dragged into the war. Capitulation soon followed and the country was occupied and dismembered. At the time of Germany's attack Crnjanski was in Rome. He was given diplomatic immunity and was allowed to make his way to a neutral country. He went first to Portugal and from there to London. At the end of the war he could not return to Yugoslavia where the Communist Party took over government. His pre-war activities made him a *persona non grata* to the new regime and he was to remain in London for almost 25 years.

Crnjanski's life in London was that of a poor *émigré* from Eastern Europe, unable to return home because of the Communist regimes which took power there. He was not alone in this position. He tried to continue as a writer in the tradition of Joseph Conrad, but his command of English was never adequate to the task and he had a variety of low-paid jobs. At home, he was publicly vilified as a creature of the previous regime, his books were no longer published and his name and all reference to his work dropped from school and university curricula. But then political changes were introduced in Yugoslavia which were to have far-reaching consequences and to effect Crnjanski personally. Following the quarrel between Yugoslavia and the Soviet Union in 1948, the former was excluded from all international Communist organizations. Boycotted by Eastern Europe the country moved closer to the West, but always with a certain reserve since the Communist Party never intended to surrender its monopoly of real political power. But the change in direction led to a thaw in cultural policy and gave more space for debate. Under these conditions Crnjanski began to appear once again in literary histories and his early work was republished toward the end of the 1950s. He was invited to the Yugoslav Embassy in London as a guest where he was asked to return to Belgrade. However, he remained very fearful of what might happen should he return and it was not until 1965 and in the company of the Yugoslav Ambassador to Britain that he finally went back.

Crnjanski's rehabilitation was complete. He influenced many writers of the post-war generations who were tired of the narrow field open to literature under the Communists. As a totalitarian regime they controlled very strictly all spaces of life dedicated to producing meanings and images. Some new writers were impressed by the radical experiments of Crnjanski's pre-war work and were attracted to the non-utilitarian attitude of the Modernists toward art. Of course, it follows that this author who once was considered the *enfant terrible* of the Belgrade circle had developed into a classic of modern Serbian literature. He published a new novel in 1962, a continuation of *Migrations* called *Druga knjiga Seoba* (*The Second Book of Migrations*). The two are actually very different in theme and style, separated by more than 30 years, and may be read completely independently from one another. Then, drawing on his experiences in exile he published *Roman o Londonu* (*A Novel about London*) in 1972. The main character is a Russian aristocrat forced to flee his homeland after the Revolution in 1917. It is a very dense exploration of the mental and emotional anguish of the *émigré*, culminating in his suicide. He also wrote and published memoirs and other literature. He died in 1977, and later the *Miloš Crnjanski Foundation* was established in Belgrade to promote continued interest in his life and work.

Serbian literature of the 1920s culminated in Crnjanski's novel *Migrations* published firstly in serial form in a journal and then as a book in 1929. The action of the novel concerns the community of Serbs in what is now Vojvodina and southern Hungary in the middle of the eighteenth century. This community has played a particular role in Serbian cultural history. Prior to the migrations of Serbs at the end of the seventeenth century very few Serbs lived north of the River Sava. Indeed, the medieval kingdom was associated with places further south in Kosovo and Macedonia. Due to Ottoman pressure many of these southern Serbs migrated north, across the Sava into the Hapsburg Empire. The population of these frontier lands was badly depleted because of frequent cross-border fighting. There was land available in return for which the Serbs were expected to form the border regiments and fight off any Turkish threat. In Serbian history the migratory movement is presented as a great trek of some 30,000 families led by the Patriarch Arsenije III, and although there was a huge shift of population it is more likely to have occurred over a series of migratory waves than in one dramatic push. The new communities were allowed a certain degree of local autonomy in which to develop legal, commercial and other institutions. These freedoms gave the first opportunity to Serbs to foster a sense of modern national consciousness and identity. In the small towns of the region an urbanized community emerged, closer and more open to cultural and other influences from the world. The Christian population of the Ottoman Empire remained closed off. Most important was the freedom given to the Orthodox Church to initiate links with the Russian Orthodox Church. On the one hand, this move gave access to seminaries for training priests and to more books. On the other hand, it also heralded a new liturgical language, a hybrid of Russian and Serbian Church Slavonic forms, which removed the written language even further from the vernacular. At the time in which Crnjanski set his novel, which covers a period of a year from spring 1744, the Hapsburg authorities were concerned about this sizeable community and the privileges by which they were given a semi-autonomous status within the Empire. Moves were afoot to eradicate any sense of national consciousness and separate identity, forcing them to accept uniformity with the dominant Germanic and Catholic culture of the Empire.

Crnjanski's novel takes this background as its raw material and builds from it an image of a society at a crossroads. The two main characters are the Isakovič brothers, Vuk and Arandjel, and together they connect the parallel story lines of the narrative while symbolizing the choices before the community. They are the complete opposite of one another in build and character. Vuk is described as round and heavy, Arandjel is tall and lean. Vuk is compulsive and Arandjel is calculating. Vuk is a leader of the local community and so charged with military responsibilities. When war breaks out with the French, he is ordered to raise a regiment of 300 men and train them to take part in the campaign. His part of the story concerns us more in our intention to examine the representation

of foreigners as they march west. Vuk is a military man, devoted
to his people and concerned at what is going to happen to them
now. His father migrated from the south and Vuk dreams of returning back over the Sava to the Serbian heartlands one day, but
for the moment this is impossible. He, then, begins to think of
migrating yet again to Russia where he will be allowed at least to
keep his Orthodox faith. He does not think of Russia as a real
place, but as an utopia of happiness for him and his people, a vast
snow-covered meadow over which he will ride forever. His Russia
is a vision of salvation and a personal, inner world of safety, based
on traditions which are under threat from the Hapsburg authorities. Arandjel is a merchant, one of the new town class. He does
business in various parts of the Empire and has no desire to return south. All that wandering is counter-productive to earning
money. He has a complete antipathy for anything to do with the
military, since war is also counter-productive to commerce. His
Europe is the Enlightenment, economic progress and stability.
Arandjel stays behind looking after Vuk's wife Dafina whom he
intends to seduce. The two brothers represent the choice before
the nation at this stage of either staying and facing the possibility
of losing their cultural identity, or of overcoming this historical
burden and moving on once again. They are living both literally
and metaphorically on a borderland between two hostile forces and
between threats of menacing change.

For much of the novel the reader follows Isakovič and his men
as they march westwards and fight their battles. It is here that the
reader confronts the representations of foreign characters, and
particularly how that foreign world views the Serbs. The commanding
officers who order and direct the affairs of the regiment are all
German, and all have an opinion of the Serbs which endorses a
cult of militarism in Serbian society. The local Austrian Governor
at Pécs is preparing a speech to deliver to Vuk's recruits which
begins: 'You Serbs have always been partial to the military.'[8] He
never gets any further than this remark as he has intended to give
his speech in Serbian but his knowledge of the language is too
rudimentary. All he knows is how to curse and swear at the men.
There is here an important, unspoken element since the Serbian
regiments were created by the Austrians for defence of their Empire. Their apparent militarism is a consequence of historic events
over which they had little control. Vuk's regiment and the other
Slavonic regiments suffer humiliation from their superiors who tend

to despise them. They are put first in battle as more expendable than other regiments, they are treated more harshly and receive heavier punishments for misdemeanours, but they never receive a fair ration of food and clothing. The attitude of the commander-in-chief of the Hapsburg army, Prince Charles of Lorraine, is typical: 'Charles had been forced to deploy this army; he did not care for it. It was poorly clothed, it stank, it was impossible to command. It was continually early or late, moved according to laws he was unable to ascertain, and caused unforeseen difficulties in general' (pp. 145–6). These are poor soldiers who do not match his standards of dress and discipline. This view is contrasted with that of Vuk's more immediate superior, Baron Berenklau. He appreciates some of the very qualities of these 'wild, greasy, shaggy, mustachioed savages' because 'he did not need to bother about them, to feed or clothe them'. He was 'harsh' and 'merciless' with them: 'Unlike Charles, he found them far from disobedient; indeed, whenever he set off on a campaign with them, he thought himself on a hunt with a loyal pack of hounds he could set on anything that came his way' (p. 146). Berenklau sees Vuk and his men in a way which does not differ greatly from the view of Charles of Lorraine, they are wild and dirty. However, he attributes a different value to the same signs, playing on their bestial qualities as positive attributes in time of war.

In some of his descriptions of Vuk's men preparing for battle or in training, it is as if Crnjanski foretold how the Serbs were going to be represented in a future war, to take place after his death. The newspaper image of the Bosnian Serb soldier discussed in Chapter 2, stripped to the waist, smeared with mud, knife clasped between his teeth as he stalks through the undergrowth is relevant here.[9] In Crnjanski's novel, during their march to the front Vuk puts his soldiers through their paces training them 'to run with pistols in their hands and knives in their teeth' (p. 104). The reference to the Serb soldiers on manoeuvres or going into battle with knives in their teeth is repeated (p. 152, p. 163). More important is the detail given to the observation of their superior officers when they view these proceedings and the general consternation which this sight provokes. On one occasion Berenklau turns up to lead the Serbian regiment personally. They take up their positions close to the French line at night in readiness for a dawn attack. Again Crnjanski includes certain details which correspond to the image of the soldier in the news photograph. He writes that the Baron 'led the men in the dark, like animals, through the undergrowth' and that the following morning 'dawn found them wet and cold, caked with mire, listening to the woodpeckers in the trees' (p. 161). It seems again that the Balkan myth encourages a limited range of possible images which have survived in a virtually unaltered form over many years.

In *Migrations* the issue of point of view becomes especially important. There are two poles to the meaning of the savage; one is the primitive barbarian and the other is the noble savage. The links between these two poles are never completely severed, they are themselves in a constant dialogue with one another. Crnjanski is interested in the complexity of this exchange and so identifying from whose perspective a particular comment is made becomes a crucial element in the reading process. There are frequent references which reinforce the foreigners' point of view on Vuk and his men, particularly the ordinary soldiers, and which give negative images. Entering Pécs, the first town which the men come to on their long march, they terrify the local townsfolk:

> They entered Pécs so unkempt, so unwashed, so wet and over-wrought that they made the children cry and the women, who had rushed out of their houses to see them, run off screaming in all directions. They sang at the top of their lungs and, exhausted and ravenous, marched with so impatient a step that, surrounded as they were by silver-trimmed officers, they looked like a pack of hungry hounds led on leashes to the hunt. (p. 17)

The townsfolk run away from what they see, a large number of armed men with seemingly little discipline. This description is given from the point of view of people in a panic who bolt at the sight of men who 'looked *like* a pack of hungry hounds' [italics DN]. Baron Berenklau feels in a similar way about the soldiers recruited by Vuk. The formulations ascribed to the foreigners' point of view emphasise negative militaristic traits as indicative of primitiveness. These soldiers are alien, living in a world of their own. However, descriptions of how these same soldiers react to what they see and experience while abroad emphasise a different attitude. Their march westwards is their first opportunity to observe things they have never seen before. For example, in one town they see the clockwork figure of a blacksmith on a roof hammering on an anvil at which 'some crossed themselves and gaped' (p. 105). Their reaction is almost child-like. On another occasion when the officers attend a Catholic church service in a large and richly decorated church they 'fell to their knees under the spell of the magnificent atmosphere' remembering 'their own quaint wooden churches' (p. 40). Again, the description of a wonder born of innocence is evoked by the point of view of those soldiers who recall what their own churches look like in comparison with this one.

Crnjanski does not let this double and ambiguous image simply linger between the two poles of innocence and savagery. The West's fear of the primitive is a fear at the possible loss of civilization or fear of a return to an earlier stage. However, at the same time, the feared object becomes desired, and there exists a certain eroticism in stepping over the threshold and taking part in the primitive, like the journalist in Cetinje who described when the Montenegrins 'surged along the street, firing, shouting, singing, leaping with joy' at the news of their victory over the Turks.[10] For a brief moment he could imagine himself sharing in their ecstasy. Crnjanski introduces into his novel the deep feelings of a foreigner facing the exoticism of such 'ecstasy' in the form of the widow of Alexander of Wirtemburg. She accompanied her husband when he was sent to Belgrade as Governor during the Austrian occupation of the city in 1717–39. Vuk served on his staff there as the youngest officer at that time. The Serb officer and the Princess met first in Belgrade and now meet again. They each recall their encounter in Belgrade all those years ago and both are more than a little surprised to see how the other has aged. A few pages are devoted to telling the story of what happened between them.

She becomes infatuated with this young officer. She embodies the ambiguity of the foreign gaze falling upon the alien Other. On the one hand, she tells her husband that she regards Vuk as 'a child' (p. 126). On the other hand, she thinks of him to herself as 'the young savage from that strange land'(p. 127). The erotic aspect of the foreign gaze becomes a double and redoubled game in Crnjanski's narrative since the Princess is attracted to Vuk as a primitive force, and yet she wants him 'to think her as pure and unattainable as a virgin' (p. 127), as the embodiment of innocence. In fact, Vuk complies and when he looks at her he feels desire for her, but is afraid of those feelings since he regards her, this foreign aristocratic woman, as 'exquisite, ethereal, sublime' (p. 127). The difference between the two points of view is one of power. The foreigner moulds the range of reactions which the small culture may feel and express. The theme of Westerners transforming unusual sights and sounds of the East into a potentially erotic charge and of Easterners mesmerized by visions of splendour from the West has been well rehearsed through many novels such as Forster's *A Passage to India*. However, the significant point in Crnjanski's novel is one of positionality, that it is written with a knowledge of the nature of the imagery of primitivism which underlies this theme. It would appear that the translator of *Migrations*, Michael Heim, is well aware of the development of this motif in Crnjanski's novel. He has made some choices which may be regarded almost as interventions into his translation which contribute to the atmosphere of the foreigner gazing upon novelties in the East. As the Princess reflects on her growing desire for the young Serbian officer she recalls his moustache and its 'exotic glossy-black serpentine coils' (p. 131). The original description does not actually contain the word 'exotic', rather a more literal reading would say that this kind of moustache, the shape and fashion of it, 'was something so unusual for her'. However, the English word 'exotic' conveys this and also adds the note of mystery which is working on the Princess's imagination.[11] A little further on she recalls how in contrast to her boredom at the tedious life in Belgrade she 'yearned to bask now under the blue Oriental sky' (p. 131). The original refers to the sky by the more mundane 'eastern', but the translator's choice again reinforces that mixture of fascination underlined by the exotic Orient.[12] That being said, the translator is less concerned at Crnjanski's insistence that the Princess's desire for Vuk is a product entirely of her feverish imagination. The garrison at Belgrade is to prepare for an attack against the Turks, and the Princess is to leave for Temisvar. She thinks that she will never see the young Serbian officer again and in desperation at the thought she bursts into his room and presses herself against him. Her clothes are thin and through them she can feel 'his body trembling' (p. 133). Vuk is surprised by her entrance but there is no indication of what he is feeling. His trembling body, described from the Princess's point of view, appears to be a sexual response to her own aroused passions. However, it may be the result of fear or anger. The reader is not told. Crnjanski closes this scene by slowly building up through a series of sentences a number of details which focus on the growing sense of great emotions welling up inside the Princess which are so strong that she begins to feel dizzy. She then swoons and falls to the ground. However, the translator omits these details and chooses to summarize this closing scene in the following way: 'But just as she was about to turn and face him, she gasped for breath and slipped into a dead faint' (p. 133). This description compresses the original and by omission does not emphasize that the development of the erotic motif on the basis of the theme of primitivism is entirely the product of the Princess.[13]

Vuk Isakovič has fought all his career in the service of the Hapsburg Empire. It has been his desire all the time to liberate Serbia and lead his people home. Therefore, his service in the frontier regiments fighting the Turks, including a tour of duty in Belgrade itself, has given sense and purpose to his life. However, this war against the French in the West has no meaning for him and his men. They do not know where they are going, why this war began and what are the Austrian objectives. Furthermore, Vuk is due for promotion and he is put under great pressure by his superiors to convert from Orthodoxy to Catholicism. He takes his men as instructed but has no enthusiasm and sinks into a melancholic mood. His melancholy leads him into an introspective struggle to save himself and his nation from the stronger forces which determine the fate of history. Everything around, all things intimate and public, is empty and vacuous. Life makes no sense. Migrating once to find refuge, the Serbs are facing a similar situation and the only answer is yet another migration which will take them further away from home. But Vuk's Russia is an expression of the ideal of purpose in human existence where there is absolute freedom to be his own self.

Vuk's melancholy and utopian dream of moving away to Russia, to find 'a tranquil life, serenity' (p. 181), provides the only escape from the negative images produced by others. He is closed off from dialogue, his culture is not revealed. His psychological and emotional state is a reflection of a deep exile from the world, not a migration towards a better life. Vuk is separated from the meaning and significance of his own experience and is therefore unable to communicate it. His voice is marked in the text as different from others. The speech of foreign characters is given in modern Serbo-Croat, whereas Vuk's speech is represented in the archaic forms of the eighteenth-century liturgical language of the Serbian Orthodox Church. This intoned and sonorous language adds a metaphysical depth to Vuk's presence in the structure of the work. It also ties Crnjanski's work to that of other writers writing from the position of a marginalized group or a small culture. In her study, *Comparative Literature*, Susan Bassnett comments on the issue of exile for writers from small cultures in the following way: 'The theme of exile, of belonging and non-belonging, is a common link between writers from post-colonial cultures. Equally, the problematics of language and national identity offers another fundamental point of unity.'[14] The Vojvodina community of Serbs are facing the challenge of the future from a position of absolute weakness. They live in exile on a borderland squeezed between the Turks and the Austrians both of whom offer the threat of annihilation. The mud through which Vuk and his men have to drag themselves and their boat as they begin their journey to the West symbolizes their torments.

IVO ANDRIĆ: THE SILENCE OF THE EAST

Ivo Andrić was born into a Roman Catholic family in Dolac, close to the Bosnian town of Travnik in 1892, but was brought up by an aunt in Višegrad on the River Drina. He went to secondary school in Sarajevo where he became involved in the Young Bosnia movement. The movement was dedicated to the overthrow of Austrian rule in Bosnia. The Hapsburgs had held administrative control of the territory since 1878 but it was not formally included in the Empire. However, this situation changed with the formal annexation of Bosnia in 1908, a situation which gave great impetus to anti-Austrian feelings. The fact that the Kingdom of Serbia was an independent South Slav state, and their neighbour, acted as a unifying force amongst the South Slavs in Bosnia and Croatia seeking their own liberation; many of them, including members of Young Bosnia, were looking forward to their unification with Serbia into a single state. Serbia represented the best possibility for freedom from foreign rule. Gavrilo Princip and the other members of the group which planned and executed the assassination of the Archduke Franz Ferdinand on 28 June 1914, in Sarajevo, were all closely associated with Young Bosnia. The authorities acted swiftly following the assassination and rounded up everyone known to be associated with the organization, including Andrić, who was interned for most of the war years. He had even by this time achieved a limited literary reputation and some of his early poems were included in a 1914 anthology called *Mlada hrvatska lirika* (*The Young Croatian Lyric*).

After the war Andrić went first to Zagreb where he was a member of the editorial board of a pro-Yugoslav literary journal called

Književni jug (*The Literary South*). It was here in 1918 that he first became acquainted with Miloš Crnjanski. He published two short books of highly expressionistic prose, almost poetry in prose form, but then turned his talents in a different direction. He published his first Bosnian short story called 'Put Alije Djerzeleza' ('The Journey of Ali Djerzelez') in 1920. It was the first of many stories and novels to be set in Bosnia in which Andrić portrays the lives of Bosnia's Moslems, Serbs, Croats, Jews, and their interactions with the Turkish and Austrian powers who dominated their lives in different historical periods. His prose style bears little relationship to the experimental flurries of many of his contemporaries in the Modernist generation of the 1920s. His narratives are based on mimetic representations about his Bosnia, its landscapes and people. The highly mixed population of the region which float through his works sometimes give the impression of the whole world in microcosm. He was not under any illusions about the dangerous nature of this concentrated combination of nations and faiths living together, once writing in a short story that 'Bosnia is a country of hatred and fear'.[15] In 1920 he joined the Royal Yugoslav Diplomatic Service. It was a career choice which brought him to live in the Yugoslav capital Belgrade.

Prior to his arrival in Belgrade, Andrić used the variant of Serbo-Croat as spoken in Bosnia and Croatia. Nowadays the speech patterns of Serbia, Croatia and Bosnia are often referred to as separate languages; Serbian, Croatian and Bosnian. The syntax of all three are more or less the same, all forms for verbs, adjectives and nouns are also the same. There are some local variations which tend to reflect historical and geographic ties such that many Italian words are used in Dalmatia or Turkish words in Bosnia. There are some differences in everyday vocabulary between standard Serbian and standard Croatian, with a mixture of these differences found scattered throughout Bosnia. From the beginning of their independence in 1992 Croatia has followed an official policy of increasing this lexical variation between the two forms of speech by sponsoring new words based on Slavonic roots and avoiding international words which are also used in Serbia. One of the main distinctions is the development of a vowel sound which has produced the pronunciation and spelling of 'e' in Serbia and 'ije' or 'je' in Bosnia and Croatia; for example, the word for milk is either *mleko* or *mlijeko* depending on geographic location. It is rather like taking the standard differences in vowel pronunciation between the dialects of northern and southern England and then representing those differences in spelling. Serbo-Croat has always allowed speakers to use the spelling appropriate to local pronunciation. However, the name of the national language in small cultures particularly is an important asset and badge of distinction.

The fact that Andrić switched variants of language and that he moved to Belgrade means that his work has been associated almost exclusively with Serbian literature. Although, for writers of former Yugoslavia he is unusually associated with other places too; with Bosnia of his birth and which provides the subject matter for most of his work, and with Croatia as he was born into a Catholic family and found some early success in Zagreb. Unfortunately, his strong ties with Serbian culture have led many Croats and Bosnian Moslems to reject or limit Andrić's association with their literatures. One American academic, of Croatian descent, considers different aspects of his life in largely negative terms but which do not sit well together: 'In Andrić we have a veteran of the nationalist and mythopoeic Bosnian youth – the movement that cast forth the Sarajevo assassins – a Yugoslav integralist of profoundly authoritarian bent, a prewar diplomat, and an associate of right-wing cultural journals, who missed the Chetnik train by a very small margin.'[16] Chetniks were a Serb nationalist organization not noted for being pro-Yugoslav. Although often abroad as a diplomat Andrić continued to publish in Belgrade, including some short stories in Crnjanski's journal. These stories were his only contribution to any right-wing journal. He did not take part in the polemical life which Crnjanski enjoyed so much. Very little, in fact, is known of his personal views about literature or politics.

Andrić rose in the Diplomatic Service and was Yugoslavia's Minister to Germany when war broke out in 1941. He was returned to Belgrade where he lived out the war years in a withdrawn privacy writing his novels. When peace came in 1945 he immediately published three novels; *Na Drini ćuprija* (*The Bridge over the Drina*), *Travnička hronika* (*The Days of the Consuls*) and *Gospođica* (*The Lady from Sarajevo*). They were an immediate success. The new Communist authorities were intent on promoting the style of Socialist Realism but Andrić's novels have nothing in common with those ideas. Socialist Realism understands literature as an extension of politics with the function of presenting a positive image of what socialist man can achieve and produce. They are abject worlds of superficial happiness with stereotypical characterization. Andrić's

Bosnia is often a dark world expressed through deep and complex narrative structures. He continued to write after 1945, becoming one of post-war Yugoslavia's best known writers internationally, and received the Nobel prize for literature in 1961.

The Days of the Consuls has been described as 'the most political of all Andrić's works'.[17] The action is set in the period 1807–1814 during the Napoleonic Wars when the French established a foothold in the Balkans. Having captured the Dalmatian coast Napoleon united it with Slovenia to form the Illyrian Provinces. This nominally independent state disappeared with Napoleon's defeat when the territory was transferred to the Hapsburgs. An important part of the French Emperor's strategy was to maintain friendly relations with the Ottoman Empire. France had been a traditional friend to the Turks and this friendship became a useful tool for Napoleon in his disputes with Russia since the Turks were in frequent territorial dispute with the Russians in the Black Sea area. In order to help smooth relations with the Porte and to assist in the organization of the French presence in the Balkans, Napoleon sent a Consul to Bosnia, to the seat of the local Pasha in the town of Travnik. His Consul was the diplomat Jean Daville. He was joined by his family and continued to live and work there until Napoleon's defeat. He had an assistant called Des Fossés who was a man younger than Daville. In addition there were the Pashas who governed Bosnia and their entourages. Since Napoleon opened a Consulate the Austrians decided they must send a Consul to Travnik to keep the central administration informed about French policy there. The Austrian Consul is von Mitterer who is accompanied by his wife and daughter. Then, there are the people of Travnik themselves, the Moslems, Croats, Serbs and Jews who live in the town and its environs. This historical context supplied Andrić with the basic outline for his novel and its main character, Daville. The characters all have their historical counterparts, but here moulded by Andrić into his fictional world.

In Crnjanski's *Migrations* the mixture of points of view was important to the presentation of the foreign image of the Balkans and the power of that image. In *The Days of the Consuls* almost the whole story is told from the point of view of Jean Daville. Andrić employs free indirect discourse whereby the reader is often given a general comment which appears to come from an authorial perspective, usually a disparaging remark about the East or Bosnia, only to discover then that the remark is part of Daville's emotional and intellectual world. It is not immediately apparent from the language and grammar of the text that they are Daville's thoughts, but the structure of the text reveals that what is written is entirely from his point of view. He rarely differentiates between the use of such terms as Bosnia, the East or the Orient. For him, they all summarize the poison of this alien place in which he finds himself. Interestingly, he quite likes the first two Pashas whom he comes to know in Travnik although these are men of the East. They are rather like him in that they regard Bosnia and Travnik as an uncivilized hole but they have no choice in serving their political masters. In this way, Andrić builds up another side of the complexity of the exchange between East and West. Daville reacts most positively to the traditions of French literature beginning with seventeenth-century Classicism. The first Vizier whom Daville gets to know in Travnik is Mehmed Pasha. When he shows an interest in knowing more about the French theatre, the Consul is 'delighted'. He reads a few scenes to him from Racine's *Bajazet*. Unfortunately, Mehmed's reaction is completely unexpected. Ottoman culture has no tradition which corresponds to the conventions of French theatre and he finds the whole idea preposterous. The scenes described by Racine with conversations between the Grand Vizier and the Sultanas in the Harem 'just couldn't happen'. Like 'someone from a different civilization' the Vizier could not understand what Daville tries to explain to him about 'the meaning of tragedy and the aim of poetry'.[18] He is not able to disassociate the naturalism of the literal reading from the greater truth embodied in the lines. This transcendental truth for Daville is only achievable in poetry. He is unable to appreciate the possibility of other sources in other cultural traditions.

In *The Days of the Consuls* the voice of Daville's young assistant is often present. Des Fossés is of a very different temperament from the older Consul, being much more self-confident. However, there are similarities between them when it comes to representing Bosnia and the Bosnians in colonial discourse. On one occasion, Des Fossés finds himself very attracted to a local girl working at the Consulate. One day he makes advances to her but completely misunderstands her reactions. When he thinks, 'Here she was on him, all around him, faint with love, with the ecstasy love promises', she was fainting from fear and fell to her knees before him begging him to spare her (p. 166). He writes his final comment on this episode in his journal by noting: 'The women are usually shapely; many of them catch the eye with the fine, regular features of their faces, the beauty of their bodies and the dazzling whiteness of their skin' (p. 168). Des Fossés begins by sexualizing the exotic vulnerability of a young girl and then disperses the lack of promised fulfilment into his bland journal entry.

Andrić gives a special emphasis to language and matters of communication between the representatives of the different communities. Daville constantly requires an interpreter to mediate for him. His interpreter is a Levantine called d'Avenat who sits unobtrusively at each audience Daville has with the Pasha, all words and all sense between the two cultures being mediated by him, a third outside party. Although d'Avenat's presence is very real otherwise there would be no communication, it also functions metaphorically within the meaning of the text about the problems of communication. Des Fossés, for example, is sent to the Consulate for his abilities to communicate in Ottoman Turkish, not for any ability to communicate with the local population. He has more contact with the Bosnians and visits the bazaar noting down his impressions of scenes and learning a few words of the local 'Illyrian' language. He does this from a position of superiority with no effort to enter their world. He forms a friendship with a local monk called Brother Julian whom he met on his first arrival in the country as they happened to be staying at the same inn on their journey to Travnik. Andrić remarks how when they meet as neither knows the language of the other they have to resort to their rather poor knowledge of Italian in order to speak to one another. These issues do not entirely prevent communication but they point to its difficulty and to the problem of mediation in these borderlands of Europe where different cultural worlds meet.

Daville's faith in the superiority of French imperialism over Bosnia and the world of the Ottoman Empire is unbreakable. This faith derives from his conviction concerning the position of French culture in Europe. He thinks about France 'as the kind of wonderful, distant land of harmony and perfection one always dreamed about in rough, wild surroundings' (p. 130). His idea of France, like Vuk Isakovič's of Russia in Crnjanski's *Migrations*, is not a geographic entity. Rather, it is the epitome of all that is civilized in the world, a synonym for Europe itself. To justify his colonial discourse he gives a special place to the written word, literature and the achievements of the Enlightenment. The written word functions as a form of compensation for Daville. It has a power strong enough to control his emotions and passions. He often holds long conversations with his assistant after which he is usually left feeling inadequate. Fundamentally unsure of himself, he is unable to engage in debate with the same ease and confidence as the logically minded Des Fossés. Following one such conversation Daville returns to his study. He is unable to sleep or to think straight. Taking a sheet of paper he continues his argument with Des Fossés having found new reserves of self-confidence: 'the Consul wrote swiftly and without pausing on the white paper' (p. 112). The object of their dispute concerns the singing of the Bosnians, in particular one of the town drunks, Musa. He writes a response to Des Fossés who, according to Daville, 'even found that dreadful singing of theirs interesting'. The French Consul finds the sounds they make worse than that of whining dogs and their displays of emotion while singing exaggerated. He concludes with an image that once again combines primitivism with loss of innocence when he writes that their singing 'is, quite simply, the fury of savages who have lost their simplicity' (p. 113). He draws attention to Bosnia as a land of oral culture, which is a very pertinent sign to Daville of its primitive Otherness. And after he finishes his written, silent argument with Des Fossés, 'the Consul felt something like relief' (p. 113). It is as if he overcomes his inner feelings of inadequacy in the loops and traces of his handwriting and in the rhetoric of his own language. Writing itself represents the superiority of French culture. Daville's colonial discourse gives priority to literary cultural forms in the French style, but in his own writing he reduces his thoughts and feelings to the expression of fine words and similes.

For Daville, Travnik has no real existence. The town has for all purposes three points which are connected; they are the French Consulate, the Austrian Consulate and the Pasha's residence. Everything else has no substance and does not enter Daville's understanding. Des Fossés tries to understand sometimes, but fails to enter into any real dialogue which would show a willingness to open his eyes to the problems as they appear to the inhabitants of the region. The symbol of roads becomes very important to him in this respect. The Bosnians destroy roads on the principle that they only ever bring trouble, at best tax collectors and at worst an invading army set to conquer them. Des Fossés cannot see the sense in what the Bosnians do. For him roads represent a fascinating opportunity which will later be overtaken by railways in the nineteenth century and by air travel in the twentieth century. They represent the movement of state and trade, of expansion and power, connecting communities into a single web of communication. One day he notices that rain has washed away the side of one of the roads near Travnik to reveal sedimentary layers of history in its foundations. It is possible to discern the remains of the same road left behind by different civilizations from Roman times to the present Ottoman surface. There is nothing to show a Bosnian presence. As Daville is unable to make out an internal geography for Travnik amongst the local population, so Des Fossés cannot see their history.

The young Consul talks about his impressions of Bosnian society with Brother Julian. They converse together easily but from completely different points of view. Brother Julian notices that Des Fossés has not wasted his time in Travnik, but also that the Frenchman has no chance of understanding the realities of life and history as lived by the Bosnians. Exasperated by the divisions between the four internal communities which he identifies as indigenous to Bosnia, Catholic, Orthodox, Moslem and Jewish, Daville's assistant cannot comprehend their hostility towards each other. The monk tries to point out the simple fact that they have lived under threat of extinction for a long time, the subject peoples of alien forces, the colonized population who have no rights on their own territory. This is the reason for their mistrust of outsiders, for their extreme disapproval of the presence of the European Consuls. However, Des Fossés is determined that this is not enough, stating:

> 'How is it possible,' asked Des Fossés, 'for this country to become stable and orderly and adopt at least as great a degree of civilization as its closest neighbours, if its people are divided as nowhere else in Europe? Four faiths live in this narrow, mountainous and meagre strip of land. Each of them is exclusive and strictly separate from the others. You all live under one sky and from the same soil, but the centre of the spiritual life of each of these four groups is far away, in a foreign land, in Rome, Moscow, Istanbul, Mecca, Jerusalem and God alone knows where, but at any rate not here where the people are born and die. And each group considers that its well-being is conditioned by the disadvantage of each of the other three faiths, and that they can make progress only at their cost. Each of them has made intolerance the greatest virtue. And each one of them is expecting salvation from somewhere outside, each from the opposite direction.' (p. 217)

Des Fossés' analysis of the problems rings all too familiar following on the events and the consequences of the conflict in Bosnia in the first half of the 1990s. However, his views are those from outside, of the foreigner, who is now dictating to Brother Julian the issues which confront the Bosnians. He speaks with little understanding of the reasons why this situation has developed in this way, with no comprehension of the complexity of relationships between the four faiths within Bosnia and of the similar complexity of their relationships with foreign powers. Violence erupts because of internal fears and suspicions fuelled by outside manipulation. Elsewhere, Des Fossés focuses on what he describes as 'this deathly Bosnian silence' with which he has been in conflict (p. 114). The land is bare and taciturn holding no meaningful communication for him.

Daville expresses a similar complaint about Travnik, that it is silent to him. Turkish architecture of the streets dictate that the outside walls of the houses are blank, with no windows. All windows look inside onto a courtyard. The houses are intensely private places, unlike the salon society of Paris. He cannot understand, or read, the events which are happening around him and views them as completely alien from his own experience. He witnesses two riots which began in the bazaar during his stay in Travnik. The first riot occurs when Vizier Mehmed Pasha is recalled to Istanbul. Respectable citizens shut themselves indoors while the mob turns against the French Consulate. They attack the Consulate because it was known that Daville was friendly with the Pasha and that he accompanied him outside town as he left. They feel the threat of the presence of all foreigners and with the Pasha gone authority has also temporarily disappeared. These events are looked upon as violent and savage by Daville with nothing to explain how they unfold in the way they do. The second riot is much more bloody and begins with an impromptu execution of two gypsies in the bazaar where they are strangled to death by a crowd tugging at the ropes round their necks. An execution block is even set up outside the Austrian Consulate and Daville writes a note to his rival in a spirit of civilized solidarity against these barbarisms. However, these events remain an incomprehensible mystery to Daville.

The eighteenth century in France witnessed not only the rise of art, philosophy and the corresponding discourses in which they are expressed, but also the voices of the French Revolution. As a child Daville recalls cheering the King, but just ten years later he was working as a journalist and reporting on the deliberations of the Constitutional Assembly. The Revolution answers his general liberal politics and forms for him a smooth succession to the King, although to an outsider it might not appear to be part of a seamless flow of history. However, even for Daville events soon take on the appearance of a more frightening and bloody reality. He recalls the following scene from the period of the Terror: 'One morning, woken by a crowd shouting, he got up and opened his window wide. Suddenly, he found himself face to face with a severed head, swaying, pale and bloody, on the pike of a sansculottes' (p. 49). In June of 1792 he signs a petition alongside thousands of others expressing sympathy for the King and his family after the first attack on the palace. The purge which followed against enemies of the Revolution forced him to volunteer to fight in Spain as a way out of the difficulty. Exonerating himself, he returns to Paris and with the help of a patron is accepted into the service of the Empire. Of course, written forms of language are manipulated towards his self-deception. He writes flattering verses about Napoleon and his battles in order to maintain favour with the regime. All of these events make sense to Daville's mind having taken place in a geographical and historical context which he recognises. But he can make no link between the 'nature of Turkish terror' (p. 176) and that of the French Revolution.

The Other of the East, of Bosnia, confronts Daville and ought to open his eyes to the deficiencies of his own culture in the sense of Bakhtin's view on international dialogue. But it does not. His voice cannot penetrate and achieve true links with the representatives of the East. His colonial discourse, firmly legitimized, cuts him off from Travnik. His body floats on the surface of the historical conditions surrounding him without any depth. Not able to interrogate properly his surroundings in Travnik, he conceives the town as existing in a void with just three points of significance. The rest of the town has no substance, it is completely silent. Daville is unable to hear Travnik society. As such, he is unable to question properly his own culture. He is as cut off from the reality of France and French culture as from that of Travnik.

SLOBODAN SELENIĆ: CULTURAL DIFFERENCE INSIDE AND OUTSIDE

Slobodan Selenić was born in 1933 in Pakrac, Croatia, and grew up in Belgrade. He spent some time as a postgraduate student at the University of Bristol before returning to Belgrade and following an academic career teaching drama. He published numerous studies in the field of drama but will be remembered better for his work in literature. As an intellectual and public figure in Belgrade during the early 1990s he was involved in the turbulent political life of Serbia. He was a member of the steering committee of one of the first coalition groups to oppose the government of the ruling Socialist Party, the Democratic Movement of Serbia. He died in 1995.

His literary career began with the publication of his first novel *Memoari Pere Bogalja* (*The Memoirs of Pera the Cripple*, 1968). There followed a period of silence in which Selenić continued to write but not to publish. The thematic focus of his work would not allow publication. The author's treatment of the recent past did not correspond to the official Communist version of events. These novels appeared in the 1980s beginning with *Prijatelji sa Kosančićevog venca 7* (*The Friends from Kosančićev venac 7*, 1980), after which Selenić wrote a stage scenario based on the same work. The story is about the relationship between a sophisticated citizen of Belgrade, Vladan Hadžislavković, and an Albanian peasant newcomer to the city, Istref Veri. His next novel, actually completed in 1972 but not published until 1982, was called *Pismo/Glava* (*Heads or Tails*). It is set in 1948 and the action concerns the historical events surrounding Yugoslavia's expulsion from the international Communist movement and problems facing those who supported the Soviet Union and those who supported the Yugoslav Communists' independent line. In 1985 *Očevi i oci* (*Fathers and Forefathers*) appeared about the marriage of Stevan Medaković and his English wife Elizabeth. In addition to novels Selenić also wrote the plays *Ruženje naroda u dva dela* (*Spiting the People in Two Parts*, 1987) and *Knez Pavle* (*Prince Paul*, 1990). The first concerns events just after the Second World War and is set in a camp for political prisoners, while the latter tells of the last moments of the royal government on the eve of war in 1941. His novel *Timor mortis* (1989) also draws on historical and political themes involving Serb-Croat relations and the German occupation of Belgrade. His final work is the novel *Ubistvo s predumišljajem* (*Premeditated Murder*, 1993). This is a contemporary story about a young couple researching into events which happened in the girl's family at the end of 1944 while the events of another conflict are unfolding around them. His work is generally known for its thematic preoccupations with Serbian history, the city of Belgrade, past and present, the dramatic changes in city life with the arrival of the Partisans in Belgrade in 1944, and the clashes produced when different cultures meet.

What concerns us here is Selenić's interest in the meeting of different cultures, particularly when the Balkan and non-Balkan worlds clash. In *The Friends* the author combines a series of related issues. Most of the book is presented as if written by the character Vladan Hadžislavković as a manuscript to his friend Istref Veri. In fact, the manuscript is handed over in 1975 about 30 years after the time when the two men last met. It is Vladan's attempt to explain his perspective on their relationship and, in order to give the full side of his story, he includes in his manuscript the story of his family and their house. Vladan's family played an important role in Serbian history, became respected citizens of Belgrade, and ultimately adopted all the Western habits with which the city came into contact. He himself was educated at Cambridge where he specialized in the English Civil War. He is sophisticated and cosmopolitan in his outlook. To a foreigner he does not belong to the traditional images of the Balkans. In 1945, after the Partisans arrive in Belgrade, he befriends the Albanian Istref Veri. Istref is from the south and the last surviving member of his family. All the others have been killed as a result of a blood feud between his family and a neighbour. He has been brought to Belgrade by a close friend in order to save his life. He represents the image of the traditional Balkans. Vladan takes him into his house, instructs him in city ways, encourages him in his education and generally acts as his tutor. The story is the old story of two cultures meeting, but turned on its head; it is all taking place in the Balkans although Vladan and Istref are like foreigners to one another.

Vladan's history of his family is the beginning of a narrative about the problems of growth and development in Balkan history. It is difficult to know even what happened in the past. As a historian familiar with English history of the seventeenth century he draws comparisons between source material available with details about that century and what is available to those who are curious about the Serbian past. He enumerates how everything about life in England at that time is documented whether talking about small details of family life or the number of dead and wounded at battles in the Civil War. But of Serbian history he says that it is 'like a big hole in which complete darkness prevails'.[19] Serbia, like most of the Balkans, was under Ottoman occupation for many centuries, the only literate activity being the copying and re-copying of church manuscripts while the great majority of the population were illiterate peasants, excluded from public life. It was not until 1804 with the First Serbian Uprising that the process toward independence began. Most of the nineteenth century is taken up by a slow increase in the extent of liberated territory and the gradual expansion of sovereignty. Belgrade, for example, did not rid itself of its Turkish garrison and the presence of an Ottoman Pasha until 1867. Vladan gains most of his information from his Uncle Njegovan whom he describes as 'the real family storyteller' (p. 40). What follows is the result of a kind of oral culture. In such circumstances, Vladan in 1945 is not so very distant from that more traditional image of the Balkans.

He is particularly interested in telling Istref about the history of his family house where they were to spend a short time together. The house was begun by his ancestor Milić who intended to build a house in the style of a Turkish beg, but who changed his mind after seeing a house built in the European style. This beginning is important as the house itself lies somewhere between the Turkish Balkans and the West. It was built on the edge of the Ottoman city, on the border between the town and the countryside outside. It was intended to be one thing but grew into something else. It is a house which symbolizes the meeting point of different cultures. The house was the centre of dispute between Milić's two sons, Jovan and Mihajlo, who alternately decorated it in European and Turkish fashions. It eventually ended in the hands of their nephew Dimitrije who had a son, Miodrag, who was Vladan's father. Dimitrije went to Novi Sad in order to find a wife for his son. Novi Sad, situated in the Hapsburg Empire at that time, represented for Vladan's grandfather the most advanced and civilized Serbian city. He married his son to Valinka but the marriage was a failure. Vladan's father was a wastrel and drunkard whom his mother eventually excluded from the house which, with Dimitrije's consent, became her property. The house thus has a bastard history, not passing down in a straight line from father to son. In 1944, with the arrival of the Communists, half of it is requisitioned by the city authorities. Vladan lives in one half, to which he invites Istref, while the remainder is taken over by people who have just arrived from outside Belgrade in the chaos of the Second World War.

These enforced neighbours from the country represent for Vladan the Other, an alien world. He thinks of them in the same demeaning terms which characterize the negative traits of the Balkan myth.

They are peasants whose arrival in the city threatens his world with extinction. He thinks of the Communist authorities in the same way. They are not of Belgrade but an invading force. However, his attitude toward Istref is completely different although in cultural terms the young Albanian is not so different from those people with whom Vladan is forced to share his house. Vladan's attraction to Istref is initially homoerotic from his side, although this sexual attraction is never realized physically. Gradually Istref draws away from Vladan who becomes obsessive toward him. The Albanian falls in love with Mara, one of the other occupants of the house, which infuriates his host. In order to try and keep his attentions Vladan persuades Istref to help him translate into Serbian some Albanian folk songs and even dresses in an Albanian fashion. In other words, Vladan seems slowly to be reverting to the typical Balkan peasant from which his family evolved. It is as if the modern Balkans cannot avoid its origins, that in time of crisis, such as war, the past will inevitably return. This is Vladan's narrative and what he has to explain to Istref after all those years.

Istref, from a different perspective, experiences his arrival in Belgrade as if he is entering a different world. He recognizes the division of Belgrade into two kingdoms; one exists for him and his Albanian friends and the other for the majority of the Serbian population. When passing from one world into another: 'He always stepped over the border which separated them with full awareness of what he was doing' (p. 27). Vladan crosses the border without knowing what he is doing. His story culminates with the event which led him to quit the house and from which time he and Istref have not met. In the end, after what Vladan considers to be many provocations, his neighbours from the country build a pig-sty in the court-yard and bring in two pigs. This is the final straw for the Cambridge-educated city dweller. In a fit of rage he takes a sword which has been in the family for generations, and one night goes out and with it and slaughters the pigs. He has become that which he despises, losing all reason he behaves like a maniac, out of control, devoid of all civilized values. As Hayden White puts it, Vladan has become 'what Western man might have been at one time and what he might become once more'.[20] To make it all the more ironic, Istref, when reading Vladan's manuscript in 1975, has not only made a career for himself as an engineer, married Mara, brought up children of whom the older ones are themselves married, but he has also been elected to Parliament. Vladan and his family, who were once the cream of Serbian society, have sunk into obscurity and will die out, he having no children. But Istref will survive. The traditional image of the Balkans has prevailed, adopted all the virtues which previous generations had learnt and appropriated a new way of life. But the danger of return, especially in a culture which is itself, like Vladan, both repelled and attracted by what it had been at one time, is ever present.

In *Fathers and Forefathers* the author expands his Belgrade theme into an examination of the meaning and value of Serbian culture. Stevan Medaković is a postgraduate student at the University of Bristol in England during the mid-1920s. Here he meets and marries Elizabeth. He takes her back to Belgrade, where they set up house. His father is a wealthy businessman whose wife died, and Stevan was brought up by Nanka, whose outlook and way of life are very traditionally Serbian. He follows a successful career as an university professor, playing chamber music with friends, and introduces Elizabeth to Belgrade's intellectual, middle-class society of which he is a part. Being one of the small and select number making up Belgrade's intellectual life, he is also closely involved in the capital's political life of the 1930s, including even invitations to court. They spend the war years in Belgrade, where their son becomes involved with the Communists, much to his parents' regret. Their house is often used by him and his friends for meetings, preparing placards for pro-Communist demonstrations after the arrival of the Partisans, and they come into conflict with the simplistic culture which these young people represent. For Selenić, the end of the war and arrival of the Communists is always linked to the destruction of Belgrade's municipal structure, urban culture, and the beginning of a new Dark Age. After the war, half of their house is requisitioned and Stevan, as a highly educated legal specialist is forced to work for the new authorities in drawing up the new constitution. The novel opens with him lying in bed, some 20 years after the war, reflecting on his life with Elizabeth up to the point when their son, Mihajlo, is killed at the front.

Selenić, like the other writers discussed in this chapter, incorporates the theme of language and identity into the textual structure of his novel. We learn at the beginning that Stevan's problems with English and English customs contribute to his feelings of alienation. He recalls how his friends used to mimic his pronunciation at Bristol University, pronouncing '"th" with a Slavonic hardness' or repeated his attempts at idiomatic English at which he just fails in such phrases as 'it struck my mind' instead of saying 'it struck me'.[21] These phrases, like some others, are given in English in the body of the text with a Serbian translation appended in a footnote. As with other novels, the use of language is linked to behavioural patterns. He recalls how one student in particular, Lesley Hayes, made his life miserable: 'He, I must admit, captured so well my way of speaking, how I twirled my moustache when I stopped half-way through a sentence searching for the right word (I didn't even know that I did that until I saw Lesley doing it), how I would tug the legs of my immaculately pressed trousers when I sat down, and held my cane and gloves' (p. 13). Stevan's use of English expresses his sense of alienation and his desire to be accepted by the dominant culture. Later, when he is married to Elizabeth and they are living in Belgrade, English continues to function in a similar way. Not long after the birth of their son Mihajlo, Stevan catches sight of Elizabeth holding their baby and feels excluded from the world of mother and son. Husband and wife are beginning to grow apart, and Stevan recalls thereafter the nursery rhyme Elizabeth sings to Mihajlo word for word in English, although he has not heard it since that day (pp. 190–1).

The inclusion of English in the novel comes to represent more than a linguistic relationship between the structure of the text and the narrator's personality. He recalls words and phrases which represent a cultural Otherness, a place where he exists only on the margins since those values are in conflict with his sense of national identity. The alien language is not only symbolic of alien values but is equated with them. So, in a memory of a conversation about homosexuality, he recalls John Downing's revelation in his own words in English when he said, 'I am irredeemably homosexual' (p. 36, p. 72). The use of English by Stevan provides a textual contrast with his experiences from growing up in Serbia. It functions as a distancing device which isolates the two worlds one from the other and is thus transformed into a more extreme connotation which we may define as 'all that which is not Serbian'. In this way, his feelings of national identity are derived to some degree by a negative association with the English language.

Some lengthy passages are given in English, and some of these are taken from Rebecca West's book *Black Lamb and Grey Falcon*. For example, on one occasion West recalls a scene in a hotel room in Vienna where her husband finds her crying. She explains that she bought some dresses in Macedonia, and the hotel maid persuaded her that they would have to be disinfected. The dresses are ruined in this process and West remarks in a highly sentimental fashion that there is a vast amount of hidden natural talent amongst the peoples of the Balkans and a simplistic happiness dominates there which has been lost in other parts of Europe.[22] Her attitude remarkably reflects the Romantic inspired attitude of Sir Walter Scott's 'civilized Europe' to the Balkan cultural space.[23] However, her husband is not convinced. In Selenić's novel, their conversation is faithfully transcribed, except that Stevan and Elizabeth take on the role of the sceptical husband. The woman whom they meet in Vienna is not named, but by themselves taking on the role of sceptic, by maintaining the whole conversation in English, the passage takes on a completely different meaning in its new context. The English-woman appears simply naive. The contrast between her experience and reality is exposed. The problem for Stevan is that he is caught between two worlds: on one side England and the West, on the other side Serbia and the Balkans.

The elaboration of this theme in *Fathers and Forefathers* is linked to the migration complex and theme of exile in Crnjanski, in that this is a world which is conscious of itself having no centre, and of existing on the imaginary periphery of another dominant culture. In this instance the fictional space evokes a semiotic geography of two worlds which are poles apart. England, for Stevan Medaković, is the home of rational thought. It is cultured, sophisticated and secure in its habits and traditions which it can call its own, such as drinking tea 'at four o'clock' (p. 54). When asked by some friends to tell them something about his country so that they will be better able to understand it, Stevan at first feels awkward, until he senses the feeling of inferiority drop from his shoulders and he tells them about the hanging he witnessed in the centre of town on 4 December 1914, and the occasion when his sister was hit by a shell from an Austrian artillery piece in front of his eyes. He also tells them of the peasant he and his father met one day who warmed his bare feet by standing in fresh dung. He is carried away by the different rhythm in which history has unfolded in the Balkans. These are examples which occur to him as being the most likely to produce a sense of difference, although they only instil a protest at their extremity. He identifies with his country in a way which Elizabeth cannot understand. He remarks how he looks at the world of Belgrade and feels responsibility for the state of the people and the nation, and then he feels compelled to put on Elizabeth's English glasses with their different lenses. His world then looks a very different place: 'I have grown used to reading, seeing, being silent, defending, attacking, loving, always under the supervision of that heavenly corrector of my eyesight' (p. 149). Again, Bakhtin's ideal dialogue of cultures is not realized. Rather, the subject of the small culture is forced to an internal dialogue with himself, unable to escape his place between cultures.

Elizabeth also represents a heightened awareness of the use of language between major and minor cultures. Most of the novel is narrated in alternate chapters by Stevan and her. Stevan's chapters are his recollections while waiting in bed for breakfast one morning. Elizabeth's chapters are composed of her letters to her cousin's wife, Rachel. Rachel is, in fact, a Jewess from Belgrade, and she writes to her about all her experiences in the city, writing in Serbian in order to practise the language as much as possible. Against all literary conventions, her letters home are written in poor Serbian, as if by a foreigner just learning the language. To give an example of how this might sound, here is a section from the first letter:

> So, Rachel, I promise I write to you in Serbian language about everything though I know so awful bad. And true, this I do, from the first Beograd days I write. Every day a little, and I think always that I write to you and I send to you, but then do not send. Now, you see, at once all of it I send from arriving in Beograd until today.[24]

It has to be remembered that in the novel these sentences are written in Serbo-Croat and the quotation above is the translator's way of putting across the effect of this approach in English. It is more common in all literatures to follow the convention that foreigners are always represented as if they speak the language of the text quite naturally. However, for a small culture the issue of language and the problem of communication is a lived experience. Elizabeth's improvement in her Serbian comes about because of an important development in the narrative. She and Stevan relate to their son differently. This divergence is seen when they each call him by a different name; Stevan refers to him by the Serbian Mihajlo while Elizabeth uses the English equivalent 'Majkl' spelt phonetically in the text. Elizabeth sees him being brought up as if in England, and Stevan as if in Belgrade. The child's manners are different from others, and eventually he rebels against his mother's Englishness which distinguishes both her and him from the rest of Belgrade. In order not to lose her son, Elizabeth comments, 'I have decided to learn to speak without an accent, without English sounds. I'll take elocution classes. I'll speak like a Serb. I'll be a Serb in order to talk to Michael on equal terms' (p. 235).

The high status of language in Balkan cultures is played out in a sort of linguistic competition between Stevan and Elizabeth. For Stevan language is a vital part of identity. He says, 'Language is not given to man just for him to be able to ask for his slippers or a little more tea. By his language man, each for himself, reveals his soul, immortal with its unique qualities contained in the manner rather than in the subject of speech' (p. 323). Therefore, the national language is central to personal identity, the way of speaking and understanding is contained in the mutual apprehension of codes embedded in the collective psyche. Stevan's essentialist position in relation to language is a consequence of awareness that the language of a small culture is no help in communication outside. All sign systems and particularly language are highly charged in small cultures where the opportunities for signification are also potential opportunities to gain the recognition from abroad which is usually lacking, or to enter into a Bakhtinian great dialogue. Some of Stevan's recollections of the attitudes of distant friends from his days in Bristol reveal contrary thoughts, that life and so language has no sense of urgency. He remembers how one friend comments: 'Life after all . . . is an affair of charm, not an affair of passion' (p. 51). It is also clear that Elizabeth feels none of this urgency; her reasons for learning Serbian in the way that she does are purely personal in relation to their son. The final sentence in the novel returns to Stevan's theme why is language given to man, when Elizabeth asks him, 'Some more tea, Steven?' (p. 361). The question is phrased in the novel in English.

These novels represent different levels of interaction between characters from the Balkans and foreign characters. Crnjanski takes his characters out of their Balkan setting, while Andrić introduces a diplomat into Bosnia at the beginning of the nineteenth century. Selenić in one novel brings together a 'Westernized' Serb and a 'Balkan' Albanian, and in another novel takes an Englishwoman to live in Belgrade. Crnjanski's world is characterized by exile, Andrić's Bosnia by silence and Selenić's Belgrade by the gap between East and West. However, each novel establishes the problem of language and identity in the small cultural milieu, and also in various ways reveals the complexity of the dialogue between dominant and minor cultures. The small environment is in a constant state of anxiety in relation to others. The Other is a feared necessity, since recognition is an essential pre-condition for existence. The small culture is conscious only of its semantic space being created from outside and that the room for interaction is minimal. With no participation in the great dialogue the small culture is in a state of exile, in a space beyond the frontier, beyond communication. The foreign gaze has only a limited horizon of constructions concerning the Balkans which it applies rigorously, excluding the region from an European sense of modernity. Questions of identity in the Balkans, usually considered in the light of their national or regional traits, are inextricably linked to questions of modernity.

In Crnjanski's novel the two brothers symbolize the choice between tradition or the future. The eighteenth century was a critical time for Europe. Life was in expansion on all fronts. The Enlightenment and changes in thinking were a part of rapid wholesale changes in living. The agrarian revolution, the beginnings of the industrial revolution, the French Revolution with its slogan of *liberté et égalité* signalled huge social, economic and political transformations. All these factors passed by the Balkans with hardly any echo except for a few individuals on the northern fringe in Croatia and Vojvodina who travelled abroad and picked up some of the atmosphere. Crnjanski's two brothers embody the choices before those small nations. On the one hand, Vuk represents a traditional vein formed from the myths of heroes and loss, while Arandjel represents a potential future in an urban world of trade and commerce. It is indicative that Daville, the representative of the European way of life in Andrić's novel, cannot see nor hear the town of Travnik. Similarly, Des Fossés cannot contemplate the way in which the Bosnians destroy roads. To him they are the arteries of modern life which connect settlements together and enable the production and exchange of goods. They also enable the circulation of ideas and consequently are part of the process of constant social and cultural transformation which is characteristic of the modern world. All Selenić's novels contain the same theme of cultural differences and the city. Vladan Hadžislavković's house in *The Friends* contains elements of both East and West, Turkey and Europe. It represents the violence of an Asiatic past and the security of an European future, except that in the Balkans the two are involved in a very complex dialogue which is in turn symbolized by the relationship between Vladan and Istref. Such is the complexity of this exchange that there is no security of identity and it is Vladan who slaughters the pigs in the courtyard, reverting to a primitive level, and Istref who by 1975 has been elected to Parliament. In *Fathers and Fore-fathers* we see a Belgrade which has a developed municipal infra-structure, but which nevertheless cannot entirely rid itself of a feeling of anxiety when placed under a foreign gaze. However, that city way of life is destroyed with the arrival of the Communists. As in other novels concerning this period in history the requisitioning of people's homes is symbolic of that destruction. For these reasons, the link between questions of identity and questions of modernity is highly important in the Balkans. Therefore, I want next to examine city development in the region, taking Belgrade as a particular example before looking at themes in city literature and the sense of crisis expressed in narratives about the recent Yugoslav wars.

4 Modernity: Urban Culture and the Balkans

CITY LITERATURE IN THE WEST

Europe's sense of modernity developed during the eighteenth century when the Enlightenment began to shape the new idea of Europe. At the beginning of the century conditions were not so different for the vast majority of Europeans, in that the feudal order had left a legacy in which the largest single group were peasants whose lives were hardly open to economic and social transformation. While the possible life expectations for a peasant living in a small village in rural France at the beginning of the eighteenth century may not have differed very much from their Balkan counterparts, a distinct gap between them was opening up by the end of that century. The West was subject to the influences introduced by the philosophical and intellectual trends of the Enlightenment, by advances in agricultural technology, changes in land tenure and changes to the political order which hardly raised an echo in the far south-east. At the same time, the West witnessed the beginnings of a demographic revolution in the emergence of large urban areas. Urbanization was one of the most significant transformations of European society. The effect was felt and seen not only in social relations and economic organization, but also in the possibilities for imagining new ways of living. Such transfers of populations from village to town did not always happen voluntarily, but were forced by changes in land tenure or the over-population of the rural areas. Urban living conditions were poor, cramped and squalid. However, the effect of this demographic reorganization coupled with advances in technology, changes in the political order and the remodelling of the European mind dominated by Rationalism and then Romanticism was to open up a renewed sense of modernity. The state was converted from a mechanism to control the rigid pattern of duties and obligations which regulated social order into a series of institutions intended to promote the sense of national community. The idea of a community bound together by similarities in historical experience and a shared language was reinforced by these same institutions which demanded allegiance to the same government. The functions of state and determinants of social order were transformed. City spaces grew hugely in the West during the eighteenth century. Increasingly, the countryside was regarded as a hinterland which was to supply the new productive centres with their raw materials. Social life became regulated by systems of exchange which drew the inhabitants of cities into greater inter-dependency; professional associations, mercantile and administrative classes, and the urban labour force. When the balance of power broke down, the authorities were to come across the rule of the mob. It is impossible to imagine the French Revolution unfolding in hidden mountain passes, its tone is of the streets and public demonstrations for change. The city is the space which links together the experience of modern living in Western Europe.

The urban environment has come to dominate modern consciousness in the West. It dominates our idea of space and spatial organization. Even flights of nostalgia for a pastoral idyll in the countryside are products of the urban-organized mind aware of the materials and structures which daily influence the senses. The local urban geography is a space full of energy which enhances changes in systems of ideas and productive processes. As we go through each day the city speaks to us. When discussing the urban environment as a semiotic system, Roland Barthes writes, 'The city is a discourse and this discourse is truly a language.'[1] We have become so adept at communicating with the rapidly changing scenes of everyday existence that our reading habits have become completely automatic and we stop to register the depths of meanings which surround us in the streets. Umberto Eco divides urban architectural spaces in such a way that he moves from 'primary functions (roof, stairway, window)' which are not fully fledged signalling systems since they do not mean so much as they perform a basic function such as facilitate movement within the space or protect it from bad weather. Then, he describes a series of hierarchies with strong connotative functions such as 'ideologies of habitation (common room, dining room, parlour)' and 'functional and sociological types (hospital, villa, school, palace, railway station)'.[2] Eco's differential system shows that the naming of significant types of space has levels of denotation and connotation covering functional and metaphoric language. In short, the spaces of urban architecture fulfil a poetics in the close symbiosis with the consciousness of the populations who not only live in them but through them too. However, a culture which names its living spaces differently, which apportions different values to certain spaces and therefore to different activities, may not be recognized as taking part in the modernity project. So, the naming of space is as significant as the naming of a character in a novel or other piece of narrative fiction. The personal name stands for the aggregate of personality traits which are summarized as forming that character, while the naming of space summarizes many aspects of modern urban realities.

Urban space has come to symbolize all modern hopes and fears. On the one hand, it is a metaphor which expresses most clearly progress, order and the advantages of the technological first world. On the other hand, it is an impersonal, vast machine which has an unlimited appetite and is able to release unlimited potential for both consumption and production. The city is both the rule of law and the rule of the mob, a dynamic and flexible space. All these views of the city excite the modern imagination in such a way that it has become the symbol of what we consider modernity. Moreover, these views internalized as socially determining constructs become themselves more than symbols of streets and public places; they become signs which direct modern understanding of the world. The semiotics of the city are encoded within all codes for making sense of the outside world. This modernity is Western, while the cosmopolitanism of the urban space is a justification of its transformation into an universalizing image. Public spaces and private lives clash with each other and curiously underline the many paradoxes of modernity. For these reasons the city is more than the sum total of its buildings: 'Cities thus become more than their built environment, more than a set of class or economic relationships, they are also an experience to be lived, suffered, undergone.'[3] There is a close relationship between the city environment and modern sensibility which Charles Dickens, for example, illustrates in his anthropomorphic descriptions of London as in the following scene from his novel *Martin Chuzzlewit* (1843) in which he focuses on the appearance of Todgers's boarding house. The city of London 'hemmed Todgers's round, and hustled it, and crushed it, and stuck its brick-and-mortar elbows into it, and kept the air from it, and stood perpetually between it and the light'.[4]

The first English novels and the discourse of the Enlightenment associated with the emergence of Europe's sense of modernity appeared about the same time. Indeed, the novel is a quintessential urban form. It presupposes characters whose lives interact intensely

with others across a broad range of social backgrounds and the
ability for characters to change their circumstances either materi-
ally or spiritually which, in turn, presupposes an environment which
encourages and offers a heightened potential for transformation.
A number of literary critics and historians have linked these changes
to the emergence of the new generic form of the novel. The history of urban development in the West is very closely linked to
developments in literature, such that it would appear that representations of city life and the urban experience are part of the
West's narrative of its modernity.

    J. Paul Hunter places the beginning of these mutually reinforc-
ing transformations in ways of living and literature in the seventeenth century where the conditions were created which would
stimulate new reading habits since 'England had changed so sub-
stantially during the seventeenth century from a rural culture to
an urban one – or rather, from a culture that took its values from
a rural past into one that looked toward modernity with eagerness
and anticipation'.[5] For Hunter, the novel of the eighteenth century
is a response to city life, and in particular to life in London. He
describes the ambiguity of these experiences: 'The other side of
the excitement and challenge of surroundings bursting with a sense
of expansion, complexity, and mystery is uncertainty of one's own
place in a drama whose range has no precedent and whose distri-
bution of parts was often incomprehensible.'[6] Ian Watt, in his book
The Rise of the Novel, focuses on the same period as Hunter, and
on the relationship between the burgeoning form of the novel and
city life, with a slightly different slant. The novel which for him
summarizes many aspects of London and the new social order which
was being created is *Moll Flanders*, which first appeared in 1722.
Moll's fortune and social standing fluctuate, and although social
mobility may seem a term which hardly fits the life of crime and
prostitution to which she takes, nevertheless her crimes are urban;
so also is the system of law courts and punishments which she meets.
Watt discusses the life and career of Defoe's heroine in terms of
the social and cultural context of eighteenth-century London in
relation to 'the rise of individualism' and 'modern urban civilization'.[7] Her life joins London as the metropolitan imperial capital
with its colonies when she is deported to America as a bonded
slave. The colonies are like a rural hinterland which provides the
centre with resources. In Moll's case, during her life in the colonies to which she is sentenced for her crimes, she enters into an

incestuous marriage and is provided with resources forming the basis of her next fortune. Although sexual order breaks down in the more remote spaces, well removed from civilized society, the primitive world of the colonies represents other advantages.

There are passages in *Moll Flanders* in which the heroine takes us through the streets of London with great precision as if reading from a map of the streets. On one occasion she finds a little girl alone and manages, unnoticed, to steal from her a small necklace before sending her home, after which she makes her escape:

> I went through into Bartholomew Close, and then turned round to another passage that goes into Long Lane, so away into Charterhouse Yard and out into St. John Street; then, crossing into Smithfield, went down Chick Lane and into Field Lane to Holborn Bridge, when, mixing with the crowd of people usually passing there, it was not possible to have been found out.[8]

On the one hand, the streets here named by Moll can more or less be followed today which attests to the continuity of urban geography. It provides a basis of stability from generation to generation. On the other hand, this and other passages from the novel combine the anonymity of life on the streets with the bustle and activity which denotes the common purpose to which the inhabitants of such a complex social organism are committed. Therefore, Moll Flanders, thief, can pass undetected in a crowd. Charles Dickens continues the tradition of describing the city as purposeful anonymity in his novel *A Tale of Two Cities* (1859):

> A wonderful fact to reflect upon, that every human creature is constituted to be that profound secret and mystery to every other. A solemn consideration, when I enter a great city by night, that every one of those darkly clustered houses encloses its own secret; that every room in every one of them encloses its own secret; that every beating heart in the hundreds of thousands of breasts there is, in some of its imaginings, a secret to the heart nearest it![9]

Characters in these city novels do not meet all their fellow-citizens, but they know they are present and can imagine the totality of their secret lives.

The urban experience is a collective one, a great dialogue which takes place not only between people and people but also with the structures and buildings which line up along the city streets. Lewis

Mumford in his monumental study of the city in human history has characterized this aspect of the city as its 'materialization' commenting that 'the buildings speak and act, no less than the people who inhabit them; and through the physical structure of the city past events, decisions made long ago, values formulated and achieved, remain alive and exert an influence'.[10] They are participants in the collective purpose, the holders of the traces of the past and the reasons why the collective came into being. At the same time, there is an ambiguity in this purpose since it is greater than any individual and greater than the sum of the city's inhabitants. Its history is constantly moving and changing, and it presents a challenge to newcomers who arrive to exploit the opportunities which it offers. The theme of the newcomer who is either overwhelmed or who takes up the challenge is a common theme in Western literature and is a vehicle for expressing the ambivalent image of the city. The story of Balzac's novel *Old Goriot*, first published in 1834, is a typical example of the outsider from the countryside coming into the city, facing the complexities of the chances it offers and facing its threats. Such a challenge can provoke expressions of near-hatred when Rastignac whispers to Paris at the end of the novel, 'It's war between us now!'[11]

The central position of the urban landscape in modern consciousness deepens with the twentieth century. The Futurist challenge of the machine age was typical of many reactions at the beginning of this century. Also, much avant-garde art of this period continues to express the sense of threat contained within the image of the city. The city is the icon of technological progress and of intense social experience. Raymond Williams describes the modern city almost as a textual marker in his essay 'The Metropolis and the Emergence of Modernism' when he writes, 'It is now clear that there are decisive links between the practices and ideas of the avant-garde movements of the twentieth century and the specific conditions and relationships of the twentieth-century metropolis.'[12] In their introduction to their book on urban experience in modern literature, *Unreal City*, Edward Timms and David Kelley make the following remark:

> The images of the city examined in this book reflect a heightened subjectivity of perception, as well as dynamic patterns of historical change. These writers take the pulse of city life and touch the nerve of urban anxiety. There is no stable centre to be found either in the city or in the civilization which it epitomises.

Thus the city ceases to be pictured as a social environment and is transposed on to an existential plane. The metropolis ultimately becomes a metaphor – a dynamic configuration of the conflicting hopes and fears of the twentieth century.[13]

The city, then, can be taken not only as a space of living but also as a significant space which determines significant areas of experience and imagination. Reactions to the city in art and literature have always been double-edged and ambiguous. It is a space associated with myths of genesis as with Romulus and Remus, but also associated with myths of fall as in the tower of Babel. These images have been re-invented and reinforced in many ways over time. Paul Aster's *The New York Trilogy* contains a character who takes a walk each day around the centre of New York. Each walk when traced on a map of the city streets would produce a rough approximation of the shape of a letter. He continues his daily perambulations until he spells out 'THE TOWER OF BABEL'.[14] The modern city portrays great chaos and great order, the attraction of anonymity and collective purpose, human achievement in public buildings and human misery in slums. It is both a utopia and a dystopia.

Representations of the city over the last 200 years have stressed various facets of human interaction with the urban environment, from being its creator to being its slave. The cityscape has been used as a setting for action, as a symbol of human achievement, as an incarnation of anonymous forces of evil, and its architectural signs have been integrated into the semiotics of literary texts. In his book *All That Is Solid Melts Into Air* Marshall Berman presents a study of representations of modernity in the city literatures of Paris, St Petersburg and New York. Common to such literature is the expression of a critical moment when urban dwellers face the challenge of being 'moved by a will to change – to transform both themselves and their world – and by a terror of disorientation and disintegration, of life falling apart'.[15] It is this experience, often contradictory, which Berman finds characteristic of modernity and which he finds highlighted in city literature. He comes to the conclusion that this view of modernity and its representation is an universal image:

To be modern is to find ourselves in an environment that promises us adventure, power, joy, growth, transformation of ourselves and the world – and, at the same time, that threatens to destroy everything we have, everything we know, everything we are. Modern environments and experiences cut across all boundaries of geography and ethnicity, of class and nationality, of religion and ideology: in this sense, modernity can be said to unite all mankind.[16]

Berman's analysis of different types of imaginative writing on the city, about Paris, St Petersburg and New York, underlines the truth of the ambiguous nature of the city image as an index of modernity. However, the question remains whether his view is justifiably an universal image, whether there is not a greater variety of experience and therefore of representations of that experience?

Given the West's dominant view of Eastern Europe as rural it is symptomatic that Western discussions of the city in literature should generally exclude it or treat it as different. In his essay on the cities of Modernism, Malcolm Bradbury remarks that when thinking of Modernism we cannot help but also think of 'urban climates' and goes on to enumerate these important cultural centres as Berlin, Vienna, Moscow, St Petersburg, London, Zurich, New York, Chicago and Paris.[17] These are the urban climates most 'seen' in evocations of the literary atmosphere between 1890 and 1930. Prague, here not mentioned, is sometimes also included because of the place of Kafka in European literature. However, since he wrote his works in German he is usually regarded as not belonging to the Czech literary tradition. The two principal Russian cities included by Bradbury are frequently treated with some qualification when analyzed which sets them apart from the metropolitan areas of the West. Marshall Berman's book contains general chapters on, for example, 'Marx, Modernism and Modernization', and also chapters on specific writers such as Baudelaire in the chapter 'Modernism in the Streets'. However, when he comes to his chapter on St Petersburg in literature as an expression of modernity he chooses a title with the oxymoronic sounding 'The Modernism of Underdevelopment'. Raymond Williams in his book *The Country and the City* also treats the expression of the city in Russian literature as essentially different to its expression in Western literature. Comparing Dostoevsky with some dominant figures from Western literature of the nineteenth century he notes that Balzac reveals 'the social intricacy of the city' and Dickens offers us an image of 'a smothered sense of society'. This is the social character of the city with 'its essential and exciting isolation and procession of men and events' which, as Williams points out, 'came to predominate in much Western literature'.[18] On the other hand, Williams remarks that Dostoevsky's image of the city emphasizes 'the elements of mystery and strangeness and the loss of connection'. Dostoevsky's evocation is not social in character but is characterized by 'a spiritual acknowledgement'.[19] In the remainder of this chapter I shall turn to examine some of the historical and social developments which have influenced the urban model in the Balkans, particularly in relation to Belgrade, and the consequent pattern of anxieties which emerge from those developments.

URBAN CULTURE IN THE BALKANS

During the Middle Ages, before the conquest of the Turks, the Balkan peninsula was divided between the two civilizations represented by Rome and Byzantium. In other words, the chief cultural influence in the region was from the then most urban and sophisticated centres of Europe. The Serbs modelled their medieval state and society on the Byzantine model, taking from them matters important to all areas of life from dress, to court etiquette and the codification of laws. During the fourteenth century Serbian power in the Balkans reached its height and in territory the state covered most of present-day Greece as far south as the Peloponnese, Albania, Bulgaria, Serbia, Montenegro, Hercegovina and southern Dalmatia. Its centre was further south than today's concentrations of Serbian population and was located around Kosovo and Macedonia. Although at this time they were the strongest power in the peninsula the Serbs never actually managed to take Byzantium. During the fourteenth century Serbian domination waned due to internal power struggles and so the army which confronted the Turks at the Battle of Kosovo in 1389 was severely weakened. Some Serbian lords even fought on the Ottoman side. The battle was not conclusive, but thereafter the Christian Balkan population could never mount sufficient forces to stop the advance of the enemy.

As the Ottoman armies advanced into the Balkans, urban life passed into the hands of the new colonial administrators. Much of the urban Christian population 'chose to withdraw to inaccessible mountains where they founded new settlements'.[20] This factor helps to explain the uneven dispersal of different ethnic groups throughout the region. The Serbs were most affected in this respect because of the territory which they occupied. From the south they moved firstly into the mountain regions of Bosnia. Then, when the Turks conquered Bosnia, they were forced further north again into the

Slavonia and Krajina regions of Croatia. The attitude of the new authorities towards their Christian subjects was virtually to ignore them insofar as they were given the right to rule their own communities through the organization of the Church, but that did not mean they were regarded as free or the equals of their Moslem overlords. The Christian population had obligations and duties but no rights. At times large numbers of Christian families would be moved if necessary to repopulate a border region which had emptied as a result of local tensions or war. This kind of change particularly effected the Serbian areas, since they occupied 'the shifting frontier between the Ottoman Empire and central Europe'.[21] The most dramatic migratory waves came at the end of the seventeenth century when large groups of Serbs moved north and crossed over the River Sava and Danube into Vojvodina. This demographic shift is often celebrated in Serbian histiography as the result of Patriarch Arsenije III leading 30,000 families to escape the Turkish terror and has been the subject of songs, paintings, and narratives such as Crnjanski's novel *Migrations*.

Ottoman interest in where cities ought to be situated followed a different set of priorities from previous practice. Concentrations of population had previously grown up around monastic centres or around areas of economic activity such as mining. Monasteries too provided a basic stimulus to economic activity in their surrounding hinterland. However, the new authorities determined that cities were to fulfil other functions. They grew around important nodal points in the imperial system. Cities were regarded as military and administrative centres, linked to the Porte, and expressly concerned with maintaining Ottoman power against the local population and with the protection of trade routes. They were to keep open the roads and highways for trade and military purposes. The direction of the transport system changed to accommodate greater exchange between the Empire's provinces in Asia and the Adriatic coast, crossing the peninsula from east to west. New cities were founded and previously small centres acquired more importance, while the once established centres began to decline. Slowly the Christian population returned to the urban centres. By the second half of the sixteenth century Moslems were a majority of the urban population although the demographic pattern was not spread evenly over the whole of the peninsula. Athens, for example, had a Christian population 'comprised from 90 to 100% of the population' while Sarajevo was one of those 'entirely Muslim cities'.[22]

Ottoman rule dictated not only the main functions of Balkan cities, from which Christians as a disenfranchised population were largely absent, but also their architecture and design. In the languages of the city, the functions of urban signs differed greatly between these cities and those of the West. Ottoman influence in the Balkans produced a distinctive type of urban culture. Houses consisted of compounds in which the extended family lived. On marriage, a new wife would move to her husband's house and become a part of and responsible to his family. The blank walls of the compound faced onto the street while family life was directed inwards, towards a central courtyard, with a gate between it and the outside world. They were intensely private places with strict etiquette regarding rank within the household and the admittance of outsiders. City life did not happen on the streets but in private. However, this is not the intimate space of the salon, but an enclosed space which was tightly controlled both physically and symbolically. The streets were not evident in a Western sense. Not only were they not evident because of the very different functions of space, but also in a more literal sense in that houses were not built with the intention to allow the movement of traffic between them. It is little wonder that both Daville and Des Fossés find a terrible silence in Andrić's Travnik. The Consul and his assistant cannot read the signs of the city. It remains for them a closed book. Another of Andrić's novels, *The Bridge over the Drina,* tells the story of the Bosnian town of Višegrad during some 400 years. As a novel it has epic proportions in its movement through history and its story of the fate of a whole community which is divided, like Travnik, between the four faiths. However, it has hardly ever been described as a city novel. There is no public life. We confront the community's collective memory stored in its stories and songs, but everything happens in an architectural vacuum with no descriptions of Višegrad houses and streets. The bridge which dominates the town fulfils a highly symbolic function within the structure of the work which supersedes its function as meeting place and the setting for all important events. There is no other public space in the novel.

Western visitors to the Balkans could not distinguish between Moslem and Christian areas of towns. The internal order of rooms in a house, the kinds of dress which were regarded as town clothes rather than peasant clothes, city life as a whole in the Balkans evolved under a Turkish Ottoman role model. Christians began to move into the towns but Western visitors were often under the impression that the whole urban population was Turkish. The cities fulfilled different functions from their counterparts in the West and looked differently. Travellers even used to have great difficulty in recognizing them as cities. Todorov describes that the Western traveller 'rarely failed to note the absence of fortress walls in Balkan settlements as the basic difference setting these cities apart from Western Europe', and that 'the absence of multistoried stone buildings puzzled them no less'.[23] Very few buildings possessed more than one storey. These towns not only looked differently but they were also governed by completely different types of political and social structures. Urban populations were registered separately from rural populations as there were enormous differences in tax laws. Ottoman cities in the Balkans were ringed and enclosed by elaborate legal and financial codes which showed a clear distinction between urban and rural areas. The state maintained a very heavy presence in regulating town life, such that 'it lacked the unified municipal structure so characteristic of the European city'.[24] During the eighteenth century, as cities were expanding in the West and new productive processes opening up new areas of employment, cities in the Balkans became increasingly centres of consumption. F. W. Carter points to 'the inadequate performance by urban centres of certain manufacturing and exchange functions'.[25]

The traditional Balkan urban experience differs in many ways from Western models. It is primarily a private rather than public space in which the city whispers and hides. It appears to lack the conditions which promote the essential vibrancy and ambiguity of the city image in the West. It is a space which controls the surrounding region and links that region to the central political power. It is the defender of the status quo rather than a challenging environment for the newcomer. It does not exist as a symbol of the continuity and change which speaks to each generation anew. The city represents a cultural role model imposed from the outside, but which gradually assimilated the local population.

The Balkan region is not alone in Europe in having an urban culture which was based on foreign models. Much the same can be said for most of East-Central Europe which also experienced a colonial past. Major cities were centres for Hapsburg and Ottoman administration and garrisons in order to maintain imperial power and justice. Prague at the beginning of the nineteenth century was a German-speaking city. The majority of people with authority in commerce, education, administration, and the legal and medical professions were German speakers. The city's large Jewish community, of which Kafka was a part, also tended to speak German. Czechs only achieved a majority in the city at the end of the century. Even then the majority language in all matters of government continued to be German as the territory remained a province of the Hapsburg Empire. The situation in the Magyar sector of the Empire was no better:

> While Hungarian had replaced Latin as the official language of Hungary in 1844, as late as 1856 German was decreed to be the compulsory language of secondary education. Even in 1873, when Buda, Óbuda and Pest formally united into Budapest six years after the Ausgleich, less than half of its population was Hungarian.[26]

Conversely, the area of Croatia in the northern part around Zagreb and including the port of Rijeka were ruled from Budapest. There was a local parliament or *sabor* in the nineteenth century with limited powers where the language spoken in the first half of the century was Latin while Hungarian and German were the main languages of education, administration, trade and law. The subject peoples of the Hapsburgs and Ottomans went through a process of national awakening in the nineteenth century, beginning with work on modernizing orthography and codifying grammar, similar to the work of Vuk Karadžić amongst the Serbs. Initially intending to foster a sense of national consciousness against colonial rule, everywhere these movements developed explicit political programmes aimed at national liberation. Although often regarded as revivals of rural traditions and folk customs, it would equally be true to see them as part of a struggle for control of municipal structures, and therefore of government and culture. Following decolonization of the region, after the First World War, the map of Eastern Europe was completely transformed. New states such as Czechoslovakia, Poland, the Kingdom of Serbs Croats and Slovenes made their appearance, and their major cities which were once the provincial capitals of territories on the periphery of large Empires became seats for the government of independent states and national cultures. The European urban model contains a variety of different historical experiences some of which have been suppressed and their stories, consequently, written out of the narrative of modernity.

It is quite easy to see how the development of city life in the Balkans contributes to the general myths in circulation about the region. The image of Balkan militarism is a rural model. Just as

the French Revolution could not have happened outside the claustro-
phobic streets of metropolitan Paris, so the Serbian and Montenegrin
heroes of the folk ballads, and their living embodiments in the
nineteenth century, could not exist outside their mountain fastnesses.
As a result, Serbian and other Balkan cultures possess a heightened
awareness about the distinctions between rural and urban imagery.
This is not simply a matter of individual texts but of the whole of
literary history as a meta-narrative about the national past. As
Anthony Smith in his book *The Ethnic Origins of Nations* points
out: 'For small nations, their culture and history have become both
means and ends of their existence, and the more they feel threatened
by the technological superiority and economic dominance of large
nation-states, the more salient and vital is their distinctive culture.
For it defines their very *raison d'être* as a separate unit.'[27] Literary
history offers a picture of national history, a national narrative.
The idea of a national narrative has been discussed with reference
to other cultures too. In his essay 'What is the History of Literature?'
Jonathan Arac considers the sometimes tense relationships between
literary fictions and history in the American case. He points to
J. Fenimore Cooper's works of the 1820s about the colonial origins
of the state on a path to independence, and although they are not
discussed in detail by Arac it would be fair to assume that he is
referring to such novels as *The Spy* (1821) and *The Last of the
Mohicans* (1826), through to the later slave narratives of the
nineteenth century.[28] The shape of literature in the past is transformed
into an account of the ideals of the collective in the present. Other
literary narratives can be constructed for all literatures, but it remains
true that the cultural image of the nation shaped by patterns of
literary history is a vital part of the smaller culture's presentation
of itself both to itself and others. Serbian literary and cultural history
is divided into two opposing views; one of which represents an urban
image for the source of Serbian modern identity and another which
focuses on a rural origin. Two examples from around the time of
the First World War will illustrate the differences.

The urban view is emphasized in Jovan Skerlić's book *Istorija
nove srpske kniževnosti* (*History of Modern Serbian Literature*). He
concentrates on the development of an urban class in the towns of
Vojvodina during the eighteenth century, away from the Ottoman
occupation south of the River Sava, in an environment more open
to cultural influences from elsewhere in Europe.[29] The second half
of the eighteenth century is characterized by the influence of the

Enlightenment on the Serbian community of Vojvodina. The most important figure in Skerlić's historical scheme is Dositej Obradović. Educated in the monastery of Hopovo, he left the life of the cloisters in his teens, quitted Vojvodina and began a life of extraordinary travels across Europe. He lived in many cities including Leipzig, Paris and London where he would learn as much as possible about the language and culture of those places. On his return to Vojvodina he published his autobiography, *Život i priključenija* (1784), in an explicit attempt to educate his fellow-countrymen about the wider world.[30] His didactic approach is compatible with all the traditions of the European Enlightenment. He opened the battle to reform the alphabet and introduce the vernacular as the standard literary norm. His life and work have the appearance of a more cultured and literate origin for modern Serbian culture which far from participating in the construction of the Balkan myth opposes it and offers a view of cultural history based on Rationalist principles and learning. It is not surprising that during the years of Communism in the former Yugoslavia this view did not receive official backing. Dositej's connections with the church and the middle-class voice of the small Serbian urban communities of his day did not lend themselves to the narrative of which the Communists wanted to be a part.

Around the same time that Skerlić was proposing his literary history, Pavle Popović offered an alternative view in his *Jugoslovenska književnost (Yugoslav Literature)*. His view does not entirely oppose Skerlić's. He points out the importance of new influences from the West in the second half of the eighteenth century and attributes great value to the work of Dositej Obradović. However, Popović emphasizes two particular features of this period which underpin the modernization of culture. One is the development of the Yugoslav Idea bringing together Serbian, Croatian and Slovene literatures, previously separated, as one of the progressive signs of the times. The second, and more significant for Popović, concerns the blossoming of folk poetry and the role it was to play in later literary developments. He keeps returning to the influence of the oral traditions in the formation of a modern literary idiom and to the work of Vuk Karadžić.[31] His model links modern Serbian culture with a national source, rather than the pan-Europeanism of Dositej Obradović. This dilemma between two different origins has continued through the twentieth century and has been a factor in drawing up the agenda for the debates about the nature of Serbian cultural identity. Popović's version found favour with the Yugoslav Communists. The tone of his language focuses on the link between cultural and national political evolution. The source of culture lies with the oppressed peasantry of the Ottoman Empire, fighting for their freedom. The wider image of the coincidence between the emergence of a modern literary idiom and the revolutionary struggle for liberation based on the internal strengths of the people corresponded to how the Communists wished to present themselves within the national narrative. However, at the essence of the debates about cultural identity lies an ambiguous relationship towards the outside world and towards the origin of the national narrative.

More recently, others have returned to this point as Serbian nationalist feeling increased during the 1980s. The media, particularly television, bombarded the population with messages that Serbia had to return to its roots. Similar messages were being expressed throughout former Yugoslavia at the same time. Each constituent national community felt that its individual identity had been undermined by the decades of Yugoslav Communism. The paradox in the Serbian case is that the agenda for establishing authentic roots had been a part of Communist cultural policy. Questioning the state-sponsored search for the national past, Predrag Protić has remarked that Serbian Romanticism's dreams about the medieval Serbian Empire, Kosovo and the national cult of Saint Sava were 'an intellectual construction which belonged only to the most conscious part of the nation', that is to the intellectuals and not to the mass of the people.[32] Protić leans heavily in favour of Skerlić's model of an urban source in which the singer of folk songs was not a founding father of national identity, rather he was nothing more than an 'entertainer who told happy and sad heroic fortunes and misfortunes to a public who, more or less, had an ear for them'.[33] The theme of cultural history reveals a continuing feeling of anxiety towards the dichotomy between what is foreign and what is authentic. All such narratives are constructs of different approaches to the issues of identity and modernity. If we make two lists in the spirit of Dubravka Ugrešić's attempt to show the constructions of East and West we can put on one side 'narrow' themes of national tradition, oral culture, peasant traditions; in short, this side of the equation is heavily enshrined by the positive images of the Balkan myth. The other side of the equation is heavily influenced by the anxiety produced by the negative values of the same mythic structure and opposes it by emphasizing the source and evolution of cultural

identity in the broad themes of cosmopolitan, literate culture, urban traditions, in short the essence of all that is considered European.

BELGRADE

The history of Serbia's principal city provides further illustration
of why the city space in Serbian culture represents an agitated space.
Belgrade was an important city for the Turks because of its position
on the border with Austria, strategically favoured with rivers on
two sides, the Danube and the Sava. Access to the Danube also
made it an important trading city. It was an administrative and
military centre from where the Pasha ruled with a large garrison
and a strong fortress. The walls of the city stretched as far as today's
street called Francuska ulica, with a broad defensive ditch on the
outside. The fortifications dropped down both slopes leading to
the two rivers. There were three gates into the city, the Varoš-
kapija, the Sava-kapija and the main gate, Stambol-kapija. The main
gate stood roughly in the space between the National Theatre today
and the statue to Prince Mihailo which stands on Republic Square
at the top of Francuska ulica. The city fulfilled all the traditional
functions of an urban settlement in the Balkans under Ottoman
domination. It represented the Sultan's strength and domination
over the region. It also looked across the Danube and Sava to the
north and west, so being an important defensive position against
the Hapsburg Empire.
    The geographical position of Belgrade was an important factor
for the Serbs too. It was not a natural choice for the Serbs as their
capital. Historically, the medieval Serbian Empire had its developed
centres further to the south in Priština, Prizren, Skopje and Ohrid.
More recently, the Serbs over the Danube in Vojvodina had emerged
as the most urban communities and their towns although small held
European-style infrastructures for legal and financial dealings. They
were cultural centres also with a local intelligentsia educated in
the universities of the Austrian Empire. During the First Serbian
Uprising, it was essential that Kara Djordje and his insurgents capture
Belgrade in order to deny the Pasha the safety of the strongest
fortress in Serbia. The city was eventually captured on the night of
29 to 30 November 1806. But apart from the military and mercantile
considerations, the position of Belgrade held huge symbolic
significance for the Serbs. The city lies on the periphery of the

new Serbian state which began to emerge in the nineteenth century, but as it looked westwards it signified the Serbian desire for Westernization and inclusion into the European cultural space, throwing off the centuries of Ottoman rule. Its position also offered a view of the lands occupied by the Austrians across the river and symbolized the desire for the unification of all Serbs into one state, although the status of the city remained in doubt for some decades.

Kara Djordje immediately set about making Belgrade his capital and installing the rudimentary institutions which he needed to run his small principality. Dositej Obradović came from Vojvodina to Belgrade as first Minister for Education. Obradović was one of the first in a long train of educated Vojvodina Serbs who came to Belgrade to help staff and run the new administration. They regarded Serbia south of the Sava and Danube as the Serbian heartlands, and that the formation of an independent Serbia there could only help their search for liberation from Austrian rule. They brought with them their different dress and manners which were modelled on German customs, while the Serbs in Belgrade and to the south tended to accept the traditional Turkish role model for years to come. Kara Djordje's rebellion was eventually defeated to be followed by the Second Serbian Uprising, 1815–17, under Miloš Obrenović. He was more successful in his policies which, unlike his predecessor, included patient negotiation and compromise with the Turks. Gradually he managed to achieve a certain local autonomy from the Sultan. However, the Belgrade Pasha and the Turks of the town who formed the majority of inhabitants were very suspicious of the growing Serbian confidence. Plots to assassinate Miloš began to circulate in the city. In fear for his life Miloš left Belgrade for Kragujevac where he felt safer and could count on the support of the local population. The area around Kragujevac had been the centre of both uprisings against the Turks. For a number of years Miloš remained wary of coming to Belgrade. A significant shift in Turkish opinion was won with the Russian victory over them in 1830. Wanting to help its Slav ally in the Balkans, the Russian government coerced the Sultan into giving Miloš greater autonomy. Their action included the issue of a note or *hatti-sherif* to the effect that all Turks not involved with either the administration or the local garrisons should leave Serbia. This decree was qualified in a second *hatti-sherif* of 1833 which gave local Turkish inhabitants five years to leave Serbia except for Belgrade which was declared to be an Ottoman town forever. In 1835 Miloš was forbidden from

transferring the Serbian capital and seat of his government from
Kragujevac to Belgrade and the Turkish authorities declared that
Belgrade belonged exclusively to the Sultan as 'imperial territory'.[34]
It was only in 1842 that Belgrade became the centre of Serbian
administration when in a palace *coup d'état* led by Toma Vučić
Perišić the Obrenović dynasty was ousted and Aleksandar Karadjor-
djević installed as Prince.

Belgrade continued to be a centre of Ottoman administration,
although the Serbs retained considerable local powers. There was
little urban development at this time except for the few buildings
erected by the Serbs outside the city walls and, thus, away from
the Pasha. The Serbian political elite was divided and in the grip
of constant crisis during the 1840s and 1850s. The situation was
successfully managed by Vučić Perišić who fell from power only in
1859 following another *coup d'état* when Miloš Obrenović returned
as Prince. Vučić Perišić was arrested and imprisoned where he soon
died, probably poisoned. Miloš was already old and he died himself
the following year to be succeeded by his son Mihailo. The young
prince had lived abroad for many years, and was the first ruler of
this semi-autonomous province to be educated in the West. The
years to his assassination in 1868 were characterized by very turbulent
relations with the local Pasha and Turkish garrison. In 1862, following
an outbreak of rioting against Ottoman authority in response to
which the Turkish garrison fired their cannon on the city, the Great
Powers intervened to prevent matters getting out of hand. They
were particularly concerned lest they should themselves become
involved in local quarrels. Under foreign pressure the Pasha and
his garrison were forced to quit the country in 1867. Sovereign power
was still held in the Porte, but it had no official representation in
the capital. With the Turkish population leaving the city along with
the Ottoman administration, Belgrade finally became Serbian.

Many travellers from the West who saw Turkish Belgrade describe it as a typical Oriental city. Narrow, crooked streets were
hemmed in by high, blank walls enclosing courtyards and gardens.
Shops were open to the street with their owners sitting in front.
The journalist Harry De Windt, author of the book *Through Savage Europe* in which he declared his poor opinion of the Balkan
Slavs, visited Belgrade during the wars of the 1870s. He recalls
arriving there: 'A tedious river journey brought you, from East or
West, to a squalid, Eastern-looking town with ramshackle buildings
and unsavoury streets . . . A truly dreary place was Belgrade in the

seventies, for everything was primitive, dirty, and comfortless.'[35] However, the inhabitants of the city were themselves aware of the legacy bequeathed them by Turkish occupation and that they had been politically and culturally part of that Empire for a long time. From the middle of the century the Serbian authorities sponsored its talented young people to go and study abroad in universities in Austria, Germany and Russia. They returned home to work as doctors, lawyers and engineers, intent on establishing the lifestyles and civilization of the West. Emilijan Josimović put forward plans for demolishing the Ottoman aspect of Belgrade and replacing it with buildings in the style of European architecture. The houses of the Turkish quarter on the slope above the Danube were pulled down and Belgrade acquired its first modern appearance. The area became known as Dorćol. Its streets were planned according to a grid system running in parallel lines from the top of the hill to the river, intersected by other streets running at 90 degree angles to them. In the last quarter of the nineteenth century the whole city was being redesigned with wide boulevards and large public buildings. Such was the transformation that even those Westerners who did not hide their disdain for the Balkans could not help but comment favourably on what Belgrade had become. Harry De Windt, for example, remarks:

> Rip Van Winkle, after his long sleep in the Katskills, can scarcely have been more astonished at the altered appearance of his native village than I was at the marvellous improvements which less than thirty years have worked in Belgrade. In 1876 a dilapidated Turkish fortress frowned down upon a maze of buildings little better than mud huts and unpaved, filthy streets... To-day it seemed like a dream to be whirled away from the railway station in a neat *fiacre*, along spacious boulevards, with well-dressed crowds and electric cars, to a luxurious hotel.[36]

The city was completely transformed from when De Windt first saw Belgrade in 1876 to his later visit in 1907. It was the capital of a much-enlarged state which had expanded its territory to the south. Serbia, from 1882, was recognized as an independent kingdom with no further connections to the Ottoman Empire. It had acquired an University and a Royal Academy. It was connected to both the East and the West via the railway, an important stop along the east-west route. It modelled itself on the latest fashions and ideas from Vienna, Paris and London. The culture of the region was looking steadfastly westward, and the Serbs were intent 'to cause the disappearance from their country of anything which could recall the old Moslem domination'.[37] The transition from an Oriental to a Western world happened very quickly and unevenly. Many traces of the Ottoman legacy continued to persist. These traces functioned in some ways like the fear of primitivism in Victorian society as described by Hayden White. The Ottoman legacy was what Serbian culture had once been and what it might become again. Belgrade as the meeting place between East and West was buried under layers of the Balkan myth which functioned to remind both Westerners and the indigenous population that the Oriental past was only recently left behind, and that transition into a new order was but a fragile step.

For many foreigners and visitors the politics of this emerging society were dark and threatening. In 1903 the city witnessed the brutal murder of the unpopular King Aleksandar Obrenović and his wife Draga. They were stabbed to death by their own palace guards and their bodies then thrown from the windows of the palace into the park below. The whole of Europe was shocked at this instance of regicide, perhaps reacting more to the thought of how easy it can be to remove the legitimate power in the state than to the cruelty of the attack on the royal persons. Most visitors comment on the threatening air of suspicion which pervaded the city. De Windt describes it as a police state which 'is an impossible place to live in, for even foreigners are subject to the most vexatious police regulations, the Press is muzzled, and harmless citizens are imprisoned for months together on mere suspicion of ill-favour towards the reigning dynasty'.[38] The author of *An Observer in the Near East* puts the sense of threat into the context of recent changes in the ruling dynasty coupled with outside, mainly Austrian, attempts to destabilize the country saying, 'The capital is, of course, a hotbed of political intrigue, and all foreigners arriving are suspected of being secret agents.'[39] Rebecca West also repeats the notion of Belgrade being a centre for international spies. She comments on the people around the table at lunch one day in Belgrade, adding, 'It is said that Belgrade is the centre of the European spy system, and it may be that some of these people are spies.'[40] The new Belgrade remains an ambiguous space and a city caught between competing worlds: only now the difference is not between East and West, but between the open world of modern civilization and an underworld of spies and intrigue where nothing is as it might appear.

It was not only foreigners who recognized a semi-Oriental atmosphere in the town and the clash of different cultures. As we have examined earlier, Western attitudes are irresistible to the inhabitants of the Balkans themselves, as if by adopting them the move towards the West becomes more complete. Lena A. Jovičić in her book from 1926, *Pages from Here and There in Serbia*, gives many little portraits of her country. Writing after the First World War she cannot ignore the severe damage caused by the years of enemy occupation and the fierce fighting which occurred when the city was retaken. She then goes on to describe 'the extraordinary building epidemic' which took Belgrade over in the aftermath of war, which meant not only reconstruction but also that 'a new city was raised'.[41] The urban and commercial infrastructure was rebuilt and the last vestiges of the Turkish town were removed. She remarks on many aspects of life in Belgrade of the 1920s and how it was changing. New shops were built which augmented the function of storing, displaying and selling goods. Facades were changed, more elaborate shop signs introduced, 'plate glass windows' were added.[42] These shops were not only centres for commercial exchanges but were signs of the transformations on the streets with more light and people browsing, walking around the cityscape, life on the streets. However, being very aware of the other image of Belgrade and Serbia, she also comments on the foreign gaze searching for evidence of the Orient:

> Those perhaps seeking in vain for a note of the Orient, or some picturesque touch of the East, will be disappointed with the streets of Belgrade, but in the market place there is all the colour and animation, all the bustle and stir, including the confusion of many voices, which seem at last to fit the picture one looks for in the Balkans.[43]

Who is the 'one' of whom she speaks? Again, Belgrade is felt by those who live there as a contact point between East and West. However, it seems an ambivalent meeting place. On the one hand, the two worlds may rub up against each other in some kind of fruitful Bakhtinian dialogue. On the other hand, rather than Belgrade as a metaphoric bridge, in a later book Jovičić describes Belgrade as the point at which 'the gap' between East and West opens up.[44] In this case, Belgrade is ever in danger of falling into the chasm between. It is a space, in Berman's terms, which 'threatens to destroy everything we have, everything we know, everything we are'.[45]

Belgrade's urban infrastructure, rebuilt after the First World War, gave it an air which came to resemble other European cities of similar size. The major daily newspaper was *Politika*, founded as an independent voice by the Ribnikar family in 1904. A brief glance at the issue published on 6 April 1941, just as Yugoslavia was about to be dragged into the Second World War, confirms the European and cosmopolitan feel of the city. Much of the news is taken up with events of the Second World War around the world, but there are also adverts for products sold around the globe. There are articles on Hollywood films, fashions, and cartoons, including Donald Duck, renamed as *Paja Patak*. A brief synopsis of the cinemas advertising that day will be illustrative for these purposes. Amongst the cinema houses with names such as *Balkan* and *Drina* there are others called *City* and *Rex*. Films from Russia, Spain, Hungary and especially America are on release: *Hollywood Cavalcade* with Buster Keaton is on offer at the same time as *Beau Geste* with Gary Cooper. Bette Davis, Shirley Temple and Mickey Rooney were all present. The city and its inhabitants were as fully informed as anywhere else in the world of events at the beginning of the globalization of popular culture.

War has been a constant handicap to Belgrade's urban development. The Second World War brought greater physical destruction than ever before. The city was heavily bombed by German forces in 1941, and then again in 1944 when it was treated by Allied bombers as an occupied area. Finally, with the aid of the Red Army, the Communist-led Partisans liberated Belgrade after much fighting in the streets as they slowly made their way from house to house. The Communists quickly established their hold on all important functions in the city and in the government of the state. The war had been particularly fierce and cruel, and the Partisans were not in a mood for compromise when they first entered Belgrade. Orders against suspected collaborators were instant and on one night, 27 November 1944, 105 members of Belgrade's intelligentsia were shot. Many of these deaths were undoubtedly the settling of personal scores and old vendettas, removing some who might seriously oppose the regime and others whose presence would be a reminder of the bourgeois past which the Communists wished to eradicate. The Communist Party of Yugoslavia's goal was the absolute concentration of all aspects of power in their hands. This aim was incompatible with autonomous municipal structures of city government which sealed the urban community together. In some senses the town began to revert to an evolutionary stage more in common with the years of Ottoman domination. They not only took over positions of authority, but also the homes of the formerly rich and powerful. They confiscated large houses in the fashionable parts of town such as Dedinje and made them their own. Many of the Partisans came from rural areas and immediately began to introduce different habits of speech, dress and manners. They controlled public life in the city, and their monopoly stretched to all public spaces. They even attempted to control the private space of each citizen. They destroyed the infrastructure which had taken many decades to build up and for which again some decades had to pass by before there was any return to a sense of city community.

Belgrade was again destroyed by the nationalist euphoria and war of the late 1980s and early 1990s. Although not physically involved in the war, Belgrade was hit by waves of refugees, as were the new capital cities of Zagreb in Croatia and Ljubljana in Slovenia. However, international sanctions which were raised against Serbia and Montenegro, the new Federal Republic of Yugoslavia, isolated the country completely. The city again began to deteriorate in the hysteria created by these abnormal circumstances; a sudden drop into great poverty, high unemployment, rampant inflation at a record some estimate to have reached 3 billion per cent at its height towards the end of 1993. Transport, health and all other systems were unable to operate. There were no goods in the shops, no money in the banks, government was corrupt and the only productive sector was the mafia illegally importing petrol and luxury goods for sale to war profiteers. Everything had to be smuggled in from abroad and was sold on the streets through rackets. The city, like the rest of the country but perhaps more intensively, was thoroughly criminalized.

URBAN ANXIETIES

The following photographs are introduced here in order to illustrate internal cultural differences, what Lena Jovičić refers to as the 'gap' in Belgrade, and what may be regarded as one of the major sources of certain anxieties concerning representations of modernity to be found in Serbian cultural identity. They illustrate a civilization of great contrasts. Changes in the urban lifestyle in Belgrade and in Serbia at large occurred at a rapid rate which helps to explain the precarious relationship between East and West in the Balkans and the anxiety aroused because of the proximity to that pre-modern past. The first portrait (Plate 1) is of Toma Vučić Perišić, opponent of Miloš Obrenović. The photograph was taken sometime between 1850 and 1856. He is dressed in a Turkish style complete with fez. It is a simple face-on pose with no background or other objects to help contextualize who the man is. His environment is empty. It is to be compared with the second portrait (Plate 2) which is of Prince Mihailo Obrenović who ruled Serbia after the death of his father, Miloš. The two portraits were taken by the same photographer, Anastas Jovanović, and in the same decade. Prince Mihailo leaves a completely different impression from the first photograph. The Prince is sitting in a relaxed and thoughtful mode, leg crossed over, one hand resting on his lap while the other supports his temple with his elbow on the table. Next to him, on the table, there is a map, some books and a statue of a medieval Serbian knight; signs of the ruler, with his territory, wisdom and strength. A portrait of the Prince's father is hanging on the wall behind them all giving an air of legitimacy to the Obrenović dynasty. This tableau of the instruments of power is overburdened with signs and is aesthetically framed with a flowing curtain. The curtain begins its descent from the upper corner of the portrait, over the head of Prince Miloš, and drapes down behind and just to the right side of Prince Mihailo. The frame of flowing material is completed by the tablecloth on the Prince's left side falling to the floor. Prince Mihailo himself is dressed like a wealthy, fashionable Westerner. The two portraits visualize the Serbia of Toma Vučić Perišić clothed in the legacy of the Ottoman past, standing in the image of the pre-modern, rural past. Mihailo Obrenović has his photograph taken as he looks into the Serbian future, an image of European modernity. Different styles of dress, of life and of thinking overlap.

Plate 3, taken in 1876, focuses on a workman and a boat by the River Sava in Belgrade. The boat is made of roughly hewn wood and is connected to the riverbank by a simple plank of wood. There is a small boat pulled onto the bank which is of an elementary design. A large pile of wood, chopped ready for use, is on the left of the picture and towards the house. It is presumably intended for heating as there is no sign of any other form of power for the house. The workman in the centre is wearing traditional style clothes with baggy trousers (*čakšire*) and peasant shoes (*opanci*). He is also smoking a long-stemmed pipe. There is no sign of any paving

1. Toma Vučić Perišić, between 1850 and 1856.

2. Prince Mihailo Obrenović, *c.* 1859.

3. The river bank of the Sava in Belgrade, 1876.

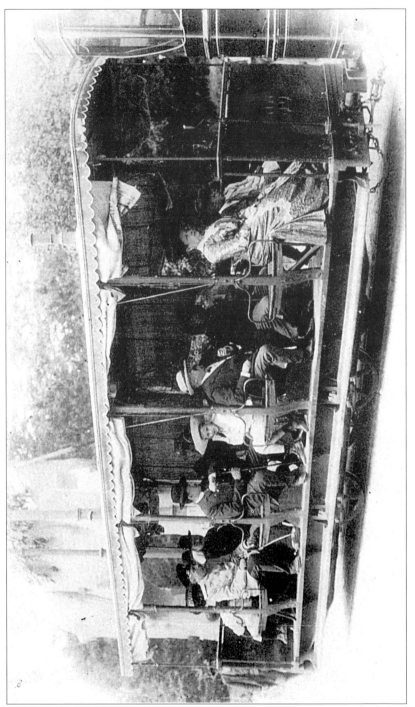

4. A Belgrade summer tram, between 1900 and 1910.

5. *Teferič* (Turkish term for outing in the country), c. 1880.

6. A family outing to Soko Banja, *c.* 1908.

7. A girl from Niš, *c.* 1880.

8. Anna Marinkovíc, 1906.

around the house and the whole area is covered in mud. This is the decade in which Belgrade began its transformation from a Turkish Ottoman town into an European city. The results of those efforts can be seen in the next photograph (Plate 4), a picture of a Belgrade summer tram taken during the first decade of the century, perhaps just 25 years after Plate 3. This open tram is coupled to a closed tram, the back of which can be seen on the right of the picture. Electricity has arrived and is providing a modern transport system, essential to the infrastructure of any large city. Behind the tram, trees line the road, which gives the impression that this is a broad boulevard. The passengers are all clearly dressed in what would have been normal wear in Edwardian England at this time, all with hats. The straight-backed lady on the front row with two children by her side is looking straight ahead. She seems like a governess or matronly aunt with her charges. The small boy sitting halfway down and looking curiously at the camera is wearing some kind of sailor suit with boots. The photographs show a difference in the level of civilization which it is difficult to believe occurred over such a short space of time. The workman in Plate 3 seems to belong to a world much further away than a mere 25 years.

The next pair of photographs give a similar impression and were taken with a similar gap of time. Plate 5 was taken in 1880 and Plate 6 in 1908. They are portrayals of outings into the countryside, but the clothes and appearance of the two groups indicate a completely different type of relationships between people and a completely different outlook on entertainments. The photograph from 1880 has the title 'Teferič', which is a word taken from Turkish to mean an outing into the countryside like a picnic. The three figures are dressed in a lavish Eastern style and are sitting on cushions, just visible behind the woman on the right. They symbolize relationships between people based on highly ritualized manners, when a woman in marriage was given over to her husband's family and her own family no longer had any responsibility towards her. Family life was run on strict patriarchal principles, with a head of household whose authority in all questions was final. Plate 6 has the title 'A Family Excursion to Soko Banja' – a spa in Serbia. The whole family has gathered, from grandparents to grandchildren. Judging from the age of the figures seated at the front they could be the families from two sets of grandparents related by marriage. They are dressed as members of a prosperous, urban, modern society. They are people who make their living by trade or profession. Some wear uniforms, which indicates their place in a society with a complex system of hierarchy and subordination distributed according to and reinforcing factors of social class, gender, education, wealth and profession.

The final two portraits (Plate 7 and Plate 8) are of two very different worlds. The first was taken about 1880 and is of a young woman from the town of Niš, Serbia's second city. The town became part of the principality of Serbia in 1878, prior to which it had been in the Ottoman Empire for 400 years. The picture symbolizes the extent to which the dominant, in fact the only, urban role model in the Balkans was Ottoman Turkish. She is dressed from her voluminous skirts to her slippers in a Turkish and typically urban fashion. Her clothes indicate that she is not from a village. She is sitting on some kind of bench over which has been draped a rug with traditional designs on it. She is looking straight ahead, her body turned away and hidden away behind the shapelessness of the clothes. Her somewhat severe expression renders her a rather asexual figure. Plate 8 is a woman from a completely different era. Her name is Ana Marinković and the photograph was taken in 1906. Her Christian name has been written at the bottom of the photograph but not in Serbian. Her name is spelt as 'Anna', whereas Serbian orthography does not allow for double consonants. The spelling follows a French or English style, indicative of the large numbers of young people of her generation who either studied in the West or had private tutors at home for foreign languages. As Serbia was liberating its territory from Ottoman rule Western styles in clothes would arrive very quickly and a middle class begin to form, paying careful attention to fashions as can be seen from Ana Marinković's gown. Her bare shoulders and neck, her eyes cast down and her delicately coiffured hair give her an air of innocent and seductive beauty. This appearance, compared with the young woman from Niš, implies not just a change in outward appearance but a social and cultural transformation from the inside. Ana Marinković thinks and feels differently from her fellow-countrywoman who lived 25 years earlier. However, the change was a revolution which happened overnight, as also seen in the other examples. A world came into being with little time to consolidate itself, aware of its newness and hence its vulnerability. The narratives analyzed in the next chapter bear witness to a type of urban anxiety which fears the loss of the civilization it has won and returning to what it once had been. These representations of city literature from the Balkans are not only a part of Berman's agitated sense of modernity, but also serve to broaden our under-standing of the critical urgency of modernity for Europe's smaller cultures, in which developments occur more rapidly and transfor-mations more radically than in dominant and more stable cultures.

5 Representations of City Life

The history of urbanization in the Balkans, and particularly in the Serbian territories, leads us to expect different emphases in representations of city life from that region. The function of the city under the Ottoman Empire as a place largely of consumption rather than production differed from the West where the city is regarded also as a powerhouse of production. The signs of the city, the relationship between urban and rural areas, and the collective endeavour which the city represents differ between the West and the Balkans. But, although we should expect a different type of city literature, such representations from the Balkans continue to offer narratives about modernization in order to reveal the critical moments of modernity as in the West, albeit with different emphases. I shall present in this chapter three aspects of the representations of city life which point to both differences and similarities with Western literatures. The first concerns the novel *Nečista krv* (*Tainted Blood*) by the writer Borisav Stanković, published in 1910 and set in a small southern town some time after its liberation from Ottoman rule in 1878 and its incorporation into the expanding Serbian state. The second part of this chapter focuses on a series of novels about Belgrade life from 1910 to the beginning of the Second World War, and the eventual resurrection of this theme some decades later. The chapter closes with an examination of two works by the same author, Svetlana Velmar-Janković, both of which concern stories about Belgrade but with a new, sharpened concentration on the meanings of the city space in Serbian culture. These novels taken together not only reflect contemporary developments of urbanization, but in their recurring thematic images they also reveal an underlying sense of agitation about what the city represents in the cultural and historical life of the region.

BORISAV STANKOVIĆ: THE DEATH OF THE ORIENTAL CITY

Borisav Stanković was born in the southern town of Vranje in 1876, just two years before its incorporation into Serbia. Many of his literary works, short stories, plays and novels are set in the town of his childhood. He was educated there, in Niš and in Belgrade where he found employment as a civil servant and where he also published. He lived in Belgrade at a time of rapid Westernization, as the photographs examined at the end of the last chapter show, whereas he was brought up during the time of transformation from an Ottoman to an European urban role model. He was one of the few writers to remain in Belgrade during the Austrian occupation from 1915 to 1918 when he also continued to work in the government administration and to write. Consequently, he was publicly condemned after the First World War as a collaborator and as an unpatriotic element. He became increasingly isolated and in this atmosphere stopped writing. He died in 1927.

Nečista krv is his most famous novel, and was translated into English by Alec Brown in 1932. The translator took certain liberties with Stanković's original text, usually to shorten a passage, but it is sufficiently accurate to capture the flavour of the original, and sometimes the freedoms which the translator allowed himself are of interest in themselves for the way in which he received and understood the work. The title of the translation is *Sophka*, whereas Stanković's title would be more literally rendered as *Tainted Blood*. Sophka is the name of the main character of the story, the daughter of Effendi-Mita. Her father's family are wealthy Serbs who have been highly respected by Turks as well as their co-nationals for some generations. The first sentences of the book make reference to the family by their house: 'The family was old and the house was old. It seemed their house had been there ever since the town existed.'[1] This opening, taken from Brown's translation, is not a literal one, since in Stanković's original version there is no reference to 'the house was old'.[2] Brown's intervention may be considered redundant, although it does emphasize a link between the family and the house. The house represents the family, the two terms are almost synonymous. The house represents the wealth and status of the family and protects it from the outside. Life goes on inside the walled compound rather than on the streets outside. The house becomes an important symbolic element in the novel. The important point established at the beginning of the work is that the house, and by extension, the family, are given an almost mythic status in relation to the town since the two come into existence at the same moment. Sophka's family story is the story of the founding fathers of that community.

Family history begins with Hadji-Triphoun. He is Sophka's great-grandfather who acquired the appellation 'hadji' after he returned from his pilgrimage to Jerusalem. The term is normally given to Moslems who make a pilgrimage to Mecca, and transferring the honour to a Christian is a sign of the family's wealth and position in both the local Serbian and Turkish communities. He dresses in the style of the Turks, receives guests in Ottoman style and decorates his house in that style. The world of his civilization is Ottoman. From the beginning, in Stanković's story, the relationship between Serb and Turk in the district is one of complicity, in stark contrast to the stereotypical image of Serbian resentment, resistance and hostility to Moslem rule. Hadji-Triphoun's crucial contribution is his decision to make a public display of the family's wealth, which was hitherto hidden away to avoid the extortionate taxation policies of the Turks. He adds another storey to his house and makes the whole upper floor a luxurious room for receiving guests. This addition means the house is more visible than most in town where single-storey buildings predominate:

> He built a portico, vaulted and strong as a keep; and he raised the storey of the house and covered it with carved timbers. He filled the rooms with priceless carpets, and with ancient and precious eikons from the Patriarchate of Ipek and the Monasteries of Mount Athos and the Monastery of Rilo; and on shelves round the white walls of the rooms he laid out silver washing vessels and golden holders for the little coffee bowls. At the outer gate he put a mounting stone of marble, so that when he rode out on his famous horses he should have something worthy of his house to set his foot on. (p. 20)

These changes represent a turning-point by which the family announces its sense of security from the power of local Turkish authorities. He heralds a new era in the history of the town, a point of which myths are frequently made.

From the time after Hadji-Triphoun Sophka's family begins to lose the fortune which he built up. They are forced to sell off land which they owned in order to pay debts. It is as if the family becomes soft when each generation is given wealth which they did not have to earn for themselves. The last phase comes with Sophka's father. He is sent away to Istanbul for his education, but when he takes over from his father he is unable to keep the family estate together. He saves face by selling off property to a former employee, who guards the secret of the family's downfall. The final straw comes with the liberation of the town and its becoming a part of Serbia. The new state introduces a different legal and commercial system based on Western models. The period which Stanković reflects in his novel is the Europeanization of the former Turkish territories with a Serbian population. The story of Serbian independence and expansion in the nineteenth century is also the story of its Europeanization. When Miloš Obrenović first gained limited autonomy for Serbia, he needed men with education to run the state administration. Serbs from over the Danube, schooled in Austria, crossed the border into the newly independent state and took up these positions. They regarded themselves 'as distinguished bearers of Western culture, destined to administer the illiterate and "half-savage barbarians" of the Principality'.[3] The local Serbs called them 'Švabe', a derogatory term for 'Germans', for their European style of dress and manners. As time passed and Serbia included new territories within its domain, this process continued with the same reactions at each stage. From the north came administrators whose function was to change the way of life of the region. Sophka's father left for Turkey because of them and the new ways they were sent to introduce:

> But with the end of Turkish sovereignty came civil courts and litigation; with much ado as to settling matters with the churls and determining what lands were whose; which the lord's, which Turkish, and which to be the churls'. Then it became evident that in the end nothing of their property would be left; in which the most cruel thing to Sophka's father was that he, Effendi-Mita, would have to go to court and take oaths and squabble, and that with whom? – with those that were but yesterday his churls! (p. 55)

Effendi-Mita leaves his wife and daughter to manage what is left of the family's possessions, occasionally sending some money home. The title *Tainted Blood* is a reference to the story of the family's degeneration.

Sophka is the main character of the novel and the one who

sacrifices herself for the sake of her father. She grows up deeply linked to her largely absent father. The family is sinking further down, although her mother manages to keep up the appearance of a well-to-do family. When they have nothing left to sell except their house, Sophka's father returns accompanied by a visitor. The visitor is Gazda Marko who represents a very different sort of Serbian culture from Sophka's family. He has come from over the border to the south, a region still under Ottoman occupation. He became wealthy there but has been forced to move to town, and Serbian territory, as a result of a blood feud with an Albanian neighbour. Sophka fancies that Gazda Marko has come to buy their house, seeing how he 'took stock of the house all the time, drinking it all in' (p. 116). In fact, he is looking for a bride for his young son, Tomtcha, and Sophka is to be his purchase. While he examines her house it is Sophka who is the real object of his gaze. Sophka, and what she represents of the last traces of Serbian-Ottoman urban culture, is symbolically linked to the house.

All important events in the development of the story, until after Sophka's wedding when she leaves her own house to live in that of Gazda Marko, occur with reference to this house. She imagines that she sees reflected in the external appearance of the house a great deal of what she is thinking and feeling. On returning from the ritual bathing at the local bath-house, or *amam*, she contemplates the house with its 'odour of death'. The roof has been repaired with money obtained by her 'sale'. The new tiles look like 'meat' or 'flesh'; it is her flesh (pp. 194–5). This close relationship between Sophka and the house is seen again a few pages later on the day of the wedding. She is standing on public display: 'on show in the downstairs large room, a waiting statue' (p. 218). The whole scene is described from her point of view, from the corner of the room in which she is standing. When the time comes to leave, her progress across the room is described and then, at the threshold, 'her veil caught on the latch of the door' (p. 220). It is as if the house is trying to prevent the final fall of the family; Sophka's marriage to a young boy of about 12, to a family whose way of life differs radically from the refined manners of her own town family.

An important function of the house in the text is that its internal geography represents a vision of orderliness. Order is reflected in the carefully chosen details of the layout of the internal geography of the house and yard:

The yard in front of the house downstairs had long been wa-
tered and swept. The paved paths from the gate to the house
showed white. At the well water was trickling out of a bucket
and glinting in the sun as it dripped over the stones. The grass
round the well, about the courtyard, and even among the stones
of the paving showed in dark patches. Their garden, behind the
house, fenced off from the courtyard, was green, and the spar-
rows were twittering under the eaves. (p. 82)

The description closes with the sight of Sophka's mother sitting 'at
the bottom of the steps, immediately adjoining the kitchen'. She is
preparing food and looking into the kitchen to make sure that the
dishes cooking on the stove do not spill over the sides of the pans.
In another episode Sophka's mother and father are entertaining
Gazda Marko in the room upstairs, a space which is reserved for
guests and important meetings, while Sophka and the family servant are downstairs. The division between spatial functions is
deliberately expressed and repeated many times. The episode opens
with the statement: 'Then upstairs, in the great guest room, they
sat down.' We read how the servant is preparing food 'downstairs',
that dishes had to be arranged on trays 'to take upstairs', that Sophka
took the tray which she 'carried upstairs and into the room to them'.
The episode closes with the comment: 'Upstairs dinner began' (pp.
117–18). Each part of the house and courtyard is divided from the
others, and through these divisions each part gains its own function which defines it and adds to the overall sense of the house as
a symbolic space of order.

This ordered space is specially protected by the large gate built
by Hadji-Triphoun. The arrival and departure of guests and visitors
who come through it are carefully detailed as in: 'The boy went;
the gates were closed behind him ... She did not even hear the
gates open and their Magda, like one very much at home, slip in'
(p. 90). It regulates the flow between the family and the outside
world, so that once inside, 'They then were absolutely isolated, walled
in by the walls of their house and the courtyard, and felt themselves
at liberty to do exactly as they pleased' (p. 72). Their gate comes
to bestow the quality of an inner sanctum to the house and courtyard.
This spirit of liberation and security allows Sophka access to her
own physical presence and inner spaces of emotion and feeling, as
when she goes out on one occasion to check that the gate is properly
closed: 'And then, on her way back from the gates, it came. She

felt that same enjoyment of her own flesh that she felt winter evenings when shut in alone' (p. 98). The house, like the culture it represents, is based on a highly elaborate etiquette governing all aspects of behaviour and on respect for privacy. Freedom within this framework is the reward of the order of civilization.

On her arrival at Marko's house after the wedding Sophka deliberately eyes the gate into the courtyard. Her fears are allayed when she realizes that this symbolically significant object 'even seemed to be familiar' and is described in terms reminiscent of the one built by Hadji-Triphoun being 'high and strong-built, a keep in itself' (p. 230). However, as with other things in Marko's house, she soon finds out that the symbolic and literal functions of the house may be completely different here. The function of the gate in Marko's house is not a force of protective security. The gate closes behind him, leaving him alone with total authority over the space within. Far from being a symbol of inner freedom, it is a prison gate which Marko calls to be closed during the wedding feast: 'The gates, come, the gates, shut the gates, bar the gates, no one shall come in' (p. 247). Of course, barring the entry forbids people to come in, but also forbids them to leave, it traps them. Later, carried away by alcohol, mutilating themselves, people begin to jump over the walls in order to escape. The walls around the house and the gate do not so much regulate contact with the world outside, rather they close it out. It is in this confined space that Sophka begins to realize the gulf between herself and their world. They lived in mountains, separated from the world, not part of society but 'scattered about the mountains and grazing grounds' (p. 251). She watches as the feasting and drinking drags on over days and an orgy erupts, with the participants unconscious of the taboos of family ties: 'there was no more old or young, nor wife or daughter, nor uncle or aunt, not any other relationship either uniting or dividing' (p. 250). Observing these events in fear Sophka eventually 'saw daylight now through those unbelievable stories of what "peasants" did' (p. 251). She is coming to realize what is waiting for her; her new husband is too young so Gazda Marko will claim seigneurial rights over his daughter-in-law.

Another important distinction between the geography of the two houses is the lack of differentiated space at Gazda Marko's. From the beginning we are given the detail that Hadji-Triphoun 'put a mounting stone of marble' by the gate, whereas Gazda Marko, we are told, 'rode up to the kitchen threshold' (p. 156). There are no clear divisions between different areas of the house and courtyard. After Marko orders the gate to be closed the house seems dominated by one 'great room' in which: 'The fires in the kitchen were banked ... Fires burned too round the house, and even down by the stables and byres' (p. 248). The whole house, inside and outside, becomes a single space. As the feast progresses, the guests become wilder in their behaviour, while at the same time the borders between different parts of the house, where there ought to be a differentiation of functions, begin to dissolve: 'Now all boundaries ceased to exist. Large room and kitchen became one tipsy sea; and in their hotness they threw off garment after garment' (p. 249). As divisions within the house dissolve so do the divisions between accepted and taboo behaviour. The restraints of civilization are represented by functional differentiation in the internal geography of living space.

The two worlds of Sophka and Gazda Marko are separated by an immeasurable gulf. That division is the difference between an urban, Ottoman civilization, and Marko's rural, aggressive boorishness . The two worlds know little about each other. The town soon learns that Marko brought his family to town from over the border in the Ottoman Empire in order to escape a blood feud: 'His native village was there, not far over the new frontier, just on the other side of the Monastery of the Holy Father – a poor village in a dour land – small houses of stone, stone roofed' (p. 162). Marko's universe is beyond the frontier, an unknown waste land, but now approaching and threatening the centre of the known, civilized world. It is stressed that Marko's part of town where he has bought his house is unlike the part where Sophka lives. It is 'recently built, not properly town yet – where peasants lived, people coming in now to the town from the surrounding villages, or come as refugees from Turkey' (p. 120). There are many references to Marko's house which he bought in town and where he continues living with the same Spartan lifestyle as he was used to over the frontier. He had carpets and cushions but these were usually kept out of sight. Stana, Marko's wife, is described in clothes which position her closer to her peasant origins: 'The only part of her clothing which suggested town was a blouse, a costly silk one, but out from under it always stuck her coarse peasant shirt' (p. 168). She cannot adjust to the town. Marko and his people from the village behave awkwardly in the company of people from the town, displaying the worries and anxieties of people not schooled in certain refinements.

But the gulf which separates these two worlds cannot be reduced to a difference of social class.

On her arrival at Marko's house, Sophka looks around at Marko's guests and she begins to romanticize their peasant appearance, simply dressed, healthy from living outdoors. Her musings on the subject are described over some two pages by Stanković, but the translator omits much of the description in an effort to summarize the scene. However, this meeting of the two worlds as they gaze upon each other is not far removed from how the civilized foreigner observes the primitive Balkans. To Sophka, these wild people from the mountains resemble characters from the old songs and stories. She considers a possible role for herself, unaware how close to the truth she might be: 'She was a famous beauty, taken off to a castle and concealed there – and these men of Marko's had gone marauding and had found her and had taken the castle, and destroyed it, and seized her, and now they were here with her, halting to rest' (p. 236). As the celebrations continue the descriptions of Marko's guests begins to change as if they are going through a process of regression: 'the attempt to follow town customs in music and dance was finally abandoned and their own wild mountain habits had sway' (p. 238). When Sophka begins serving the men with drink and kissing their hand in a ritual performance which was no longer practised in the town, she notes how they 'began to behave like children in their pleasure' (p. 243). As time goes on and the gate is barred Sophka 'began to feel horror, and a trembling of fear' (p. 251). At this point she has gone through the range of expressions about wild men as heroes from imagination, like children in their simplicity, and now like savages.

Marko's plan to take his daughter-in-law is considered normal practice in the villages, but is a custom unacceptable to the town. Marko knows this, and that his attempt is an attack on a level of civilization which had taken centuries to build. Sophka is saved from Marko by the local matchmaker, at which Marko takes off back to the frontier lands from where the news eventually comes that he has been killed. It seems that the town has reasserted itself. Sophka becomes mistress of her husband's house, bringing into it that same order which she had known at home:

It only needed a hand to manage it; and Sophka was that hand. Carpets woven and cushions dyed and embroidered were laid over the floors and their harshness disappeared. Large shelves

of strong wood held bright *sakhans* and *tepsias* and the kitchen
was warm and inviting. The whole house gradually changed; comfort came where there had been Spartan misery. (p. 281)

Her downfall, when it comes, is at the hand of her father once
again. He reminds Tomtcha, now a grown man, that his marriage
was a business deal between the two fathers, and he wanted the
money promised. Tomtcha, like Marko before him, rides off to the
frontier leading a life of violence, only occasionally returning to
town where he abuses and breaks the spirit of Sophka. At the close
of the novel Sophka and her children, many of them sickly, drag
themselves around the spaces of the house with no differential function to divide up the internal geography. The servant eventually
comes and joins her sitting by the fire in the kitchen. All decorum
and respect for order is gone. Sophka spends less of her time in
the house and frequently visits her neighbours, idling away time:
'through the whole day, once started, she might go from house to
house' (p. 301). However, the translator misses an important detail that Sophka on her daily rounds to her neighbours no longer
enters or leaves the houses through the main gate, that vital symbol of order and security.[4] Her world has been destroyed.

Sophka taken in this reading is a narrative about the end of an
era. Serbia has expanded southwards and includes territory formerly belonging to the Ottoman Empire where Ottoman customs
and manners represent the pinnacle of urban civilization. This is
Sophka, her family and her house. This community is weakened
and their energy already sapped. However, Vranje has been transformed into a new frontier town which is most at threat from refugees
and others fleeing over the border from Turkey to the south. They,
like Gazda Marko, represent conquering barbarians come to tear
down the walls of civilization. They are not newcomers challenged
by the opportunities of the urban environment. This is a confron-
tation between order and chaos which the city proves incapable of
resisting. Put another way, it has already been noted that the new
Serbian state was intent on eradicating all vestiges of Ottoman rule.
The decline of Sophka in order to make way for something completely different is a necessary symbolic act. Thinking of the
photographs examined at the end of the last chapter, we can say
that the image of the girl in Turkish dress from Niš has to be
removed to allow for the introduction and upbringing of Ana
Marković. Stanković's novel is a part of the tradition of city literature

which expresses modernity's critical moment poised on the brink
of destruction, as described by Berman. The critical moment here
threatens a radical loss of a complete civilization. Sophka is one of
those who faces 'a radical threat to all their history and traditions'.[5]
Stanković's urban setting may not coincide with the city literature
of London, Paris, Petersburg and New York in all particulars, but
the strong distinction between urban and rural, of civilization under threat from the outside, the potential for dynamic development,
and the semiotic meanings of architecture belong to the total European experience and expression of modernity.

From its publication Serbian critics have experienced problems
in accommodating Stanković's work in general and this novel in
particular. His thematic focus falls on the end of a way of life based
on an Ottoman role model, and the destructive forces that such a
huge social transformation brings in its wake. Stanković's great
contribution to Serbian literature is acknowledged, and his sub-
tlety of character portrayal and of depicting the broad historical
moment are recognized. However, such praise is usually accompanied by a slight reservation or qualification which distances his work.
In 1914 the critic Jovan Skerlić summarizes Stanković's work concerned with the lands of Old Serbia, saying that he was a poet 'of
an exotic world', who describes Vranje 'of the old days' before
modernization, in which are mixed 'Eastern sensuality and Slavonic
sensibility' and where 'the battle is fought between East and West'.[6]
The general impression has changed little in more recent times
with comments to the effect that he is a regional writer whose work
expresses 'love for bygone days and the patriarchal way of life and
at the same time a deep resistance towards modern life and a rejection of town life'.[7] Ivan Šop in his book *Istok u srpskoj književnosti*
(*The East in Serbian Literature*, 1982) rightly observes that in Yugoslav literatures 'the problem of the relationship with the Orient
appears differently than in other European literatures'.[8] The relationship does not arise as a result of literary influences but because
of historical ties and connections which are particularly complex in
the Serbian case. For all that, Šop includes Stanković amongst those
whose work projects 'the authentic experience of the East'.[9] The
critics are uncomfortable with Stanković's 'Orientalism'. The concern with identity and modernity is transformed into a fascination
with the burden of the past. However, for Sophka the world of
Marko and his people is as exotic and far removed as she is exotic
and far removed from the world of Stanković's reading public in

1910. He traces with her the process of modernization, the chaos of the end of an era, the turmoil of values, the end of the Ottoman world in Serbia. The loss of Sophka's world was part of the design of those who wanted to establish a Westernized Serbia, her destruction is a necessary part of that other historical narrative. Rather than writing about Vranje before modernization, Stanković is an author who puts the story of Serbia's modernization at the centre of his novel.

THE RISE AND FALL OF METROPOLITAN LITERATURE

In the same year that Stanković published his novel *Nečista krv*, another novel about a very different city environment appeared. Milutin Uskoković published his novel *Došljaci* (*The Newcomers*, 1910). He is the first to take contemporary Belgrade as a setting for the action of his work. Jovan Skerlić comments on this important aspect of Uskoković's novel: 'In *The Newcomers* he has given the hitherto best Belgrade novel, with faithful reproductions of various Belgrade scenes, troubled life in a young capital, the feverish struggle in a society not yet properly ordered, beautiful and vibrant descriptions of the Belgrade landscape.'[10] Many others repeat Skerlić's sentiments about Uskoković's achievement in this respect. Some go further than Skerlić in recognizing that Belgrade plays a more active role in his work. Uskoković focuses on the new way of life which the development of Belgrade as a metropolitan centre offers. It has none of the comforting intimacy of a small-town atmosphere. Belgrade itself is a 'key symbol' in the representation of the clash between urban and patriarchal cultures of the new Serbia.[11]

The Newcomers concerns the arrival of Miloš from a small town in Serbia. He, like many others, is attracted to the dynamism and opportunities which the city gives to those willing to take risks and seize the moment. Coming from Užice, he is employed as a reporter on a Belgrade newspaper. He is sent out to cover the suicide of a young woman who killed herself for love. At the scene he meets Zorka, a slightly older woman. This is one of the first novels in which sexual attraction forms a motivating factor in the action of the story. The two are attracted to each other and begin a secret affair. They meet in the parks around the city, confident that in a city of that size they are unlikely to be recognized by a casual passer-by. The city permits the kind of clandestine liaisons which small-town and village life do not. This is a city of limited ambitions amongst those who are truly talented, and which is otherwise driven by the pettiness, jealousies and rivalries of the less talented. Miloš writes a play which is hugely successful, and in which Zorka recognizes his resistance to the idea of their marriage. As an act of extreme self-sacrifice she commits suicide by throwing herself into the Danube. Miloš decides that Belgrade is an environment which is too hostile to newcomers such as himself, encouraging depravity, dishonesty and the break-up of family life. He is defeated by the city and wants to return home. At the end of the novel he walks with a friend to the railway station. On the way he observes crowds of people filling the streets in which: 'The large shop windows of the fashionable Belgrade stores were luxuriously illuminated.'[12] This is a world in which life spills out into the streets, parks and public places in all corners of the city. The crowds fill the streets with anonymity and with the self-satisfaction of a culture which exists only for the moment, not thinking about tomorrow. Belgrade takes an active role in determining the limits of human agency. Characters are forced to confront the challenge of the city, adapt to its values, grasp its culture and struggle to understand the multi-accented cityscape.

Other novels were to follow in the 1920s and 1930s, such as Rastko Petrović's *Sa silama nemerljivim* (*With Immeasurable Powers*, 1927), Branimir Ćosić's *Dva carstva* (*The Two Empires*, 1928) and his *Pokošeno polje* (*The Mown Field*, 1934), and Stevan Jakovljević's *Smena generacija* (*A Change of Generations*, 1939). These works reflect the consequences of rapid urban and commercial development which would leave people caught between the traditions of two cultures. Much of the action in these novels is motivated by the conflict between traditional patriarchal values and the demands of urban living made on the newcomers to the city. They represent the metropolitan aspect of city literature, analogous to developments seen in Western literature. Characteristic themes in these novels highlight the break-up of close family circles, damage caused by value systems based on money and greed, illicit and erotic affairs. The story of *The Two Empires* is based on the conflict between two worlds. The hero is the son of a secondary-school teacher whose ambition is to make a name for himself and thereby to enter the city's high society. His actions are not the result of his character but are conditioned by the circumstances in which he lives in Belgrade. He begins a love affair with a married woman through whom he hopes to further his aims. During this period he also befriends her husband, and he is caught between desire for her and a sense of moral obligation arising from this friendship. The solution is found only when the three of them are staying away from Belgrade and its corrosive influence, in a monastery. The hero is helped by one of the monks to confront his conscience and to return to Belgrade cleansed from desire and the corruption of the city. Such novels, perhaps at times sentimental in tone, continued to appear to the beginning of the Second World War. By the appearance of Jakovljević's *A Change of Generations* this kind of 'Belgrade prose' was at an end as a creative source for imaginative literature. The characters in his work are wooden, their actions mechanical and predictable. The story relies on plots and sub-plots which have been well rehearsed earlier.

After the Second World War cultural and literary life in Yugoslavia came under the direct influence of the Communists. From the beginning of their rule they were highly aware of the role which all forms of representation may have in forming public opinion. Europe's smaller nations are particularly conscious of the many histories which make up the past and that these histories are written by the victors. The afterword in a literature text book intended for schools and published in the early 1950s opens with this sentence: 'There is no doubt that in our new system of schooling literature represents one of the strongest ideological means in the building of a socialist personality.'[13] The Communists required from literature two specific tasks; one was to show the path to Socialism by positive messages and stories, the second was to represent the Partisan victory in terms which would justify the Communists' monopoly of political power. Literature and literary history were the ideological tools of a totalitarian regime. In these early years the Yugoslav Communists followed Stalinist practices in government and quickly denounced pre-war writers who were known anti-Communists, such as Miloš Crnjanski. The emphasis was placed on narratives about the war in which Partisans were shown consistently in a good light, while their enemies were portrayed as instinctively evil types. Novels about the city, particularly following the tradition of 'Belgrade prose', were distinctly not encouraged.

Novels about the metropolis whether it be Belgrade or elsewhere tend to depict certain kinds of social organization. All the voices of the city represent different social groups and different class interests. Characters may be upwardly or downwardly mobile, but action is motivated within a moral framework which tends to value material success coupled with an individual humanism. The life of the city is the collective endeavour of all inhabitants, which is a sum far stronger than the sum of its individual parts. Life is public, anonymous, unfolding on the street. This is not an image of a society which will accept control of all facets of manners and behaviour. The Communist aim was to spread its net through all aspects of city life, to stunt its anarchic tendencies, to bring into its control not only public life, but also the private lives of citizens. Whatever was thought privately was made a matter of public concern. This kind of totalitarian regime demands the right to prohibit images which support individualism and pluralism. Therefore, city literature under the Communists remained dormant for some years.

Literature about Belgrade began to appear again during the late 1960s. One of the first of these novels was Dragoslav Mihailović's *Kad su cvetale tikve* (*When Pumpkins Blossomed*, 1968) set at the end of the war in a deprived area of the city. Characters use the language of the streets and their mental and emotional horizons are fixed by the harshness of daily life.[14] Mihailović's novel was one of many at the time which intended to use literature as a vehicle for expressing the brutal realities of life. The narrator is the main character of the story who recalls the time of his youth when he was involved in a street gang. While away on military service, his sister is raped, as a result of which she commits suicide. He discovers that the rapist is the leader of his old gang. He plots revenge and eventually kills him before escaping to Sweden where he has lived ever since. This and other novels of the late 1960s with strong social themes are evidence of a change of direction in the Communist Party's attitude towards cultural policy, but the Party never relinquished all its original attitudes. When Mihailović dramatized his novel and it was put on stage he experienced political difficulties and the production did not have a long run. Later writers in the following decade also turned to the representations of Belgrade in their prose works. One of them was Borislav Pekić with his novel *Hodočašće Arsenija Njegovana* (*The Pilgrimage of Arsenije Njegovan*, 1970). His evocation of the city transforms its history, streets and buildings into metaphors. It is a highly symbolic work out of necessity since it reflects on those issues towards which the Communists were most sensitive such as the traditions and values based on civic pride, the city's commercial expansion, property ownership and the pluralism of a society which acknowledges difference of citizens and their right to dissent. Although his treatment of the city and its meanings for Serbian culture are necessarily subdued, later works approach these issues more openly and vigorously.

Pekić's novel has been translated into English with the title *The Houses of Belgrade*. The two titles of both the original and the translation convey the twin facets of the narrative. On the one hand, the story is narrated by and concerns the pre-war rentier, Arsenije Njegovan, who has not left his flat since 1941. It is now 1968 and he decides to step outside into the street again and to visit the houses which he used to own before the arrival of the Communists. He believes that they are still his properties. His walk around Belgrade is a pilgrimage, a visit to symbolic shrines which he worships in his memory. He was and continues to be obsessed by his houses, even developing a philosophy of ownership: 'Between me and my possessions a relationship of reciprocal ownership operates; we are two sides of one being, the being of *possession*.'[15] He looks upon the physical presence of the houses with the eyes of a true believer, sometimes too pious in his tendency to forgive himself all sins in pursuit of his religion of possession. His stepping beyond the walls of his flat is also a pilgrimage in the symbolic sense of a journey of self-discovery. His reflections on former times give the impression of a figure trying to come to terms with the past. The houses as shrines also occupy a central thematic role in the text. He gave each of them a name and considers their architectural features and interior design as if traits of their personalities. He invariably regards these houses as feminine, and his image of them as hollowed-out statues for habitation adds to their womb-like appeal. He describes them as they are being built as if they are being ripped from mother earth. They are the embodiments of life cycles from birth and development into maturity; what he does not see is that he is now visiting them in the decay of an advanced old age hastened by the effects of Communist rule. Pekić's novel heralds a return to 'Belgrade prose' as narratives in which the cityscape plays an important role in the semantics of the fictional world. However, this example and later ones by other writers have little to do with the pre-war series of novels; rather, they hark back to certain preoccupations which first became evident in Stanković's work.

In his thoughts Arsenije Njegovan recalls stories about his grandfather, Simeon. He helped Emilijan Josimović in his proposal to demolish the old Turkish quarter of Belgrade, now known as Dorćol, and replace it with houses built in the European style with streets planned according to a grid pattern. Knowing the contents of Josimović's plans, Simeon invested in some financial speculation, buying up parcels of land which were going to be essential for the realization of the intention to construct an European Belgrade on the ruins of the Turkish city. For Njegovan his grandfather simply showed himself to be an individual of vision who participated in the construction and allocation of space whether it be for parks, ornamental gardens, thoroughfares, private houses or government buildings. The city is an amalgamation of all these functions which need to be ordered within the cityscape. His family, therefore, are associated with the transformation of Belgrade for which they 'stood out, distinguished by a European orderliness; they built up Gospodska and Pop-Pantina Streets (now Brankova and Marshall Biryuzov Streets)' (p. 143). Opposed to them there remained large parts of the city where 'Asiatic chaos still reigned' (p. 144). Njegovan's grandfather is written into the myth of the foundation of modern Belgrade in a way which is reminiscent of Sophka's grandfather in Stanković's novel *Sophka*. Simeon's Belgrade represents the overcoming of the alien past, rebuilding a new civilization more desired than what existed before. The city is the symbol of a modern, European world and all associated values which stand in contrast to the collectivist uniformity imposed by Belgrade's Communist rulers after the Second World War.

Njegovan has not left his flat since the end of March 1941. On that day he was walking through the centre of Belgrade on his way to an auction to buy a property with which he had fallen in love. On the way he comes across a large crowd of demonstrators. He is not aware of the facts surrounding these events, but he is in the middle of a *coup d'état* against the regent, Prince Paul. The Prince had signed a pact of friendship with Hitler to allow the transportation of German troops across Yugoslavia to reinforce Mussolini's forces in their campaign against Greece. The popular groundswell of opinion against the pact was supported by an odd collection of groups including high-ranking officers in the army, the Orthodox Church and the Communist Party. The particular crowd which he comes across is being addressed by representatives from the Communist Party. Njegovan recognizes certain sentiments being expressed with which he is in full agreement, namely an attack on bankers and the evils of the capitalist banking system. He is against these institutions and their financial practices because he despises their lack of understanding for the symbiotic relationship between owner and object owned in his philosophy of ownership. For him this is an intimate relationship, for a banker it is a financial transaction. At first, the crowd listens to Njegovan assuming that he is speaking from a Communist perspective, as they realize that his point of view stems from an attitude towards property rights which runs directly counter to their own ideology the crowd pushes on and Njegovan is badly injured as a result. He makes his way home but has been so badly shaken by the violence of the streets that he does not leave his flat until 1968, on which occasion he also is a witness to demonstrators on the streets. They are student demonstrators, but their purpose is again obscure to Njegovan and he assumes that he is once more seeing a total breakdown of order. He considers that social collapse is due to a fault in urban design: 'The workers' suburbs have been located in an encircling belt which grips the commercial heart of the city like a vise. This has concentrated the proletariate in breeding grounds of revolt and destruction' (p. 175). Njegovan offers an example of the disorienting effect brought about when the signs of the city are misrecognized.

As Njegovan walks around Belgrade, unaware of all the changes since the Communists came to power, his thoughts begin to exercise a defamiliarizing effect on the city. Not realizing that private property was requisitioned after the war, he thinks that his properties are still his. He meets with former caretakers and rent collectors whom he looks at through his pre-war lenses and assumes that they are still working for him in their old capacities. As he reflects on the public buildings lining the city centre streets he cannot imagine their function under Communism. His mind keeps returning to the municipal institutional infrastructure from before the war. To him these buildings continue to fulfil the same roles and house the same administrations from 30 years ago. He uses the pre-war names of streets. These streets still exist but with new names which reflect the total change of regime, values and culture introduced at the end of 1944. Belgrade was transformed from an Ottoman to a Serbian city, destroyed and rebuilt, transformed by the Communists and created again. Names have not altered the physical geography but they are surely as much a sign of the disappearance of the old town of property owners and all that they stood for as the actions of Simeon Njegovan and Emilijan Josimović in the Turkish quarter of the 1870s. Now streets are named after the Communist builders of a new society.

The physical presence of the city and its history fall under Njegovan's defamiliarizing gaze, questioning its existence as if from another culture removed in time and space. His personal vision, consistent and logical within its own internal system, exposes the fragility of the city as an affirmation of modernity and identity. Pekić approaches Belgrade on a symbolic level, its abrupt changes and transformations altering the shape of the city as a cultural space. The city comes to represent a strange experience of life with no centre, where history keeps slipping through Njegovan's fingers. The buildings and materiality which make the urban environment are not in this case the collective record of a community, but a discordant choir of voices. Njegovan dies at the end of his pilgrimage. Like Sophka in Stanković's novel, he represents a generation and culture which no longer has a place in the new world. The critical moment arrives and wipes away the traces of what has been, renaming and reinventing the city.

SVETLANA VELMAR-JANKOVIĆ: BELGRADE RE-PRESENTED

Two works by Svetlana Velmar-Janković explore further the meaning of the cityscape for Balkan forms of modernity based on elements found initially in Pekić's novel. The first work is named after the old Turkish quarter of Belgrade, Dorćol. Velmar-Janković published her cycle of short stories *Dorćol* in 1981, which was also the beginning of the last decade of the country founded after the Second World War. The year of publication came shortly after the death of President Tito, a time when many literary taboos were broken. The main targets for these new works were the Communist myths about the Partisan movement which they had created as part of their justification for rule after the war. The Partisans, in these myths, were not only the natural victors over traitors and occupying forces, but also an army which committed itself to high moral standards to protect innocent civilians. It was time to rewrite the official history, to describe what happened in Belgrade when the Communists arrived and to give the city back its history. As Pekić has intimated in his novel, for the Communists all collective memory of the society which existed before the war was contaminated because it was not of their creation. So, giving the city back its history in these fictional representations was highly significant. Many of these later narratives about the city also include more broadly topics from Serbian history, the history of Belgrade being a metaphor for the development of the independent state in the nineteenth century. Velmar-Janković's *Dorćol* is a series of interrelated stories about some of the main historical actors involved in Serbia of last century.

Dorćol has a highly symbolic structure. Each story in the collection is the name of one of the streets in the district. The streets are named after figures from Serbian history who were involved in events from the First Serbian Uprising to the withdrawal of the Turks in 1867. Vasa Čarapić, Uzun-Mirko and Zmaj od Noćaja are figures associated with Kara Djordje's unsuccessful First Serbian Uprising; Gospodar Jevrem, Gospodar Jovan and Kneginja Ljubica are the two brothers and wife of Miloš Obrenović; Dositej Obradović and Kapetan Miša also have streets named after themselves in Dorćol for their respective contributions to the early cultural and commercial life of Serbia; while other figures representing various aspects of this period also appear. The stories are organized around a rough geographical principle that as the reader reads each one he is taken on a journey. The first story is named after the street which borders the district, 'Francuska ulica'. The next few are streets at the top and bottom of the slope as it faces the Danube, while the remainder cut across them in an east-west direction. Their order in the text gradually leads into the district until the last story, 'Stara čaršija', where the centre lies at the crossroads called in Turkish *dort jol* from which the name Dorćol is derived. The crossroads were formerly a site for executions.

Each story begins by introducing the eponymous historical figure after whom the street is named. They are all spectral images who unseen tread their eternal paths, every day the same, down their street, observing the life of modern Belgrade, reflecting on their historical roles and looking out for other spirits who used to live on their streets. Their individual reflections coincide and conflict building up a complex picture of Serbian culture. There is a fundamental dichotomy between the figure of Kara Djordje and that of Miloš Obrenović. The former is regarded as a heroic figure finally defeated by the greater numbers of the Ottoman forces, forced into exile, from where he was betrayed into Miloš's hands and murdered. Miloš Obrenović used cunning and stealth to achieve his aims of increased autonomy from the Turks, turning against his fellow-countrymen whom he suspected of not supporting his tyrannical rule. This is the beginning of cycles of success, deceit and betrayal which typify the representation of Serbian history presented here. Miloš's brothers ally themselves to Toma Vučić Perišić in order to force Miloš into exile; then he turns against them. Human agency is a limited factor in a culture which focuses attention on inevitable repetitions of internal conflict. There are numerous other details in the text which draw attention to the constant return of destructive forces. In the story about the incident which leads to the Ottoman withdrawal from Belgrade, there is a description of the 1862 Turkish cannonade on the city, immediately followed by reference to later bombardments in 1915, 1941 and 1944: 'The bombs exploded, truly at intervals, yet nevertheless one after the other (it is still not 1915, nor 1941, nor 1944, but it is a beginning).'[16] The street named after Vasa Čarapić is at the head of another called 29. novembra (29th November Street) in honour of former Yugoslavia's Republic Day. However, the date also coincides with the taking of Belgrade on the night of 29 and 30 November 1806 by Kara Djordje's forces when Vasa Čarapić perished in the assault. The narrator remarks on this coincidence simply that historians could say that their subject confirms 'that some dates are repeated'(p. 61). History is not governed by relationships of cause and effect, which denies the possibility of collective continuity. All that remains are isolated lives and memory.

Isolation is a dominant theme in Velmar-Janković's work. The characters seek out other historical figures where their streets intersect or yet others whose lives are associated with their streets. Gospodar Jevrem waits in vain each day for Vuk Karadžić and Dositej Obradović but he never meets them. On seeing the figure of Nikola Pašić, a prominent Serbian politician from the beginning of this century, he wants to put to him a question about Serbian politics and the cycles of ruin which seem to characterize the history of the city. He asks, 'Is it possible without treachery?' (p. 26) However, he receives no reply as Pašić is deeply distracted by his thoughts about another historical era. Each character is isolated in the age which gave birth to them, and different eras can only catch faint and distant sounds about events in which they were not involved. The statue of Vasa Čarapić from his vantage point is able to watch the people of modern Belgrade crossing the road in front of the National Theatre to Republic Square. He notes a connection between the alternating green, red and yellow traffic lights and the movement of the pedestrians from which he concludes that the people are somehow dependent on the lights. His view from the past is unable to read the signs of the modern city, rather like Njegovan's more consistent defamiliarization of the cityscape. All that exists are unexplained parallels between different ages which link them together. For example, Uzun-Mirko once worked as a tailor's apprentice in Belgrade before the First Serbian Uprising, and on the site of the shop where he worked there now stands a branch of the modern textile company 'Srbijateks'. The buildings of the city administration which he visits in 1843 to qualify for a derisory pension are occupied by a similar institution during the Second World War in 1943. The chemist's shop owned by Savka Kaljević is still a shop, but instead of her smiling face the customer is greeted by a plastic doll 'in a light raincoat' (p. 36). The passage of time is illustrated by transformations which serve to cut off and divide different eras. The city does not speak the same language. As its semiotic systems change the city outstrips its inhabitants, leaving them behind. It becomes a design of streets, a vast network of thoroughfares along which lives pass but with no other significance.

Velmar-Janković's image of Belgrade is an image of sinister ambiguity. The centre of the quarter focuses on a crossroads which was called in Turkish times *dort-jol*. Executions used to be carried out on this spot in a peculiar manner. We are told that the condemned man would be led out and decapitated while still standing. The head flies from the shoulders and the body of the prisoner 'already dead, still alive staggers towards non-existence' (p. 211). The transformation from life to death is the passing of a frontier in which, for a brief moment, opposites co-exist. Such is Belgrade, never permitted its full development before being arrested again. The city's history is a narrative of identities which co-exist in a confusing pattern expressing both civilization and primitivism at the same time.

The other work by Svetlana Velmar-Janković to be examined here is her novel *Lagum*, published in 1990 just before the break-up of Yugoslavia. It takes the form of a fictional autobiography tracing the years before the Second World War in the life of a Belgrade middle-class family, how they experienced the war and their fate when the Communists took over. The work has been translated into English with the title *Dungeon* (1996). The original title is more accurately a reference to underground tunnels such as those which run beneath the old Turkish fortress of Kalemegdan in Belgrade. One of their uses was to serve as prisons. The word evokes connotations of capture by an alien power, internment and claustrophobia. The story is told by an old lady in her eighties. She leaves behind the story of her life wanting it to be 'a mark'. She describes her imprint existing, as she describes it, 'In the snow. In the ocean waves. In the sand. In the darkness of outer space'; thus, giving a sense of a constantly moving, slippery, irrecoverable environment.[17] It is an account of events from before the Second World War, the war years and the consequences of Communist rule. Her life stands for all the other lives turned upside-down by the chaos of this century in Belgrade. Her name is Milica Pavlović, married to Dušan Pavlović, a distinguished art critic and Professor at the University of Belgrade. They led a very comfortable life before the war. Their stability is threatened firstly by the Germans in the occupied city and then by the Communists who arrest Dušan Pavlović on their arrival in Belgrade. Most of their flat is requisitioned and Milica Pavlović is left with one small room for herself and two children. She often searches in her memory for those difficult times, on each occasion filling in a little more of the details. She also narrates her life after the war. Denied at first any kind of job or income, she eventually is given work as a translator from French. Her children grow up and become successful in their chosen fields. She even gets to know those who changed her life and forced her out of her own home. She writes her story in 1984 shortly before her death.

The story has certain echoes from Stanković. Milica Pavlović is a woman left by herself to face the destructive energies of an outside force coming into her city as Sophka had to face Gazda Marko. All the powers of history conspire in one moment to threaten her existence. However, unlike Sophka, Milica Pavlović overcomes her tormentors. Leaving her manuscript to the Partisan officer who led the small detachment of Partisans who arrested her husband, she squeezes from him his comments on his past actions which are invariably apologetic. She tries to take the mask off the official histories, the lies about the past which remained buried for so long after the arrival of the Partisans. With them the world was created anew. Milica associates this with the immediate change in language which they introduced. The immediate changes which she notices are the abundant use of the imperative and in particular the loss of the polite form for 'you' (*vi*). This word contrasts with the familiar form *ti*. Traditionally the polite form is associated with town life and is largely absent in village environments. It is used when speaking to strangers, it shows a certain respect such that one would use it to an older person or superior at work. It is not a term of subservience, rather it establishes a discreet distance which would be out of place in familial surroundings or with friends. Like many of the details in the book this one too symbolizes a much more momentous transformation. It is not just the loss of a pronoun, but the erasure of a way of life. Milica Pavlović, the middle-class wife and mother, has to disappear, not being part of the Communist order. She indicates the huge transformation by quoting the significance of language for the whole process of creation: 'In the beginning was the word' (p. 175). Such is the gap between that day when her husband was taken away and her pre-war life that she looks on the events of 1939 as if they were 'many centuries ago' (p. 179).

The Pavlović's flat in Belgrade is a highly symbolic space. When thinking about the past, Milica sometimes remembers moments of 'well-ordered inner space, idyllically embodied in the flat' (p. 91). Her furnishing its rooms and caring for it reflect her inner strength and poise. Its loss, on the other hand, when it is requisitioned, reflects the denial of her space and life in the new order. This denial of her individuality is taken a stage further when she is finally allowed to work as a translator, but only from the confines of the room which was given to her and under an assumed name. She has no public and acknowledged existence. She is absent from the city and its new life. The transitoriness of the world is given a specific symbolic space in the internal geography of the flat. One of the rooms faces away from the sun and being cold and dark has not much function. Milica dubs it the 'winter garden' from the beginning. She regards it as a 'transitional room' (p. 75), but wants to give it 'the role of a space for pausing' (p. 76). It remains an ambiguous place, not really suited for living in, not fully integrated into the flat as a whole, not even a part of the present time. Milica wants to maintain elements of both its 'primitiveness' and of its 'elegance' (p. 76). This means to hide something of the former and to try and enhance features of the latter. Her attitude bears a resemblance to the development of Belgrade itself entering the modern age. On the one hand, there was the desire to eradicate the traces of the Ottoman past. On the other hand, there existed a critical imperative to put on show all the signs of European civilization. So, the 'winter garden' is dressed in pieces of Chippendale furniture shipped in from England. The room is like a window-dressing, an imitation of a real room, a sign of the fragility and freshness of the values of the Pavlovićes' new Belgrade. It is significant that when Milica is led away from the drawing room to the room allotted for her use, which was incidentally the room intended for a live-in maid, she passes through the 'winter garden'. A few days later she arranges a meeting with another Partisan officer which takes place in the same transitional room. She remarks that it is now 'emptied' (p. 178). This functions as another sign of the loss of her world, the one she and her husband were active in creating, but which has now been voided of all significance.

In November 1944, when the Communists arrest Dušan and demand that Milica abandon their flat, the Pavlović family are written out of Belgrade life. They are not allowed to survive as reminders of the past, since the world begins anew and 'nothing alien had any business to exist' (p. 180). For Milica, while staring at the past, history is chaotic and frightening. She recalls a short period when she taught in a grammar school, where she found the boys to be rebels:

> These spontaneous rebels were interested above all in political events, because Europe was already convulsed by the exercises in violence that had begun, the Kingdom of Yugoslavia was shaking with sound and fury (did that title of Faulkner's not apply to almost every moment of our crazy century?). And I had constantly to invent ways of interesting my pupils in works of literature and, even more demandingly, in questions of grammar and syntax. (pp. 95–6)

The broad canvas of politics is changed at each new 'moment of our crazy century'. The victor rewrites the truth of the past, inventing a continuity for himself to justify his presence now. On the other hand, the created worlds of literature represent a counterpart to history, a realm of narrative order above the forever disappearing reality of the present. Milica's memories in her narrative, describing episodes with mounting details, concentrate her recollections about events into tight patches of intense light by which the narrator is trying to see the sense of the larger event. After her husband is taken away the former caretaker of their building, now a Partisan, is left in the flat with her. She does not know where her husband has been taken nor why the caretaker remains with her. Like the 'sound and fury' of the century crashing down, there seems no reason. But the narrator focuses all her attention on the memory of the caretaker's shoe as he sits in the hall, watching her. It is a 'heavy shoe' or 'boot', in a 'worn state' but still managing to exude an air which is 'half-military and half-police' (pp. 28–9). It sits there, at the end of the left leg crossed over the right, swinging, pointing at her when she appeared in the hall. Milica describes it as evil. The article is the worn shoe of the peasant and the boot of the new police state. It is the condensation of that day in November 1944 when all was lost. Such details fix a reality in the fiction and emphasize the urgency of events not only for their public but also for their private meanings. The consequences of the war were total and for everybody.

Betrayal is a theme to which Milica constantly returns in different ways. Her husband, Dušan, begins to work with the German authorities in Belgrade in an effort to save as many innocent lives as possible. Over the border, in the Independent State of Croatia, Serbs are being killed every day by the Ustaše, the Croatian Fascist Party intent on eradicating all traces of a Serbian presence. Dušan is able to go over the border and bring back with him people interned in camps waiting for death. The reasons are 'various pretexts, which could not possibly have convinced the Germans themselves' (p. 42). However, since his actions could be taken as an act of collaboration, his wife considers him a traitor even though his actions save lives. He brings one of the people whom he saves home to live with him and his family. She is a peasant girl, a Serb from Croatia, arrested by the Ustaše and surely to lose her life. Zora lives with the family as another daughter. But, when the Partisans come for Dušan, she is amongst them as one of his accusers. She then takes over their flat as her own. Milica has similar feelings towards the caretaker who for years had helped all the middle-class families in their building in their daily lives, now he is more of a gaoler. The Partisan officer in command when her husband is taken away and to whom she leaves her manuscript is formerly the Armenian grocer from the corner of their street. His comments on her descriptions of what happened half a century before reveal a consciousness in conflict with itself and a division between what individual Partisans thought was right and how they acted at the time. He remembers that he felt something which now 'seems like shame'. He hears a voice: 'What are you doing, it asked me, what crime has this woman committed. And these children. You know she's done nothing. You of all people' (p. 115). Pavle Zec, Dušan's younger colleague from the University, was a Communist before the war. Milica hides him from the authorities during the war without her husband's knowledge. He then refuses to help them when he is an important figure in the new administration. Everyone seems to have been implicated in telling lies and making masks for the new order. History, when we look at Velmar-Janković's work, is a chain of deceit which requires the collective memory to be periodically extinguished, leaving behind only personal memories and traces.

In conclusion, we can examine now a certain similarity between Velmar Janković's image of Belgrade and Berman's description of modernity in American literature during the 1970s. Berman emphasizes the pivotal role in American literature during this decade of writers from America's ethnic minorities confronting their histories and family memories in the struggle to establish an identity for themselves not submerged in the majority culture. However, he shies away from those works which 'present extravagantly idealized versions of the familial and ethnic past'.[18] The more fulfilling narratives are those which set out to examine the roots of their culture, not to identify with the past as a substitute for the present, but to recognize that the past can never be recaptured. What happened and is gone may represent images, myths and a life at radical variance with today. He makes two points which closely link the American works which he discusses with *Dorćol* and *Dungeon*. The first point is that when turning to this difficult past we find ourselves in a world of ghosts, like the streets of Belgrade. Berman says, 'This means that our past, whatever it was, was a past in the process of disintegration; we yearn to grasp it, but it is baseless and elusive; we look back for something solid to lean on, only to find ourselves embracing ghosts.'[19] Belgrade, like the American city for its cultural minorities, is not a space with its evolutionary links intact. It can hardly be compared with Lewis Mumford's optimistic view of the city as a physical structure in which 'decisions made long ago, values formulated and achieved, remain alive and exert an influence'.[20] Berman's other comment concerns the theme explored by some writers 'to re-enact the very tragic struggles that drove them from their homes in the first place'.[21] Velmar-Janković, Pekić, Stanković and other writers too all expose the collapse of political, social and moral order which drove their narrators and characters from their homes. Such novels about city life are in search of lost roots, destroyed by the invasion of a primitive and uncivilized world from just over the border. Never far away, this other world looks as exotic, threatening and dangerous to the city dweller as the Balkans appears to the outsider. As an expression of modernity, these narratives cross the boundaries of any critical moment. The moment of crisis is pervasive and dominant, in which identities are in constant transformation. Life on the streets is open and exposed. Thus the writers examined in this chapter look for an idea of self in the signs and symbols of private space, turning inward to try and establish order and continuity.

6 Discourses of Identity and Modernity in Times of Crisis

In this final chapter I examine two more novels and a film which take issues of identity and modernity and rework them. The works in question are *U potpalublju* (*In the Hold*, 1994) by Vladimir Arsenijević, *Ubistvo s predumišljajem* (*Premeditated Murder*, 1993) by Slobodan Selenić, and the film *Podzemlje* (*Underground*, 1995) directed by Emir Kusturica. All three are narratives connected with the wars in former Yugoslavia during the early 1990s. To varying degrees they include the motifs of retreat into a private space and the fear of primitivism which are two of the basic elements within the complex of identities in the central Balkans. They are narratives which represent the extreme experience of war and the disintegration of a society and country. The mass destruction of the present is associated with other historical events which lead to evocations of cycles of destruction. They are about the disappearance of a world which was home to so many for so long and the accompanying rekindling of fears and uncertainties. Or perhaps the fears and uncertainties have never really disappeared, and their underlying presence was a cause rather than effect of war and hostility. These narratives are more intense in their treatment of contemporary events which sometimes appear confusing without the benefit of hindsight to discern them in the light of broader historical patterns. There is a sense in which these works question the reality of what is happening now, trying to find a perspective from which to view and make sense of events. However, the enormity of the war, its causes and consequences, defy attempts to establish a point of view which will incorporate the cataclysm into a neat story. Consequently, they are works with dense textual structures, which have stories embedded within stories and films within films. This technique suggests alienation, as if characters are not fully involved in the immediate events of the present.

VLADIMIR ARSENIJEVIĆ: WAR BY TV

Vladimir Arsenijević is a young writer whose first novel, *In the Hold*, was a huge success on publication and won numerous literary prizes in Yugoslavia, including the 1994 NIN prize for book of the year. Its topical theme, covering the three months early in the Serb-Croat war at the end of 1991, led to interest expressed by publishers abroad and it has now been translated into some major European languages. The book is divided into three parts each one named after the month in which the action takes place; October, November and December as the Serb-Croat war escalates. The narrator, like the author himself, is somewhere in his mid- to late-20s when war breaks out and he records how the war influenced the lives of his generation in Belgrade and how they tried to live with it, or not, as the case may be.

Belgrade lived in a strange atmosphere towards the end of 1991. The city was suddenly hit by an unexpected poverty with high inflation and shortages of food and goods. The situation was to become much worse over the following years as the war grew. Many people could not believe that war had broken out, and it seemed alien from the experience and expectations of the majority. War was being pursued in Croatia. The towns of Vukovar and Dubrovnik were besieged and bombed, and there was a massive call-up of the army reserve in Serbia. In September of that year columns of tanks left the capital, rumbling out at night, taking the road to Croatia. Army reservists, mainly young men under 30, lived in fear of being sent to the front. Typically, call-up papers would be served at night, sometimes after midnight. If the one for whom the papers were intended was at home, they would be served immediately and the recruit would have to report the following day for active service. More usually, anyone knocking on a door late at night would be ignored for as long as possible; otherwise another member of the household not eligible for military service would open the door. The army had to obtain a signature for receipt of the call-up papers from a member of the household to prove that the recruit was still resident at that address. Such a signature would suffice to show that the papers had been legally served. Typically, family members would claim no knowledge of the whereabouts of those due for active service at the front. Following this initial failure the army would try a variety of ruses to serve the papers. Postmen would deliver them as registered letters which would require the recruit to sign for them, establishing his residence at that particular address. However, it was not unknown for postmen to point out the danger to more unsuspecting recipients of registered letters. Telephone calls were made from round the corner to try and trick the person into answering and showing that he was at home at that moment. Many people avoided answering the door or telephone for many months. Others went into hiding in their own city to avoid being found. They did not dare stay for too long in one place and so keys of flats of other people willing to help circulated from hand to hand. The fear of being sent away to fight caused many to leave the country to face an uncertain future abroad, while at home the government branded them as traitors and threatened them with prison should they return. Thus, alienation was complete for those who failed to comply with going to the front for a war they could not understand.

Arsenijević's narrator focuses on the younger generation as he goes through the mayhem which the war brings. In his limited historical experience he reflects on the life they led before the war. This is a retreat into a vision of better days. He and friends benefitted from Yugoslavia's political and economic system which made their lives freer and wealthier than their counterparts elsewhere in Eastern Europe. They were from a country which did not impose all the restrictions on personal freedom which the youth from other East European countries experienced. They were the products of a more open society which enjoyed its own youth culture. The narrator reflects on all that was positive and ordinary in their lives and expectations for the future in a time of peace, before 1991. He has a job which he does not much care for but it provides him and Angela, his pregnant wife, with a small flat and the daily needs of life. His brother-in-law, Lazar, is a member of the Hare Krishna sect who wears robes and has his head shaven. He regularly calls on his sister and her husband on Saturday afternoons when they sit, talk and smoke marijuana. Then, he is caught up in the call-up for the front and to the narrator's amazement accepts the situation and leaves for the front where he is killed. The narrator is forced to ask himself what he would do in a similar situation. One of his old friends, Dejan, returns from the war having lost an arm in the fighting. After visiting him in hospital, the narrator meets him again by chance in the street when Dejan begins to outline his ideas of how he will make a living in the future. His plans show a mind which is becoming unhinged. Their relationship and Dejan's eventual suicide is a central part of the growing sense of incomprehensibility expressed by the narrator and of the increasingly eerie quality which comes to dominate the cityscape. The narrator perceives a gap between himself and the events taking place around him, and feels the problem of distinguishing between normality and abnormality. He is being torn away from contemporary urban reality. He traces his growing psychological burden through private thoughts and emotions. But, as the text unfolds, these sometimes trivial events assume universal, apocalyptic proportions. Belgrade is being overtaken by a dark and anonymous force. The signs of this terror are based on the lack of continuity with the world before 1991, nightmarish visions, and the growing and unfocused sense of guilt described by the narrator.

The narrator is confused by the unbridgeable gap separating the world in Belgrade before and now during the war. He thinks of his friends who have been mobilized and sent away to the front. He knows what has happened to some, killed or wounded, but nothing of others. He intends to call their parents, wives or girlfriends, but cannot bring himself to say anything, as he finds himself doubting those friendships from the past: 'What, I wondered, what if, for one reason or another, we were never as close as it had seemed?'[1] His inquiries, in those circumstances, may seem obtrusive. Constant changes are taking place, transformations of people's lives from living to dead, from friend to stranger, people dying on both sides, fleeing the country and choosing exile. Life is hidden and covert, no longer unfolding in public on the streets. The narrator recalls how his friend, Dejan, used to be a member of a band:

> He played in a band called GSG 9, after the elite West German anti-terrorist commando corps GSG 9, and they looked great then, bare to the waist, muscular, depilated, sweaty and serious, surrounded by computers and strobe lights, and while two of these guys mixed reports of mass deaths and great catastrophes, Wagner, Stravinsky and the sound of cities being shelled, Dejan, shaved bald, sweating more than all of them, played his set of drums, standing, as though he were inflicting punishment on them. (p. 25)

The group epitomized the cross-cultural society of Yugoslav youth culture in the 1980s. They made a record in Maribor in Slovenia, played concerts in cities of Croatia, Serbia and Macedonia inside former Yugoslavia, and outside in Austria and Italy. Wherever they played their audiences were made up of 'thin little urban girls in

Doc Martens' (p. 25). This was a youth culture uniting Europe on a mass scale. Dejan, once an ambitious drummer and left with one arm, soon to commit suicide, is a symbol of the changes and disappearance of the old world which will never be resurrected again. All connections between this Belgrade at the end of 1991 and previous Belgrades have been cut.

The sense of change is accompanied by an obvious sense of danger. One of the immediate dangers felt by the narrator is to be mobilized. He watches a scene in which his nightmare is played out. Woken one night by banging on their neighbour's door he looks through the spyhole into the corridor of their block of flats. There he sees two men, one in an army uniform and the other in plain clothes. The former is spitting all round on the floor. They interrogate the neighbour for the whereabouts of his son but he keeps replying that he does not know and they turn to leave. Passing the narrator's door, the one in uniform suddenly puts his eye to the other side of the spyhole 'as though he knew I was on the other side'. The magnifying lens immediately presents a disfigured image of his face: 'His face began to stretch, he looked as though he were going to pour himself down his own nostril, and then explode' (p. 74). These and similar nightmarish visions reveal the gaps in reality as they begin to open up and crack asunder the impression of a seamless existence in which individuals live collectively in the city, lives passing by other lives with an unspoken but shared purpose.

The reality gap is partly the result of the psychological burden and unfocused sense of guilt felt by the narrator and shared throughout the whole of the paranoid city. At first, he describes himself 'wedged in the gap between weariness and guilt' (p. 6); adding later that he sees himself 'calm in the face of the impending catastrophe, like a calf blinking meekly before the sentence of the butcher's hammer' (p. 7). This is 'a guilt which eluded definition' (p. 7). He remembers his participation in the March demonstrations of that year, recalling the days spent on the public square in town, seeing them as a waste of time. Their anti-government action was too late as they already lived and walked about 'in the place which had been deprived of all sense' (p. 28). At the end, the narrator and Angela, although they too once thought of emigration and exile, shut themselves away in their private world to wait for the arrival of their baby. In this inner sanctum the narrator feels 'in the hold', secure from the storms above in their private and enclosed space. However, the space is ambiguous since it is also where slaves or convicts would be kept and the narrator remarks, 'We felt as though we were in the hold of a ship, condemned to the roles of the obligatory culprits for all suffering' (p. 94). The consequence of this burden leads him to the illusion that the war is not really happening, that everything is governed by the logic of a supreme irrationality, and finally to an apocalyptic vision of Belgrade's cityscape.

The title page proclaims that Arsenijević's novel is a 'soap opera'. The soap genre is associated with precisely the opposite subject matter to Arsenijević's novel. It is concerned to dwell in the ordinariness of life, making plots out of trivia and stories which never end. However, his story relates the ordinary experience of an extraordinary time. A typical soap opera juggles a number of story-lines at the same time. Each story-line impinges on so many of the characters. Minor characters in one story are already part of other stories in which they will have a major role to play. Each episode seen on television is not a complete story, discrete unto itself, but serves to further the development of so many of the plots and sub plots, supposedly reflecting the movement of real people through life. Arsenijević develops his stories in a similar way. Over the three months covered by the novel, Lazar is called up, goes away, and his body is returned for burial. The narrator visits Dejan in hospital, meets him in the street, and later he hears of his suicide. In an ironic reworking of the characteristic soap-opera focus on family life, in which traditional role models are idealized for providing stability, he recalls how Angela beat her drug habit in order 'to meet up with her true nature, to become what she had in fact always wanted to be – *a housewife*' (p. 37). In the period covered by the book Angela's pregnancy is progressing and she and the narrator are preparing for their baby's arrival at home. Strands of narrative segment weave themselves around other strands. The trivia of everyday life fast become intermingled with the incomprehensible events and consequences of the war. The great tragedies of the war, death and collective lunacy are highlighted when told through the everyday banalities of soap-opera type conversations and family meetings.

The narrator frequently refers to the fighting in terms of television, film or theatre, as if it comprises a fictional world embedded within his world. From the beginning he considers that Lazar's decision to accept his call-up into the army and go to the front is the result of thinking that in a childish way the war is not real, that he has a 'cowboy and Indian perception of Serbo-Croat mutual slaughter' (p. 19). The outbreak of war is described as if a play with an overture, a 'classical bloody tragedy' of which 'the play had actually only just begun' (p. 23). The use of such terms reinforces the sense of unreality which the war holds for the narrator and his generation. They are slipping into something which cannot be a case for genuine concern since knowledge about it is at first only brought home by TV news as an alienating series of images, flickering on the screen, bathing the viewer in a soft blue light. He comments that 'in a way, that was all TV' and not the real world (p. 24). Television bombards the population with nightly images of frightened refugees and mutilated bodies. But, this world on the screen, insubstantial, perhaps the modern equivalent to Dorćol's ghosts, exists and it is irrecoverably linked to the Belgrade viewer. Watching the destruction of Vukovar, the narrator is aware somewhere in his consciousness that it is not impossible for them to catch sight of Lazar in his soldier's uniform amid the rubble, corpses and drunken unruliness of Serbian soldiers. The war is distanced and near at the same time, unknown and yet visible. Arsenijević's narrator finds himself sucked into an unbelievable world which is positioned on the brink of utter loss, with no way backward or forward, where the war is trivialised as an everyday part of life's soap opera.

At Lazar's funeral the narrator realizes that the war and its consequences have removed any necessity for personal responsibility and moral action. The funeral is essential to the family, but the narrator describes events with a feeling of distance and uninvolvement. A number of events concerning those officiating, such as one man bumping into a rubber plant and then falling to the floor, give the impression of a farce unfolding, not the dignity of a funeral rite. Leaving the room, the narrator is followed by one of Angela's female relatives who could not stop herself giggling at the antics inside. They walk together through the cemetery. She looks like a film star to him, and slowly he begins to imagine that they are acting in a film: 'leaning against the cracked canvas with the panorama of the old cemetery, according to the code of an East-European dream, I broke all the rules – I kissed her' (p. 56). Theirs is a brief sexual encounter and when they return to rejoin the family crowd the narrator is expecting the finger of God to name his guilt, but nothing happens. There is no retribution. The war transforms the sense of morality which regulates social communication. In a world where there is no responsibility towards others, individuality is lost and the narrator often summarizes and categorizes people around him, such as all those names of friends who have left the country are 'the Vanished' (p. 28) and even the woman in the cemetery is simply 'the Relative'(p. 56). The episode closes on a note which spells the end of social order with the ominous phrase: 'Everything is possible' (p. 58).

The city is overcome by the power of irrationality. Events happen in random sequence with no explanation, such as the man who pushes his face against the narrator's spy-hole. Some questions are only resolved by chance meetings. Angela does not know where Lazar has been sent. Visiting army HQ and the Hare Krishna temple where he used to go, she can find no-one who knows his whereabouts. By chance, she meets an acquaintance in a bus whose brother is also in the army and is posted to the same unit as Lazar. After visiting Dejan in hospital, the narrator meets him again by chance in the street. He later hears of his friend's suicide via another casual meeting with a mutual friend. Nothing seems to happen, or to have ever happened, as a result of human will and agency and nothing turns out according to design. Lazar's funeral provides a typical example of this transformed world. The narrator's parents attend because they loved the boy, although he comments that their love was 'for no apparent reason'. Later, at the funeral feast, the dignity of the occasion is suddenly lost when the guests 'following a strange impulse . . . began singing an old song about unhappy love, faded roses, and snow' (p. 62). In this strange world governed by an irrational logic, it would seem that Lazar's Hare Krishna teaching that everything depends on 'karma', provides a perfectly adequate explanatory framework for why he is going to fight (p. 14). Nothing has its place any more and ordinary life is simply incongruous.

At times, the narrator focuses intensely on the enormity of what is happening. These moments stand out by their suggestion of an anger and bitterness which is otherwise suppressed by a psychological self-defence mechanism to survive. His generation has been attacked by a catastrophe of biblical proportions living in 'the last moments of a sick world' (p. 29). The apocalyptical tone is heard elsewhere when Belgrade is described in terms of Sodom and Gomorrah as the 'kingdom of conspirators, murderers and politicians' (p. 18). The city has been deceived, the youth have lost their past and future, and everything which is precious and valuable is indistinguishable from the surrounding Balkan mud. All sense is lost, and all that remains are the words hanging in a vacuum without their meanings. Collapse of the old order is complete when it seems impossible to communicate anymore. The narrator tries to name the anonymous forces directing fate as Executor or Commander (p. 18). They are unseen powers steering the turn of events which has spilled out of control. Human agency disappears. At one point this anonymity controlling the city takes on shape. Walking down one of the main streets in the centre of town the narrator suddenly finds the scene in front of him ripped open:

> In the glare of a sudden and all-pervasive vision that split the ordinary street scene before my eyes, I caught sight of all of us, running, while the ground beneath our feet was breaking up and opening with a terrible cracking sound, and out of those depths came the unbearable stench of the centuries which, in our inertia, we had omitted to use in a dignified way, a great, slimy pulsating monster was mocking us from in there, unconcerned about the horror which we were conjuring up with our irresolute movements, and our desire not to be. (p. 48)

Belgrade is transformed into a city of sin where punishment is indiscriminate. The incomprehensibility of the monstrosity of what he is facing in that time and that place forces the narrator to see himself and others on the border between reality and unreality. He is distanced and detached, not taking part in the story but watching the monster appear from below the street as if on TV. He converts the reality of what is happening into images taken from a horror film. He is not only watching the danger and the efforts of others to escape but also himself: 'I caught sight *of all of us*, running, while the ground beneath our feet was breaking up' [italics DN].

SLOBODAN SELENIĆ: THE PRIMAL STRUGGLE

In his novel *Premeditated Murder* Slobodan Selenić links two stories from two different wars. His approach involves looking further back than Arsenijević who is more concerned with the immediacy of the present crisis than to contextualize it within a longer historical period. One story is set in late 1992 and concerns a young student in Belgrade, Jelena Panić. She studies drama and does occasional work as a photographer for student magazines. She lives alone in her family flat, since her mother left a few years earlier, when she married and moved with her new husband to his home in New Zealand. Her mother sends occasional presents of money although these have become rarer since the imposition of sanctions against the country for its involvement in the war in Bosnia. Money can only arrive when sent via a third party travelling to the country from New Zealand. Jelena is, understandably, bitter against her mother. Her father is also an absent figure in her life, only calling Jelena when he needs to borrow money from her. She herself gives an outward impression of being a modern young woman, aware of intellectual and artistic trends around the world, wise to the ways of urban living, able to look after herself, straightforward in her speech to the point of frequent obscenities, but also vulnerable and sensitive. She needs to protect herself from the dangers of the outside world in her lonely and exposed state. Her country no longer exists since the international community has recognized the dismemberment of the state formed by the Communists after the Second World War. Students are demonstrating in Belgrade's streets against the government of President Milošević in Serbia, but to no visible effect. The war continues in Croatia and Bosnia and the sanctions imposed against the new Yugoslavia, made up of Serbia and Montenegro, have sealed the borders against all trade and contact with abroad. There are shortages of medicines and basic foodstuffs, prices are high, and the economy is dependent on black-market trading. People are desperate and society is becoming increasingly criminalized. Much of this background to those times is muted in Selenić's text which is largely narrated by Jelena herself, a survivor who is intent on getting through the crisis. It is at this point that the Serb fighter from Croatia, Bogdan Bilogorac, enters her life.

Bogdan Bilogorac is a Serb from the Krajina region, an overwhelmingly Serb region of Croatia which refused to recognize its inclusion in the independent Republic of Croatia and created their own mini-state supported from Belgrade by the Milošević government. Bogdan has been wounded in the leg and is recuperating in the Serbian capital. Jelena discovers him on a park bench and takes him home with her. Eventually, they fall in love and live a life mostly concealed from the everyday horrors of the war. However, the war is never far away and Bogdan continues to claim that it is his duty to return to the front when he recovers from his wound. His world of Krajina is very different from Jelena's Belgrade. Long-standing problems between Serbs and Croats in that area are not resolved. The Serbs form majorities in most towns and villages but they are an overall minority in Croatia and fear for their future. Bogdan's patriotism, based on this fear, is alien to Jelena's point of view. In fact, she can see no sense in his aspiration to return to the place where he was recently nearly killed for a cause which he cannot articulate, except to say that all Croats are bad. Consequently, she adopts the name Cretin for him ('Bonehead' in the translation). On the other hand, Bogdan appears innocent in relation to the cruelty of the war and the corruption which it brings in its wake. He is its victim as much as those against whom he is fighting. He recovers and intends to return to the front as dictated by his feelings of duty. The gulf between their two worlds now suddenly widens when the stark choices of fight or not fight, duty and love, life or death appear. Jelena refuses to see him off out of anger at his obstinacy to realize the futility of his actions. But, Bogdan leaves and Jelena soon receives a message that he has been killed. Full of remorse at not saying goodbye, unable to comprehend the motives for her lover's actions, she herself goes to Krajina to try and find his body to bring back to Belgrade for burial. She succeeds, and then announces her decision to leave the country forever and join her mother in New Zealand. Her life, far from the front, has been broken by the war amidst the ruins of Belgrade transformed by sanctions and the arrival of poverty and loss of hope.

Bogdan spends much of his time with Jelena helping her to research a book to be published by one of her friends. The book is the story of Jelena's grandmother, Jelena Arandjelović, or more precisely about one episode from her life at the end of the war when she had an affair with a Partisan officer, Krsman Jakšić. Unlike Jelena Panić, Jelena in 1944 is a sophisticated young lady, who was brought up in a rich bourgeois household. Her mother married the widower Stavra Arandjelović who was of peasant origins but who came to Belgrade to make his fortune and became a wealthy industrialist. His life-story has echoes of the Belgrade novels of the 1920s and 1930s when the city represented a challenge to the newcomer, some of whom succeeded and some of whom did not, but they were not stronger than the city itself. Stavra already had a son, Jovan, by his first wife. Jovan and Jelena grew up like brother and sister, although not so biologically. Their first sexual experiences in adolescence are with one another and they secretly continue their semi-incestuous relationship for some years; it has to be borne in mind that all information about them comes from a confessional diary left by Jovan with little indication from Jelena that she agrees with his version of events. However, they experience sexual desire with a growing feeling of guilt at knowing that what they are doing is not right for two children brought up as brother and sister. When Jelena decides that she can go on with the deception no longer, she calls a halt to their nocturnal meetings. From then she has relationships with other men, although Jovan never mentions any women in his life after Jelena. He grows into a snob who looks down on others and is incapable of practical life, representing the degenerate aspect of city life in the Balkans forced to confront the vitality of the newcomers. The two researchers begin their work after Jelena finds a bag containing material about the lives of Jelena and Jovan. The bag contains letters, memoirs, diary extracts, newspaper pages and other mementos of Jelena's and Jovan's telling the story of that period in their lives. Thus, each character narrates his or her own part in the overall story.

In 1944 the Partisans arrive in Belgrade and the life of the Arandjelović family is completely and irrecoverably changed. Their big house is requisitioned by the new authorities. Stavra represents the pre-war social and economic order which the Communists intend to eradicate and he is arrested as a collaborator. Jovan is also arrested and sentenced to some months of hard labour. Jelena is obliged to work for the new regime and is given a job at the Tanjug news agency because of her knowledge of foreign languages. There she meets the Partisan officer Krsman Jakšić whose advances Jelena rejects, until the day he approaches her without his usual swagger, as if a broken and tamed animal. Realizing his influence in the new system, she enlists his support to help her step-father. Jovan is disgusted by Krsman, considering him a 'Communist barbarian' and a 'mountain bandit'.[2] Krsman takes on the role of Stanković's Gazda Marko, attracted to the beauty of the civilized Jelena and wanting to possess her. The story of her attraction to him is told almost entirely from Jovan's point of view, and her real feelings are not clear. She invites the Partisan officer to their home, where Jovan is agitated by his presence. After one such visit when Krsman admits that he has been offered the Arandjelović house in Belgrade Jovan loses control and screams at Jelena:

> Every house they appropriate transforms into a barn . . . They smell of decay, they kill their ailing fathers with shovels and we plead with them to free our Stavra?! They wipe their arses with their fingers and rub them off on walls, they feed their fires with pages from the Testament, they care for their cows better than for their women because they are stronger and cheaper to feed. (pp. 129–30)

He finally falls on her and rapes her. At this point the classical Belgrade/Balkan story of the city needing to be protected from the likes of Gazda Marko or Krsman Jakšić is inverted, as in Selenić's earlier novel *The Friends*. Jovan is transformed into the violent, aggressive and uncivilized figure. One day when Krsman is invited to lunch, Jovan leaves the dining room, takes the Partisan's revolver from its holster and shoots him. He then turns the gun on himself and takes his own life. The motive for Jelena and Bogdan to research the story is to discover who is Jelena's maternal grandfather, Krsman or Jovan, the peasant from the mountains or the educated and cultured son of a wealthy Belgrade industrialist. Thus, issues of identity and modernity lie at the novel's core. The question of Jelena's grandfather not only leads us through a number of oppositions from urban to rural origins, but it also takes us through the complex relationship represented by Jovan between civilized Belgrade and the urge to destroy itself.

The new era opening in 1944 as described by Selenić is characterized by a complete change in language as in Velmar-Janković's *Dungeon*. The massive social upheaval introduces corresponding alterations in the semiotic system. Things do not mean what they did before. The latest morphology and syntax is structured around the words, dress and lifestyles of the Communists. Jelena Panić often discusses those times with the gentlemanly Mr Kojović, who was a friend of the family and worked with her grandmother Jelena in Tanjug. He tries to explain to her some of the atmosphere of those times when he worked alongside her grandmother. He speaks of the 'look' and 'allure' of the Communist Partisan, and how 'following the liberation from the Nazis, any deviation from Communist beliefs, the parameters of fashion, codes of behaviour and expression was downright dangerous' (p. 17). This means the ubiquitous uniform with a red star pinned to the cap and the poverty of language. Language is stripped of all phrases which refers to pre-war life. 'Mister' is replaced by 'comrade' since the Serbo-Croat word holds strong class connotations while 'comrade' reduces all to the same status. Jelena, while working at the centre of the Communists' information and propaganda network, flaunts all these unwritten rules of etiquette and turns them round to confront the new enemy. Jelena refuses to use the Communist formula for addressing others. These were the two forms for 'comrade': the masculine 'drug' and the feminine 'drugarica'. Instead, she inserts the Soviet 'tovarich' for masculine and Macedonian 'drugarkata' for the feminine forms.

Her colleagues at work 'suspected it was some kind of bourgeois mockery, but how could they criticize her for using the languages of our two great Slavic-Bolshevik-Proletarian brother nations' (p. 18). She goes further in this mocking style, wearing fur coats, tailored skirts and high-heel shoes. One day, wearing fishnet, elbow-length gloves to the office she is confronted by one of the comrades who asks why the gloves are full of holes. Jelena replies, 'These are the only ones I have,' adding, 'These are hard times, Drugarkata Milesa. You know how it is – all to the front, all for the front' (p. 18). Jelena inverts the Communist rhetoric used to justify shortages and to exhort the population to ever greater sacrifice for her own elegant wardrobe.

The language and codes of the Communists conceal and justify their intention to rule and to wipe out all signs of the past. They have to wipe out the memory of a different definition of life in order to institute their version of social relations. In order to achieve this goal the Communists have to control all aspects of semiotic modelling. They cannot permit meaning to flow freely from a variety of different levels. The political culture of totalitarianism, whether it be in everyday speech, clothes and fashion, literature or history, is by its very nature hegemonic. Kojović remarks on the legacy of their success in this field. He is attempting to let Jelena Panić feel what it was like when the Communists arrived in 1944. However, he is faced with the absolute impossibility of communicating how he, Jelena and Jovan experienced those times as the language has changed so much in the intervening years. The Communists created their own myths about themselves and their exploits in the war, glorified their aims and led a very successful campaign for mass amnesia. All novels, films, poems, every sphere of public life and a large part of private life had to conform to their truths and their meanings, such that it is difficult to find a point of access to that world as Kojović and others saw it:

> For example, whatever the word Partisan might imply today – even at its most objective – Yugoslav Communists who fought against both the Royalists and the Axis Powers, its meaning in 1945 was entirely different. Ah, the amount of self-adoration, hatred, the sheer volume of stories, memories, films and memoirs stored within that word in the last half-century! No, you simply cannot imagine what that word meant before your time. (pp. 11–12)

The world of the past resembles a work of fiction in which Krsman is a 'Partisan prince', playing the part of a hero. Kojović describes how Jelena tamed him: 'It was like in the movies, truly' (p. 22). The language of *Premeditated Murder* weaves between fiction and history.

The lack of distinction between fiction and history is a common theme of much modern literature and is regarded as one of the hallmarks of Postmodernism. In small cultures, however, such a narrative strategy is not driven by the desire for endless play, deliberately delaying the slippage into fact or fiction. It is part of the critical process to establish a continuing naming process, essential to those whose histories have been frequently and abruptly rewritten. There is a need to textualize and thereby confirm the transitory world even in fictional forms. Perhaps fictional worlds are more satisfying for this task since they hold out the tantalizing function to create the illusion of access into a world which is more complete than the real. For example, Jelena Arandjelović leaves behind a precise biography of her stepfather which Krsman requested in order to try and help him. This private history of one man expands into a broader description of Belgrade's industrial and commercial development in the first half of the twentieth century. Bogdan makes a complete and detailed inventory of the material which they find in the bottom of the wardrobe. It includes a page torn from the daily newspaper *Politika* and other items which add to the reality effect by their function as representative of the realia and memorabilia of a life in the past. The bag contains 31 items, some of Jelena's school works, 23 letters from Jovan addressed to Jelena and one from her to Jovan, Jelena's birth certificate, a train ticket for the London Underground, a library membership card from 1941, Jovan's confession of his relationship with Jelena, and other items (pp. 70-2). Documentation becomes a fetish in the effort to name, to fix the identity of what once was in order to understand the present. Jelena and Bogdan are coordinating these individual memories and assembling them to make a bigger history.

Selenić's aim to establish a naming process requires his characters to comment on the truth of what they are saying, to further the illusion of creating a fictional–historical world. Kojović, with all the weight of his charming personality, often repeats that he is only telling what he remembers. He admits that he once 'had to lie a little' when he was being interrogated by the Communist secret police about Jelena's and Jovan's activities during the war (p. 7). At the same time, he confirms that he has been telling Jelena 'everything as it truly happened' (p. 11). He explains how he came to know what happened in places where he could not possibly have heard or seen anything. For example, Jelena and Krsman first met when a Soviet delegation visited their Tanjug office. Kojović felt very uncomfortable since Jelena was abrupt and rude to the visiting officials and he wanted to know what they said afterwards amongst themselves. He admits that later 'Krsman told us what exactly happened' (p. 19). He also admits his information gaps about the development of the relationship between Krsman and Jelena since 'more and more often, Krsman would ask Jelena to step out of the room whenever he had something to communicate to her' (p. 85). In his diary confession Jovan comments on his own words like Kojović: 'At least, that is what I remember. I am writing as I remember it. What I don't know, I don't write. Simply recording events' (p. 52). Similarly, from the beginning, Jelena insists that her story about her grandmother is there for us to read with no editorial interference from her. She find the materials in the wardrobe and her only task is to 'put them together' (p. 3), and she finds the expert witnesses to interview so that 'the book writes itself' (p. 4). The narrative technique is intended to reinforce the illusion that as readers we are watching events unfold along their natural course.

Jovan's diary confession of his relationship with Jelena is another example of close testimony related to the events of 1944. They are supplemented by the fictional proceedings of the witnesses' statements at Stavra's trial for collaboration. Likewise, the narrative story comes to resemble a court trying to establish the facts of two cases. First, there is the question of the identity of Jelena's grandfather. Second, there is the case of Krsman's murder and Jovan's suicide, deaths which Bogdan Bilogorac re-enacts in his brave but blind return to the front in Croatia. *Premeditated Murder* uses this doubled and redoubled reality effect to search into the historical roots of a more recent crisis, to force sense out of nonsense and ascribe meaning to the meaningless deaths of so many in the Yugoslav wars of the 1990s. This essence of Selenić's narrative is deepened and reinforced by certain types of textual structures. Most of the characters function as narrators, indeed their function as characters is either to piece together the testimony of others or to give evidence. Jelena often makes references to the 'gaps' in her narrative which she is trying to fill, as if a further comment by Selenić on the status of his fictional world and desire to make it replete with the past. It is the characters themselves who produce the narrative, commenting on their own credibility or role in the filling of gaps, and also commenting on how others speak. When a character gives a written transcript, such as Jovan's diary of his relationship with Jelena, and there is no oral standard on which to remark, the physical appearance of the 'narrative' is described: 'I dumped Jovan's manuscript (single-spaced type. The paper yellow around the edges. Sheets held together with a sewing pin. No pencil corrections anywhere. A longer, narrower format than usual) back into the bag' (p. 27). All efforts are made to try and find truth, use evidence, find the connection between now and the past; in short, to provide a contribution to help overcome the effects of collective amnesia.

The parallels between 1944 and 1992 are unmistakeable as times of crisis in which an age of barbarism is on the horizon. The repetition of these ages suggests a cyclic form of history in which the small culture is condemned never to achieve its full potential, never reach an expression in which it will be able to enter into dialogue with significant others, in which it will always be closed off from its own past. There are only analogies, parallels, other narratives of crisis in which there is no reconciliation between apparent contradictions. When speaking of the people involved in the events of 1944 Kojović's statement that 'there are no innocent people in corrupt times' (p. 100) and Bogdan's that 'all these people from our book are unlucky souls in an evil time' (p. 148) coincide. Both may be true, and neither makes any difference to the crucial issue of the worlds of 1944 and 1992 falling apart. Jelena Panić compensates for this non-answer by her language. Her language is the all-inclusive heteroglossia of the streets used for irony, humour and for subverting the status quo. It is a speech style based on rapidly shifting registers, jumping from comic-strip to science fiction, mixing highly stylized literary forms with the forms of mass media. It is as if she is trying to incorporate the world, rural and urban, modern and archaic, into her discourse, racing to appropriate all possible sources of danger before they can spill out of control, trying to outstrip her world as it falls apart. However, by turning to the past the critical urgency of the present is diluted and her narrative neither reinvents the past nor explains the present.

The two stories wrap around each other. On the one hand, Jelena Panić is researching the life of her grandmother, collecting material and piecing together the events of that period involving Krsman from written documents and interviews. At the same time Jelena Panić comments on the progress of the book and tells how her relationship with Bogdan develops. On the other hand, motifs from the two are intertwined and reinforced by the structure of the text. The events of 1944 shed some light on what is happening in the mayhem of 1992 as they begin to mirror one another. Both main characters are called Jelena as if to minimize the individual nature of their identity. Both women are involved with outsiders to Belgrade whose view of the world clashes with their own. The two stories are not exact reproductions of each other, but taken together they represent a cross-section of city dweller and outsider. Jelena is the sophisticated and elegant Belgrade of the pre-war days. Jelena Panić is the modern and liberated Belgrade of the early 1990s. Both of them represent the cosmopolitanism of their own times. Krsman is the boorish peasant who despises the urban ways of Belgrade, while Bogdan is the naive newcomer cast adrift in a new world. The novel focuses on individual characters at the same time that it diffuses their characteristics into a reflection of generalized historic and social functions. War brings the threat of a return to barbarism. The old order is being destroyed and the future looks uncertain. Jovan regards the Communists as invaders not as liberators. Jelena goes abroad as an interpreter to a delegation attending peace talks in Paris. She writes back to Jovan describing what she sees of the ruined European landscape and of American and Soviet representatives who dictate the division of the spoils. She comments that their world no longer exists. Similarly, Jelena Panić's world is over too, although not yet provided with the benefit of hindsight to see any reason for its destruction. The narratives relate singular instances to reflect on collective histories.

In his book *The Ethnic Origins of Nations* Anthony Smith comments on how larger and more dominant cultures relate to the concern which smaller cultures frequently express regarding their own past and origins. He writes that there is a misunderstanding between the two: 'Those whose identities are rarely questioned and who have never known exile or subjugation of land and culture, have little need to trace their "roots" in order to establish a unique and recognizable identity.'[3] It is not a simple search for origins, but part of a process of reaffirmation of existence. The two Jelenas represent the small culture in crisis whose identity is under question. History is being rewritten during their lifetime. Jelena Arandjelović is the namesake of Helen of Troy, the figure at the centre of the conflict between the two opposing forces represented by Jovan and Krsman. The triangular relationship which holds them together is symbolically indicative of the intricate connections between different levels of civilization and primitivism in the Balkans. The etymology of Krsman's name also holds a symbolic resonance. The first syllable is the root of numerous words which are not in themselves cognate and when taken together they project contradictory images. The root *krs* or *krš* refer to the karst mountains in the Central Balkans, with connotations of 'ruggedness' and 'strength'; at the same time, they point to the verb meaning to transgress (*kršiti*). Contrary to those images of nature, power and potential aggression is the image of the cross (*krst* in Serbo-Croat). Other words connected to Christianity and baptism open with the same first syllable. Jelena Panić has inherited the name of her grandmother. Her looking back to 'roots' is a part of a much larger narrative of discovery of origins and of a primal struggle for survival. She is helped in her enterprise by the sincere and uncorrupt Bogdan, whose name means literally 'god-given'. However, she never discovers the true nature of her grandmother's relationship with Krsman, and in the end only discovers the ghosts of the past. The ambiguity of origins remains: is it Krsman or is it Jovan?

EMIR KUSTURICA: THE GREAT BETRAYAL

Kusturica's film *Underground* represents a third approach to the issues of identity and modernity as they have been modelled in narratives about the most recent crises in the Balkans. Selenić searches for sense in an historical continuum, even though the continuum is tenuous, revealing the gaps in the Communists' official history and self-glorification. Arsenijević's narrator struggles to maintain the critical moment on the brink of an abyss, watching himself and others as a distant observer, hiding in his inner sanctum. In his film Kusturica challenges historical orthodoxies and characters retreat into a private space where they are closed off from outside reality. Finally, unable to distinguish truth from illusion, they become viewers of their own fate in which they fail to see themselves. The story spans 50 years from the Second World War to the Yugoslav wars of the 1990s. The film text explores the reality of that historical experience through metaphor, allegory and symbol. The action is non-mimetic, characters do not age in accordance with the passing years, events are bizarrely unreal, and yet there exists an internal logic to the development of the plot as a whole and of individual scenes which is consistent with the extremely dense textual structure of the film. The film is epic in its portrayal of Yugoslavia under Communism and the destruction of the country, and yet lyrical in its sense of individual humanity. The script was co-written with Dušan Kovačević, who also wrote the novel based on the script, *Bila jednom jedna zemlja* (*Once Upon a Time There Was a Country*).[4] The film was received at home and abroad as a remarkable piece of cinema, and was awarded the *Palme d'or* at the 1995 Cannes film festival. This was not the first time that Kusturica had received international recognition for his work; ten years prior to this award he also received the *Palme d'or* for his *Otac na službenom putu* (*Father is Away on Business*, 1985), although on that occasion he was not in Cannes to accept the award as he returned to his then home in Sarajevo to 'help a friend lay a parquet floor'.[5] Considered because of his actions and his work to be something of an eccentric figure, he spent some time at the beginning of the 1990s in Hollywood, where he made the film *Arizona Dream* with Johnny Depp and Faye Dunaway. His exuberant style and emphasis on an evocative rather than strictly narrative approach did not find success with the American market. *Underground* also received a mixed reception because of the assumed political leanings of the director. Kusturica was born in Bosnia and worked for many years in Sarajevo. His name is typically Moslem, but he always regarded himself as Yugoslav rather than identifying with any of its individual ethnic, national and religious groups. During the war in Bosnia he did not return to Sarajevo but made the film *Underground* in Belgrade. His actions were interpreted by some as supporting the Serbian cause in the Yugoslav wars. Consequently, his film was regarded by many as being *a priori* pro-Serb. Furthermore, criticisms levelled against the director seem to emerge out of a general feeling that in times when the crisis of war is all too evident, there is an expectation that all efforts should be made to name those guilty for the killing. Kusturica's film has a broader thematic framework than the war itself. It examines the fall of Yugoslavia and the destruction of the ideals of 'Brotherhood and Unity' between all its constituent nations and nationalities on which the state was established in 1945. Kusturica's film, concerned as it is with naming, does not point a finger at individual parties, but suggests that too many individuals are complicit in creating an atmosphere which allowed the war to happen that it is not possible to name them all.

The two main characters are petty criminals, Marko and Blacky, who are also members of Belgrade's Communist Party organization. The story begins on the day when Germany bombs the city on 6 April 1941, bringing Yugoslavia into the Second World War. The air-raid sirens, approaching planes and falling bombs are first heard from the confines of the city zoo. Marko's brother, Ivan, is a keeper there and is feeding the animals. Sensing the approach of death they begin to panic. Many animals are killed and maimed in the explosions. Their cages are ripped open and the animals try to flee. In the chaos of the moment, predators turn on weaker animals and kill them. Then, we see lions and elephants roaming the streets of Belgrade. These are scenes of war in which all normal laws and expectations are revoked and in which levels of violence simply increase until they have absorbed all feelings of pity and humanity. This symbolic scene in the zoo with animals which are on the one hand caged and helpless, while on the other hand potential killers themselves, contrasts with a liberal inclusion of archive footage. Real German planes are shown on a real air-raid. The scenes showing the destroyed buildings and bodies in the streets are likewise from cine film shot at the time. Archive footage showing a German propaganda film of the entry of their troops into Zagreb and Belgrade is also used. These contrasting styles establish from the beginning one of the film's major themes about the relationship between reality and art, truth and the illusion of truth, and the effects of betrayal.

Marko and Blacky take part in clandestine operations in support of the Partisans. In fact, their operations mainly involve robbery and extortion in order to obtain money to buy arms. The members of the Partisan organization in the city resemble the good-time Mafia bosses with their molls in Hollywood gangster films about Chicago in the 1920s rather than a group of dedicated individuals inspired by the ideals of communism. They meet in cafés drinking champagne, playing cards, brawling amongst themselves over the division of the spoils. Much of the violence owes more to the conventions of 'Tom and Jerry' cartoons rather than presenting a realistic portrayal, such humour adding to the sense of non-mimetic representation and reinforcing other levels on which the film finds its true coherency. For example, during the bombing of Belgrade, Blacky is eating breakfast and becoming increasingly irritated at the sound of bombs exploding. The final straw occurs when an elephant escaped from the zoo steals his shoes from the window sill by taking them up in his trunk and a falling bomb causes the light fitting above the table where Blacky is sitting to crash down. Grabbing the live cables of the light fitting, he bites through them while electricity racks his body. The fact that the air-raid is first seen from the zoo with animals fleeing in all directions and that Blacky is an electrician by trade supply an internal consistency to these two bizarre events.

Blacky has a lover, the actress Natalia. She is portrayed as an empty-headed opportunist, whose acting is always wildly exaggerated both when she is supposed to be playing a role on the stage and when she is not. There seems to be no difference between Natalia's acting when she plays the part of a fictional actress on the stage and Natalia as a fictional character, since both cases are instances of overacting. Meanwhile, Marko and Blacky are being hounded by the occupying authorities. It is dangerous for the other members of the Partisan organization and for their families to remain at large in the city. So, Marko hides them in the cellar of his grandfather's house. They include his own brother Ivan and Blacky's wife who is pregnant. On entering the cellar she falls down the stairs in the darkness, gives birth and soon dies. Natalia takes up with a new lover, Franz, a German officer in the occupation. Blacky resolves to kidnap her during one of her stage performances while Franz sits on the front row of the theatre. His entry causes great consternation in Natalia and the other actor on stage with her. Blacky forces the actor to tie Natalia to his back as if all is part of the play. Franz is at first confused, thinking Blacky to be an actor, but finally realizes what is going on, at which point Blacky shoots him. Failing to recognize what is actually happening will be a pivotal element later in the film's structure. Following his exploits in the theatre Blacky is also forced to take refuge in the cellar while Marko steals Natalia from him and they live together in the house above. This spells the beginning of the betrayal.

The community in the cellar stay there for the next 20 years. Marko and Natalia play the deception that Belgrade is still under occupation. They relay the sounds of fighting and air-raid sirens into the cellar, Marko brings bogus messages from Tito encouraging Blacky to wait for his call to arms, and all the time they are supplied with food and other basic provisions by Marko from the house above. In return, the Partisans in their cellar make rifles which are delivered upstairs from where Marko sells them on the black market. All contact between the two levels in the house happens only through personal visits from Marko or by a lift. Blacky and the others never venture above ground. Gradually, the community develops into a fully fledged society with its own rules and rituals. The day is marked by periodic intoning of slogans against the German occupiers and for the Communist Partisans. Tito's Yugoslavia is characterized by the distinction between those above and those below ground. Those in the cellar are grateful for all the provisions handed down from above like children receiving presents, re-evoking an aspect of the primal innocents in the Balkan myth.[6]

Marko continues to further his career in the Party and the government after the war, becoming a poet along the way in imitation of the disproportionate number of writers who emerged in such circles after the war in Tito's Yugoslavia. His career is built on the lies and myths which he circulates about the exploits of himself, Blacky and Natalia working for the patriotic cause in occupied Belgrade. In his stories he portrays himself as the real mastermind behind all their successes. The disappearance of Blacky is explained by inventing a story about his capture and heroic death before a firing squad. Marko's rise to power is charted by showing archive footage of Tito and transposing pictures of Marko and Natalia into it. For example, on one old reel Tito is dancing with an Asian lady at a New Year's Eve party when Marko and Natalia appear in the same film dancing around them. The interspersing of historical and fictional figures returns Kusturica to the themes of recognition of truth and the power of illusion, playing with the identity of the actors who are acting in the film. As often happened in Tito's Yugoslavia, and to make the Partisan myths about themselves all the more pervasive, the exploits of Marko, Blacky and Natalia as penned by Marko are to be made into a film. This film-within-a-film is a central motif. The same actors play the roles of the three Partisans in the scenes from the film set. The director of the film is both a caricature of a fawning sycophant whenever Marko appears on his set and of an egotistical, petulant artist driving his actors to produce exactly what he wants.

Twenty years after the community's arrival in the cellar Blacky's son, Jovan, is getting married. During the celebrations a hole is blown in the wall and an opportunity to leave opens up. Blacky and Jovan pick up guns and run out into Belgrade's night air. Jovan has never been above ground, while Blacky is returning to the illusion that the war is still going on. They immediately stumble onto the film set based on Marko's memoirs. The actors crowding the streets above in German uniforms correspond precisely to their expectations. The two Partisans follow the actors and film crew to the next set where they are about to shoot Marko's account of Blacky's fictional execution. The conclusive proof for Blacky that he is a witness to the continuing occupation of Belgrade is given when he sees once again his adversary Franz. The same actor who played Franz during the occupation of Belgrade turns up again playing the same part, but now as a German actor playing the role. As Franz did not recognize Blacky as an intruder into the play in the theatre, now Blacky cannot recognize Franz as an actor on a film set. Instead, Blacky simply remarks that Franz has not changed at all since he last saw him some 20 years before, adding, 'That's Germans for you'. At the same time, Jovan points out that the actor playing the part of Blacky looks just like his father, to which the real Blacky remarks that all heroes resemble him. According to the historical logic of the actors and director on the film set, Blacky and Jovan cannot be observing them. From the point of view of the two Partisans, what they are observing based on Marko's memoirs cannot be anything other than pure fiction. There is a constant shifting in this scene between the world as understood to be real on the film set and the world of Blacky and Jovan from the cellar. This interplay weaves together two incompatible referential worlds which, despite the absolute absurdity of the situation, are logically combined under Kusturica's direction. The film set is substantial to Blacky as it corresponds to the lies, deceit and betrayal which he has been fed by Marko for 20 years, and he is substantial to the audience watching him as one of the characters in the narrative of a film about a community which has lived under ground during all those years unaware that the war is over. When he and Jovan attack the film crew in order to save the Partisan about to be executed, Blacky shoots and kills Franz, which he failed to do in the theatre during the war. He also saves himself, as we see the same actor playing Blacky in the film within a film shuffle off into the river still tied to his stake.

The scene of Blacky's execution attacked by father and son is played with great humour and almost slapstick farce. The director, that manic figure, exhorts the fictional Blacky to act naturally although he turns in a melodramatic role with exaggeratedly heroic gestures before the firing squad. At one point, tied to his stake and refusing a blindfold, with a look of admonishment on his face, he deliberately extinguishes with his foot the cigarette which Franz first offers to him and then drops to the ground. When Franz is shot, the director, unaware of what is happening, encourages Blacky to continue acting out the scene while with a look of shock he keeps babbling that this is not part of the script. This scene contrasts sharply with a later one set during a real war. Inexplicably, Blacky and Marko reappear in the Yugoslav wars of the 1990s. Blacky is a commander directing his artillery on a town below while Marko is in the town. He is now a gun runner and arms dealer, meeting with one of the defenders to sell them weapons. Marko is accompanied by two UN soldiers. The buyer whom he meets is acted by the real director of the film, Emir Kusturica. These events are played without humour, Kusturica playing his role realistically in contrast to the caricature of a film director in the earlier scene. In the film within a film the director played by an actor is shooting a scene which did not happen, in the later scene Kusturica the director is playing the part of an actor in a scene which all too closely resembles what did happen in the recent Yugoslav wars. Blacky is now in a real war not watching an invention about a previous war. The film within a film is linked to the present crisis by portraying the public lies which had been prevalent for so long making for decades of betrayal.

Kusturica refuses his film to be reduced to singular readings. His real war is not a mirror of the wars of the 1990s. Blacky enters the town where his troops are taking prisoners. Amongst the town's defenders are Ustaše, Četniks and Partisans; the Croat nationalist, Serb nationalist and Communist forces from the Second World War. There are UN soldiers whose role seems to be every bit as complicit in the violence as that of the others. When confronted by an UN officer Blacky addresses him by the old Communist word for comrade 'drug', and when asked who is his superior officer, he replies, 'my country'. By a strange set of circumstances, Ivan, Marko's brother, appears in the ruins of the besieged town and now knowing the truth of Marko's betrayal, on seeing his brother he beats him to death before taking his own life. Marko's last words are: 'No war is a war until a brother kills a brother.' In *Underground* Kusturica presents a narrative of corruption, manipulation, betrayal, the absurdity of war and the absurdity of the years between the wars in Yugoslavia. His innocent children from the cellar are transformed at the end into savage warmongers.

All the former inhabitants of the cellar and house above ground are dead except Blacky, who is a commander in a new war liberating a town. Marko and Natalia were killed during the fighting, Ivan commits suicide after killing his brother, Jovan died much earlier by drowning after he and his father attacked the film set. Blacky has been searching for Jovan since then, as if searching for a lost innocence, even calling his name in the smoking shambles of the town which he captured. At the end of the film Blacky returns to the cellar from which their experiences began and he sits on the wall of the well which stands in the middle of the floor. Thinking he sees Jovan's face in the water of the well in the cellar he leans over and falls in. Blacky can then be seen swimming under water, escaping the confines of the cellar once again and, joining the other characters, they swim on together. The very final scene opens with a continuation of Jovan's wedding, interrupted when the cellar wall was blown open. All the dead are now resurrected and everyone is present who was there before. The celebration is taking place out-doors on a broad swathe of ground by a river. They have been returned to nature. Loud and fast music is playing, the guests dance with an exaggerated wildness, and vast quantities of food and drink are on the table. In all the scene recalls the celebrations of Sophka's wedding in Stanković's novel when she is firstly charmed by the exoticism of the men from the mountains, only to come to the realization of the threat hanging over her.

Once, when asked why he made *Underground*, Kusturica replied that it was 'because of the last scene'.[7] The camera turns on Ivan, Marko's brother, whose presence in the zoo as keeper marked the beginning of the film when Belgrade is bombed. Like everyone else, he is now restored to youth, and has also lost his stutter which marred his speech earlier. Ivan is the only character in the film who remains uncorrupted and does not manipulate others. His role is to close the film with a different tone from the one with which the story began. He addresses the camera to announce that they will build new homes now and tell stories to their children which begin with the words, 'Once upon a time there was a country'. The film has completed the cycle from the historical reality of the air raid in 1941 to fairy stories, myths and legends underlining the thin distinction in these narratives between fiction and reality. Then the camera, as it pans back, reveals the scene of the Bacchanalian feast where everyone is oblivious to everything except their own frenzied merriment. The piece of land on which they are confined breaks away from the mainland and drifts towards the centre of the river. Kusturica's narrative begins with a danger imposing itself from outside which is transformed into internal manipulation and deceit. The film closes with a show of physical, psychological and moral isolation. The characters are blind and deaf to all other voices. There never was much scope for dialogue; now there is even less.

I began this book by examining the Balkan myth as an important constructive factor in the creation of cultural representations in the West about the south-east European peninsula, and particularly about the Slavonic Orthodox and Moslem areas of Serbia, Montenegro and Bosnia. The essence of the myth focuses on various representations of primitivism, whether they be images of the noble savage or of the threatening barbarian. Those authors from the Balkans who introduce Western characters into their narratives expose the clash of cultures and expectations encountered when the two worlds collide, revealing a range of responses to the negative projections implicit in the foreign point of view. Crnjanski's Vojvodina Serb, Vuk Isakovič, is exiled behind a wall of alienation, while Andrić's French Consul in Travnik, Daville, lays open the paucity of the foreign gaze. Selenić's characters from Belgrade, Stevan Medaković and Vladan Hadžislavković, suffer inner pain and struggle being torn between a Western voice, representing civilization, and the Balkan story of which they and their families are a part. At the same time, as Western representations of Balkan identity become internalized, the thematic burden shifts towards questions of modernity and the scope for dialogue is further limited.

In the next part of the book I turned to urban experience and representations of the city in the West as central to its understanding of modernity. In contrast, the development of urban culture in Serbia has a complicated history in which the Ottoman governing class formed the dominant role model. Eventually, in the nineteenth century, there emerged two almost parallel but incompatible worlds in those areas where the Turkish presence survived longest. One world formed itself in the mirror of the sophisticated West, while the other remained moulded in the image of its Oriental past. The former represents the future desired by the peoples of the Balkans themselves, while the latter more closely reflects the image of the West's Balkan myth. The convergence of these two worlds, underpinned by the weight of the Balkan myth, fuels fears and anxieties in the region which are characteristically expressed in those narratives which take as their main thematic focus the clash of civilization and primitivism. They are found in the city novel of the twentieth century and in recent narratives centred around the Yugoslav wars of the 1990s.

The symbolic space between primitivism and civilization in these narratives puts one in mind of Lena Jovičić's phrase about the 'gap' which opens up in Belgrade between East and West.[8] Jovičić describes that gap as an empty space where something is missing. However, these Balkan narratives fill that gap with a complex exchange. Certain themes, motifs and narrative structures are common to these novels. Beginning with *Sophka,* they are usually set at a time of great social and political transition. These periods have seen sudden and abrupt changes in all areas of public life, in which history has been rewritten, values and even language transformed, and continuity with the past disrupted. Many of the narratives studied here turn to the end of the Second World War and the arrival of the Partisans in Belgrade, intent on destroying all traces of the pre-war city. Indeed, one of the recurrent motifs of these novels is the image of the city itself. The city and the countryside represent two opposing sign structures in Serbian culture. The former is associated with cosmopolitanism, the West and civilization, while the latter is associated with provincialism, the Balkans and primitivism. The taking of the city by the conquering barbarian is a symbolic representation of the cultural anxiety felt at a return to atavism and irrecoverable loss. In moments of extreme crisis, the gaps and complex exchanges multiply even more as the novels and film examined in this last chapter show. The retreat into a private space is more extreme both 'in the hold' and in the cellar, where those below ground are cared for and manipulated by those above ground. These narratives also play with the ambiguities of the 'gap' between the borders of reality and fiction, history and collective amnesia, truth and betrayal. Taken together they express a range of images associated with the exchange between primitivism and civilization, and demonstrate the urgency to name and fix the past before it is lost forever. Kusturica tells the story of Yugoslavia after 1945 through the power of allegory and symbol. He closes the story with the community from the cellar, representatives of Yugoslav history, marooned, exiled and isolated on an island floating away from the mainland. Dancing, drinking and laughing, they embody the ambiguous role which may be either the artlessness of children or the depravity of savages. Now, as before, the Balkan myth continues to provide interpretative strategies both at home and abroad. Our understanding of the Balkans narrows, and the 'gap' between East and West becomes ever wider.

Notes

CHAPTER 1. CONSTRUCTING THE BALKANS

1. The translation has since appeared as Meša Selimović, *Death and the Derviš*, translated by Bogdan Rakić and Stephen M. Dickey (Northwestern University Press, Evanston, Ill., 1996).
2. Kiril Petkov, 'England and the Balkan Slavs 1354–1583: An Outline of a Late-Medieval and Renaissance Image', *Slavic and East European Review*, 75/1 (1997), p. 108.
3. Ibid., p. 86.
4. Gerard Delanty, *Inventing Europe: Idea, Identity, Reality* (Macmillan, London, 1995), p. 36.
5. Ibid., p. 37.
6. Ibid., p. 50.
7. Kiril Petkov, 'England and the Balkan Slavs', p. 114.
8. Maria Todorova, 'The Balkans: From Discovery to Invention', *Slavic Review*, 53/2 (1994), p. 465.
9. Cengiz Orhonlu, 'Geographical Knowledge Amongst the Ottomans and the Balkans in the Eighteenth Century According to Bartinli Ibrahim Hamdi's Atlas', in Francis W. Carter (ed.), *An Historical Geography of the Balkans* (Academic Press, London, 1977), p. 281.
10. Gerard Delanty, *Inventing Europe*, p. 65.
11. Peter S. Koledarov, 'Ethnic and Political Preconditions for Regional Names in the Central and Eastern Parts of the Balkan Peninsula', in Francis W. Carter (ed.), *An Historical Geography*, p. 312.
12. Larry Wolff, *Inventing Eastern Europe: The Map of Civilization on the Mind of the Enlightenment* (Stanford University Press, Stanford, 1994), p. 165.
13. Ibid., p. 172.
14. Kiril Petkov, 'England and the Balkan Slavs', p. 103.
15. Jovan Cvijić, *Balkansko poluostrvo i južnoslovenske zemlje: Osnovi antropogeografije* (Zavod za izdavanje udžbenika Socijalističke Republike Srbije, Beograd, 1966), p. 5 (originally published in French as *La Péninsule Balkanique: Géographie humaine*, Armand Colin, Paris, 1918).
16. *The Oxford English Dictionary*, vol. 1 (2nd ed., Clarendon Press, Oxford, 1989).
17. *The Storehouse of General Information*, vol. 1 (Cassell, London, 1891), p. 310.
18. *The Oxford English Dictionary*.
19. Barbara Jelavich, *History of the Balkans: Twentieth Century*, vol. 2 (Cambridge University Press, Cambridge, 1984), p. 106.
20. Edward W. Said, *Culture and Imperialism* (Vintage, London, 1994), p. 119.
21. Edward W. Said, *Orientalism* (Penguin, London, 1991), p. 1.

22. Ibid., pp. 1–2.
23. Milica Bakić-Hayden and Robert M. Hayden, 'Orientalist Variations on the Theme "Balkans": Symbolic Geography in Recent Yugoslav Cultural Politics', *Slavic Review*, 51/1 (1992), p. 1.
24. Edward W. Said, *Orientalism*, p. 323.
25. Ibid., p. 204.
26. Milica Bakić-Hayden and Robert M. Hayden, 'Orientalist Variations', p. 2.
27. Ibid., p. 9.
28. Mark Thompson, *A Paper House: The Ending of Yugoslavia* (Vintage, London, 1992), p. 26.

CHAPTER 2. TEXTUAL REPRESENTATIONS

1. There have been two books recently published which deal with this topic in some detail. They are Maria Todorova, *Imagining the Balkans* (Oxford University Press, New York, 1997) and Vesna Goldsworthy, *Inventing Ruritania: The Imperialism of the Imagination* (Yale University Press, New Haven and London, 1998).
2. Kiril Petkov, 'England and the Balkan Slavs 1354–1583: An Outline of a Late-Medieval and Renaissance Image', *Slavic and East European Review*, 75/1 (1997), p. 115.
3. Ibid., p. 88.
4. William Shakespeare, *Twelfth Night*, III. i.
5. Ibid., III. iii.
6. Henry Smith Williams (ed.), *The Historians' History of the World*, vol. 24 (The Times, London, 1907), p. 232.
7. Sir Walter Scott, *Waverley* (Penguin, London, 1994), p. 180.
8. Danilo Kiš, *Homo Poeticus: Essays and Interviews*, edited by Susan Sontag (Carcanet Press, Manchester, 1996), p. 241.
9. Ibid., p. 242.
10. Walter J. Ong, *Orality and Literacy: The Technologizing of the Word* (Methuen, London and New York, 1984), p. 16.
11. Quoted in Duncan Wilson, *The Life and Times of Vuk Stefanović Karadžić 1787–1864* (University of Michigan Press, Ann Arbor, 1986), p. 390 (originally published by Clarendon Press, Oxford, 1970).
12. Maria Todorova, 'The Balkans: From Discovery to Invention', *Slavic Review*, 53/2 (1994), p. 455.
13. M. M. Bakhtin, *Speech Genres and Other Late Essays*, translated by Vern. W. McGee (University of Texas Press, Austin, 1990), p. 7.
14. Charles Lamb (published anonymously), 'A Ramble in Montenegro', *Blackwood's Edinburgh Magazine*, 57 (1845), p. 33.
15. Harry De Windt, *Through Savage Europe* (T. Fisher Unwin, London, 1907), p. 25.
16. Charles Lamb, 'A Ramble', p. 37.
17. Ibid., p. 38.
18. Rev. A. C. Fraser (published anonymously), 'Visit to the Vladika of Montenegro', *Blackwood's Edinburgh Magazine*, 60 (1846), p. 438.

19. Ibid., p. 443.
20. Report from Cetinje, 2 November 1877, reprinted *The Guardian 2*, 2 November 1994.
21. Hayden White, *Tropics of Discourse: Essays in Cultural Criticism* (John Hopkins University Press, Baltimore and London, 1985), p. 178.
22. Christopher Ricks (ed.), *The Poems of Tennyson* (Longmans, London, 1969), p. 1240.
23. Sir Walter Scott, *Waverley*, p. 146.
24. Harry De Windt, *Through Savage Europe*, p. 15.
25. William Tufnell Le Queux (published anonymously), *An Observer in the Near East* (Eveleigh Nash, London, 1907), p. 6.
26. Ibid., p. 123.
27. Harry De Windt, *Through Savage Europe*, p. 42.
28. Ibid., p. 50.
29. Ibid., p. 180.
30. Ibid., p. 81.
31. William Tufnell Le Queux, *An Observer*, p. 23.
32. Ibid., p. 29.
33. John Reed, *The War in Eastern Europe: Travels Through the Balkans in 1915* (Phoenix, London, 1994), p. 21 (originally published by Scribner's, New York, 1916).
34. Ibid., pp. 51–3.
35. Jan Gordon, *A Balkan Freebooter: being the true exploits of the Serbian outlaw and comitaj Petko Moritch, told by him to the author and set into English* (Smith Elder and Co, London, 1916), p. 127.
36. Jelena Lazarević, *Engleskinje u srpskom narodu* (Izdanje beogradskog ženskog društva, Beograd, 1929), pp. 201–2.
37. Paul Fussell, *The Great War and Modern Memory* (Oxford University Press, Oxford, 1975), p. 175.
38. Harold F. B. Wheeler (ed.), *The Book of Knowledge: A Pictorial Encyclopaedia for Readers of all Ages*, vol. 5 (Waverley Book Company, London, undated), p. 2407.
39. Ibid., p. 2467.
40. Stephen Clissold (ed.), *A Short History of Yugoslavia: From Early Times to 1966* (Cambridge University Press, Cambridge, 1969), p. 84.
41. Fred Singleton, *A Short History of the Yugoslav Peoples* (Cambridge University Press, Cambridge, 1985), p. 120.
42. W. A. Morison, *The Revolt of the Serbs against the Turks (1804–1813)* (Cambridge University Press, Cambridge, 1942), p. xii.
43. Rebecca West, *Black Lamb and Grey Falcon*, vol. 2 (Macmillan, London, 1943), p. 515.
44. Lena A. Yovitchitch, *Peeps at Many Lands: Yugoslavia* (A. & C. Black, London, 1928), p. 11. The author used an anglicized spelling of her surname.
45. Ibid., p. 82.
46. Ian Traynor, 'Threat of wider Balkan inferno haunts West', *The Guardian*, 17 February 1995.
47. Mark Thompson, *The Guardian*, 31 December 1992.
48. Ian Traynor, *The Guardian*, 7 April 1993.

49. John Carlin, *The Independent*, 6 June 1995.
50. *The Guardian*, 16 March 1994.
51. Maggie O'Kane, 'Tears by the Drina when the liberators come to town', *The Guardian*, 20 April 1992.
52. Ian Traynor, 'BBC made to grin and bear it', *The Guardian*, 12 May 1992.
53. Veronica Horwell, 'Guns and roses, blood and bread', *The Guardian 2*, 12 October 1992.
54. Ian Traynor, *The Guardian*, 6 May 1992.
55. Mark Thompson, 'Interview' (with Cathie Carmichael), *South Slav Journal*, 14/1–2 (1991), p. 76.
56. Edward W. Said, *Culture and Imperialism* (Vintage, London, 1994), p. 273.
57. Dubravka Ugrešić, *Steffie Speck in the Jaws of Life*, translated by Celia Hawkesworth (Virago, London, 1992; first published in Yugoslavia in 1981); and Dubravka Ugrešić, *Fording the Stream of Consciousness*, translated by Michael Henry Heim (Virago, London, 1991; first published in Yugoslavia in 1988).
58. Dubravka Ugrešić, *Have a Nice Day: From the Balkan War to the American Dream*, translated by Celia Hawkesworth (Jonathan Cape, London, 1994), p. 11. All other quotations are taken from this edition.
59. Misha Glenny, *The Rebirth of History: Eastern Europe in the Age of Democracy* (2nd ed., Penguin, London, 1993), p. 3.
60. Dennis P. Hupchick, *Culture and History in Eastern Europe* (St. Martin's Press, New York, 1994), p. 118.
61. Philip Longworth, *The Making of Eastern Europe* (Macmillan, London, 1994), p. 7.
62. Charles Taylor, 'The Politics of Recognition', in Amy Gutman (ed.), *Multiculturalism* (Princeton University Press, Princeton, 1994), p. 25.
63. Ibid., p. 33.
64. Larry Wolff, *Inventing Eastern Europe: The Map of Civilization on the Mind of the Enlightenment* (Stanford University Press, Stanford, 1994), p. 5.
65. Danilo Kiš, *Homo Poeticus*, p. 75.

CHAPTER 3. THE BALKANS TALK BACK

1. M. M. Bakhtin, *Speech Genres and Other Late Essays*, translated by Vern W. Mcgee (University of Texas Press, Austin, 1990), p. 7.
2. Svetozar Koljević, 'The Linguistic Aspects of the International Theme in *Roman o Londonu*', in David Norris (ed.), *Miloš Crnjanski and Modern Serbian Literature* (Astra Press, Nottingham, 1988), p. 75.
3. Edward W. Said, *Orientalism* (Penguin, London, 1991), p. 108.
4. Joseph Conrad, *Heart of Darkness* (Penguin, London, 1994), p. 87.
5. Edward W. Said, *Culture and Imperialism* (Vintage, London, 1994), p. 120.
6. Ibid.
7. Ibid.

8. Milos Tsernianski, *Migrations*, translated by Michael Henry Heim (Harcourt Brace, New York, 1994), p. 34. All other quotations are taken from this edition. The publisher of the translation adopted an anglicized spelling of Crnjanski's surname.
9. *The Guardian*, 16 March 1994.
10. Report from Cetinje, 2 November 1877, reprinted *The Guardian 2*, 2 November 1994.
11. Compare with wording in Miloš Crnjanski, *Seobe*, Izabrana dela, knj. III (Nolit, Beograd, 1983), p. 106.
12. Ibid.
13. Ibid., p. 107.
14. Susan Bassnett, *Comparative Literature: A Critical Introduction* (Blackwell, Oxford, 1993), p. 76.
15. Ivo Andrić, 'A Letter from 1920', translated by Lenore Grenoble, *The Damned Yard and Other Stories*, edited by Celia Hawkesworth (Forest Books, London and Boston, Dereta, Belgrade, 1992), p. 114.
16. Ivo Banac, 'Foreword', in Sabrina Petra Ramet, *Balkan Babel: the disintegration of Yugoslavia from the death of Tito to ethnic war* (2nd ed., Westview Press, Boulder and Oxford, 1996), p. xvi.
17. Svetozar Koljević, 'Nationalism as Literary Inspiration', in Božidar Jakšić (ed.), *Interculturality in Multiethnic Societies* (Hobisport, Beograd, Založba Drava, Klagenfurt/Celovec, 1995), p. 204.
18. Ivo Andrić, *The Days of the Consuls*, translated by Celia Hawkesworth in collaboration with Bogdan Rakić (Forest Books, London and Boston, 1992), p. 130. All other quotations are taken from this edition. A more literal translation of the title *Travnička hronika* would be *The Travnik Chronicle*. Other translations of this novel are *Bosnian Story* (translated by Kenneth Johnstone, Lincolns-Prager, London, 1958) and *Bosnian Chronicle* (translated by Joseph Hitrec, Alfred Knopf, New York, 1963).
19. Slobodan Selenić, *Prijatelji sa Kosančićevog venca 7* (Svjetlost, Sarajevo, 1990), p. 38. All other quotations are taken from this edition.
20. Hayden White, *Tropics of Discourse: Essays in Cultural Criticism* (John Hopkins University Press, Baltimore and London, 1985), p. 178.
21. Slobodan Selenić, *Očevi i oci* (Prosveta, Beograd, 1985), p. 13. All other quotations are taken from this edition. The English translation of *Fathers and Forefathers* is scheduled for publication by Harvill Press, London, 1999.
22. Compare Slobodan Selenić, *Očevi i oci*, pp. 117–18 with Rebecca West, *Black Lamb and Grey Falcon*, vol. 1 (Macmillan, London, 1943), p. 25.
23. Sir Walter Scott, *Waverley* (Penguin, London, 1994), p. 180.
24. Slobodan Selenić, 'Two Excerpts from *Fathers and Forefathers*', translated by Ellen Elias-Bursać, *North Dakota Quarterly*, 61/1 (1993), p. 157.

CHAPTER 4. MODERNITY: URBAN CULTURE AND THE BALKANS

1. Roland Barthes, 'Semiology and the Urban', in M. Gottdiener and Alexandros Ph. Lagopoulos (eds), *The City and the Sign: An Introduction to Urban Semiotics* (Columbia University Press, New York, 1986), p. 92.
2. Umberto Eco, 'Function and Sign: Semiotics of Architecture', ibid., p. 74.
3. Peter Preston and Paul Simpson-Housley (eds), *Writing the City: Eden, Babylon and the New Jerusalem* (Routledge, London, 1994), p. 2.
4. Charles Dickens, *Martin Chuzzlewit* (Clarendon Press, Oxford, 1982), p. 129.
5. J. Paul Hunter, *Before Novels: The Cultural Contexts of Eighteenth-Century English Fiction* (W. W. Norton, New York, 1990), p. 97.
6. Ibid., p. 120.
7. Ian Watt, *The Rise of the Novel: Studies in Defoe, Richardson and Fielding* (Penguin, London 1972), p. 106.
8. Daniel Defoe, *The Fortunes and Misfortunes of the Famous Moll Flanders* (Penguin, London, 1994), pp. 212–13.
9. Charles Dickens, *A Tale of Two Cities* (Penguin, London, 1994), p. 21.
10. Lewis Mumford, *The City in History: Its Origins, Its Transformations, and Its Prospects* (Secker and Warburg, London, 1961), p. 113.
11. Honoré de Balzac, *Old Goriot*, translated by Marion Ayton Crawford (Penguin, London, 1951), p. 304.
12. Raymond Williams, 'The Metropolis and the Emergence of Modernism', in Edward Timms and David Kelley (eds), *Unreal City: Urban Experience in Modern European Literature and Art* (Manchester University Press, Manchester, 1985), p. 13.
13. Edward Timms and David Kelley (eds), 'Introduction', ibid., p. 4.
14. Paul Auster, *The New York Trilogy* (Faber and Faber, London and Boston, 1988), p. 70.
15. Marshall Berman, *All That Is Solid Melts Into Air: The Experience of Modernity* (Verso, London, 1985), p. 13.
16. Ibid., p. 15.
17. Malcolm Bradbury, 'The Cities of Modernism', in Malcolm Bradbury and James McFarlane (eds), *Modernism 1890–1930* (Penguin, London, 1976), p. 96.
18. Raymond Williams, *The Country and the City* (Hogarth Press, London, 1993), p. 234.
19. Ibid.
20. Nikolai Todorov, *The Balkan City 1400–1900* (University of Washington Press, Seattle, 1983), p. 13.
21. Ibid., p. 15.
22. Ibid., pp. 54–5.
23. Ibid., p. 33.
24. Ibid., p. 9.
25. F. W. Carter, 'Urban Development in the Western Balkans 1200–1800', in Francis W. Carter (ed.), *An Historical Geography of the Balkans* (Academic Press, London, 1977), p. 182.

170   *Notes*

26. Peter Sherwood, '"A nation may be said to live in its language": Some Socio-historical Perspectives on Attitudes to Hungarian', in Robert B. Pynsent (ed.), *The Literature of Nationalism: Essays on East European Identity* (Macmillan, London, 1996), pp. 29–30.
27. Anthony D. Smith, *The Ethnic Origins of Nations* (Basil Blackwell, Oxford, 1986), p. 217.
28. See Jonathan Arac, 'What is the History of Literature?', *Modern Language Quarterly*, 54/1 (1993), pp. 105–10.
29. See Jovan Skerlić, *Istorija nove srpske književnosti* (Prosveta, Beograd, 1967), pp. 49–122 (originally published by S. B. Cvijanović, Beograd, 1914).
30. Dositej was Obradović's monastic name. He was first called Dimitrije but is generally referred to by his monastic name. His autobiography has been translated by George Rapall Noyes: *The Life and Adventures of Dimitrije Obradović* (University of California Press, Berkeley and Los Angeles, 1953).
31. See Pavle Popović, *Jugoslovenska književnost* (Geca Kon, Beograd, 1930), pp. 49–68 (originally published by Cambridge University Press, Cambridge, 1918).
32. Predrag Protić, *Iz Skerlićevog doba* (Srpska književna zadruga, Beograd, 1991), p. 86.
33. Ibid., pp. 86–7.
34. Radosav P. Marković, *Pitanje prestonice u Srbiji Kneza Miloša* (Drag. Popović, Beograd, 1938), p. 40.
35. Harry De Windt, *Through Savage Europe* (T. Fisher Unwin, London, 1907), pp. 109–10.
36. Ibid., pp. 112–13.
37. Henry Smith Williams (ed.), *The Historians' History of the World*, vol. 24 (The Times, London, 1907), p. 206.
38. Harry De Windt, *Through Savage Europe*, p. 165.
39. William Tufnell Le Queux (published anonymously), *An Observer in the Near East* (Eveleigh Nash, London, 1907), p. 122.
40. Rebecca West, *Black Lamb and Grey Falcon*, vol. 1 (Macmillan, London, 1943), p. 484.
41. Lena A. Yovitchitch, *Pages from Here and There in Serbia* (S. B. Cvijanovich, Belgrad [sic], 1926), p. 82. The author used an anglicized spelling of her surname.
42. Ibid.
43. Ibid., p. 79.
44. Lena A. Yovitchitch, *Peeps at Many Lands: Yugoslavia* (A. & C. Black, London, 1928), p. 11.
45. Marshall Berman, *All That Is Solid*, p. 15.

CHAPTER 5. REPRESENTATIONS OF CITY LIFE

1. Borisav Stanković, *Sophka*, translated by Alec Brown (Jonathan Cape, London, 1932), p. 19. All other quotations are taken from this edition. Consequently, the spelling of personal and place names have been also taken from this edition, although they may now be considered

somewhat old-fashioned in the way the translator transliterated them from the original Serbo-Croat.

2. Compare with Borisav Stanković, *Nečista krv*, Sabrana dela, knj. III (IP "Beograd", Beograd, 1991), p. 5.
3. Traian Stoianovich, 'The Pattern of Serbian Intellectual Evolution 1830–1880', *Comparative Studies in Society and History*, 1 (1958–9), p. 243.
4. Compare with Borisav Stanković, *Nečista krv*, p. 278.
5. Marshall Berman, *All That Is Solid Melts Into Air: The Experience of Modernity* (Verso, London, 1985), p. 16.
6. Jovan Skerlić, *Istorija nove srpske književnosti* (Prosveta, Beograd, 1967), p. 457 (originally published by S. B. Cvijanović, Beograd, 1914).
7. Jovan Deretić, *Istorija srpske književnosti* (Nolit, Beograd, 1983), p. 473.
8. Ivan Šop, *Istok u srpskoj književnosti* (Institut za književnost i umetnost, Beograd, 1982), p. 18.
9. Ibid., p. 25.
10. Jovan Skerlić, *Istorija*, p. 463.
11. Marko Nedić, *Stara i nova proza: Ogledi o srpskim prozaistima* (Vuk Karadžić, Beograd, 1988), p. 151.
12. Milutin Uskoković, *Dela* (Narodno delo, Beograd, 1932), p. 245.
13. Produced by Pedagoški centar, *Povijest književnosti naroda Jugoslavije* (Naklada Istarske knjižare "Matko Laginja", Pula, 1953), p. 536.
14. Dragoslav Mihailović, *When Pumpkins Blossomed*, translated by Drenka Willen (Harcourt Brace Jovanovich, New York, 1971).
15. Borislav Pekić, *The Houses of Belgrade*, translated by Bernard Johnson (Harcourt Brace Jovanovich, New York, 1978), p. 63. All other quotations are taken from this edition.
16. Svetlana Velmar-Janković, *Dorćol* (BIGZ, Beograd, 1986), pp. 45–6. All other quotations are taken from this edition.
17. Svetlana Velmar-Janković, *Dungeon*, translated by Celia Hawkesworth (Dereta, Belgrade, 1996), p. 27. All other quotations are taken from this edition.
18. Marshall Berman, *All That Is Solid*, p. 333.
19. Ibid.
20. Lewis Mumford, *The City in History: Its Origins, Its Transformations, and Its Prospects* (Secker and Warburg, London, 1961), p. 113.
21. Marshall Berman, *All That Is Solid*, p. 333.

CHAPTER 6. DISCOURSES OF IDENTITY AND MODERNITY IN TIMES OF CRISIS

1. Vladimir Arsenijević, *In the Hold*, translated by Celia Hawkesworth (Harvill Press, London, 1996), p. 26. All other quotations are taken from this edition.
2. Slobodan Selenić, *Premeditated Murder*, translated by Jelena Petrović (Harvill Press, London, 1996), p. 28. All other quotations are taken from this edition.
3. Anthony D. Smith, *The Ethnic Origins of Nations* (Basil Blackwell, Oxford, 1986), p. 2.

4. Dušan Kovačević, *Bila jednom jedna zemlja* (Vreme knjige, Beograd, 1995). The film also carries the same subtitle. Quotations are taken from the English subtitles of the film.
5. Ljiljana Binićanin, 'Moje srce lupa snagom i erupcijom Balkana', *Ilustrovana politika*, 3 June 1995, p. 14.
6. This element in the cellar is similar to an earlier play by Dušan Kovačević, *Proleće u januaru* (*Springtime in January*), written in 1975.
7. Ljiljana Binićanin, 'Moje srce', p. 15.
8. Lena A. Yovitchitch, *Peeps at Many Lands: Yugoslavia* (A. & C. Black, London, 1928), p. 11. The author used an anglicized spelling of her surname.

Bibliography

Andrić, Ivo. *Travnička hronika* (Svjetlost, Sarajevo, 1976).
Andrić, Ivo. *The Days of the Consuls*, translated by Celia Hawkesworth in collaboration with Bogdan Rakić (Forest Books, London and Boston, 1992).
Andrić, Ivo. *Na Drini ćuprija* (Svjetlost, Sarajevo, 1983).
Andrić, Ivo. *The Bridge over the Drina*, translated by Lovett F. Edwards (George Allen and Unwin, London, 1959; republished by Harvill, London, 1994).
Andrić, Ivo. 'A Letter from 1920', translated by Lenore Grenoble, *The Damned Yard and Other Stories*, edited by Celia Hawkesworth (Forest Books, London and Boston, Dereta, Belgrade, 1992), pp. 107–19.
Arac, Jonathan. 'What is the History of Literature?', *Modern Language Quarterly*, 54/1 (1993), pp. 105–10.
Arsenijević, Vladimir. *U potpalublju* (Vreme knjige, Beograd, 1995).
Arsenijević, Vladimir. *In the Hold*, translated by Celia Hawkesworth (Harvill Press, London, 1996).
Auster, Paul. *The New York Trilogy* (Faber and Faber, London and Boston, 1988).
Bakhtin, M. M. *Speech Genres and Other Late Essays*, translated by Vern. W. McGee (University of Texas Press, Austin, 1990).
Bakić-Hayden, Milica and Robert M. Hayden. 'Orientalist Variations on the Theme "Balkans": Symbolic Geography in Recent Yugoslav Cultural Politics', *Slavic Review*, 51/1 (1992), pp. 1–15.
Bassnett, Susan. *Comparative Literature: A Critical Introduction* (Blackwell, Oxford, 1993).
Berman, Marshall. *All That Is Solid Melts Into Air: The Experience of Modernity* (Verso, London, 1985).
Bradbury, Malcolm and James McFarlane (eds). *Modernism 1890–1930* (Penguin, London, 1976).
Carter, Francis W. (ed.). *An Historical Geography of the Balkans* (Academic Press, London, 1977).
Clissold, Stephen (ed.). *A Short History of Yugoslavia: From Early Times to 1966* (Cambridge University Press, Cambridge, 1969).
Conrad, Joseph. *Heart of Darkness* (Penguin, London, 1994).
Cooper, James Fenimore. *The Last of the Mohicans: a narrative of 1757* (New American Library, New York, 1962).
Cooper, James Fenimore. *The Spy: a tale of the neutral ground* (Penguin, London, 1997).
Ćosić, Branimir. *Dva carstva* (Srpska književna zadruga, Beograd, 1928).
Ćosić, Branimir. *Pokošeno polje* (Matica srpska, Novi Sad, 1962).
Crnjanski, Miloš. *Seobe*, Izabrana dela, knj. III (Nolit, Beograd, 1983).
Cvijić, Jovan. *Balkansko poluostrvo i južnoslovenske zemlje: Osnovi antropogeografije* (Zavod za izdavanje udžbenika Socijalističke Republike Srbije, Beograd, 1966).

de Balzac, Honoré. *Old Goriot*, translated by Marion Ayton Crawford (Penguin, London, 1951).

Defoe, Daniel. *The Fortunes and Misfortunes of the Famous Moll Flanders* (Penguin, London, 1994).

Delanty, Gerard. *Inventing Europe: Idea, Identity, Reality* (Macmillan, London, 1995).

Deretić, Jovan. *Istorija srpske književnosti* (Nolit, Beograd, 1983).

De Windt, Harry. *Through Savage Europe* (T. Fisher Unwin, London, 1907).

Dickens, Charles. *Martin Chuzzlewit* (Clarendon Press, Oxford, 1982).

Dickens, Charles. *A Tale of Two Cities* (Penguin, London, 1994).

Fortis, Alberto. *Travels into Dalmatia: Containing General Observations on the Natural History of that Country and the Neighbouring Islands; the Natural Productions, Arts, Manners and Customs of the Inhabitans* (Arno Press and New York Times, New York, 1971).

Fraser, Rev. A. C. (published anonymously). 'Visit to the Vladika of Montenegro', *Blackwood's Edinburgh Magazine*, 60 (1846), pp. 428–43.

Fussell, Paul. *The Great War and Modern Memory* (Oxford University Press, Oxford, 1975).

Glenny, Misha. *The Rebirth of History: Eastern Europe in the Age of Democracy* (2nd ed., Penguin, London, 1993).

Goldsworthy, Vesna. *Inventing Ruritania: The Imperialism of the Imagination* (Yale University Press, New Haven and London, 1998).

Gordon, Jan. *A Balkan Freebooter: being the true exploits of the Serbian outlaw and comitaj Petko Moritch, told by him to the author and set into English* (Smith Elder and Co, London, 1916).

Gottdiener, M. and Alexandros Ph. Lagopoulos (eds). *The City and the Sign: An Introduction to Urban Semiotics* (Columbia University Press, New York, 1986).

Herder, Johann Gottfried. 'Essay on the Origin of Language', *On the Origin of Language: Two Essays (Jean Jacques Rousseau and Johann Gottfried Herder)*, translated by John H. Moran and Alexander Gode (University of Chicago Press, Chicago and London, 1986), pp. 85–166.

Hunter, J. Paul. *Before Novels: The Cultural Contexts of Eighteenth-Century English Fiction* (W. W. Norton, New York, 1990).

Hupchick, Dennis P. *Culture and History in Eastern Europe* (St. Martin's Press, New York, 1994).

Jakovljević, Stevan. *Smena generacija*, 2 vols (Izdavačko-prosvetna zadruga S. O. J., Beograd, 1941).

Jelavich, Barbara. *History of the Balkans*, 2 vols (Cambridge University Press, Cambridge, 1984).

Kiš, Danilo. *Homo Poeticus: Essays and Interviews*, edited by Susan Sontag (Carcanet Press, Manchester, 1996).

Koljević, Svetozar. 'The Linguistic Aspects of the International Theme in *Roman o Londonu*', in David Norris (ed.), *Miloš Crnjanski and Modern Serbian Literature* (Astra Press, Nottingham, 1988), pp. 75–87.

Koljević, Svetozar. 'Nationalism as Literary Inspiration', in Božidar Jakšić (ed.), *Interculturality in Multiethnic Societies* (Hobisport, Beograd, Založba Drava, Klagenfurt/Celovec, 1995), pp. 191-207.

Kovačević, Dušan. *Bila jednom jedna zemlja* (Vreme knjige, Beograd, 1995).

Kusturica, Emir (dir.). *Underground*, original Serbo-Croat version with English subtitles (Fox Video, London, 1995).

Lamb, Charles (published anonymously). 'A Ramble in Montenegro', *Blackwood's Edinburgh Magazine*, 57 (1845), pp. 33–51.

Lazarević, Jelena. *Engleskinje u srpskom narodu* (Izdanje beogradskog ženskog društva, Beograd, 1929).

Le Queux, William Tufnell (published anonymously). *An Observer in the Near East* (Eveleigh Nash, London, 1907).

Longworth, Philip. *The Making of Eastern Europe* (Macmillan, London, 1994).

Marković, Radosav P. *Pitanje prestonice u Srbiji Kneza Miloša* (Drag. Popović, Beograd, 1938).

Mihailović, Dragoslav. *Kad su cvetale tikve* (BIGZ, Beograd, 1984).

Mihailović, Dragoslav. *When Pumpkins Blossomed*, translated by Drenka Willen (Harcourt Brace Jovanovich, New York, 1971).

Morison, W. A. *The Revolt of the Serbs against the Turks (1804–1813)* (Cambridge University Press, Cambridge, 1942).

Mumford, Lewis. *The City in History: Its Origins, Its Transformations, and Its Prospects* (Secker and Warburg, London, 1961).

Nedić, Marko. *Stara i nova proza: Ogledi o srpskim prozaistima* (Vuk Karadžić, Beograd, 1988).

Obradović, Dositej. *The Life and Adventures of Dimitrije Obradović*, translated by George Rapall Noyes (University of California Press, Berkeley and Los Angeles, 1953).

Ong, Walter J. *Orality and Literacy: The Technologizing of the Word* (Methuen, London and New York, 1984).

The Oxford English Dictionary (2nd ed., Clarendon Press, Oxford, 1989).

Pedagoški centar. *Povijest književnosti naroda Jugoslavije* (Naklada Istarske knjižare "Matko Laginja", Pula, 1953).

Pekić, Borislav. *Hodočašće Arsenija Njegovana* (Prosveta, Beograd, 1971).

Pekić, Borislav. *The Houses of Belgrade*, translated by Bernard Johnson (Harcourt Brace Jovanovich, New York, 1978).

Petkov, Kiril. 'England and the Balkan Slavs 1354–1583: An Outline of a Late-Medieval and Renaissance Image', *Slavic and East European Review*, 75/1 (1997), pp. 86–117.

Petrović, Rastko. *Sa silama nemerljivim*, Dela Rastka Petrovića, knj. III (Nolit, Beograd, 1977).

Popović, Pavle. *Jugoslovenska književnost* (Geca Kon, Beograd, 1930).

Preston, Peter and Paul Simpson-Housley (eds). *Writing the City: Eden, Babylon and the New Jerusalem* (Routledge, London, 1994).

Protić, Predrag. *Iz Skerlićevog doba* (Srpska književna zadruga, Beograd, 1991).

Pynsent, Robert B. (ed.). *The Literature of Nationalism: Essays on East European Identity* (Macmillan, London, 1996).

Ramet, Sabrina Petra. *Balkan Babel: the disintegration of Yugoslavia from the death of Tito to ethnic war* (2nd ed., Westview Press, Boulder and Oxford, 1996).

Reed, John. *The War in Eastern Europe: Travels Through the Balkans in 1915* (Phoenix, London, 1994).

176   *Bibliography*

Ricks, Christopher (ed.). *The Poems of Tennyson* (Longmans, London, 1969).
Said, Edward W. *Orientalism* (Penguin, London, 1991).
Said, Edward W. *Culture and Imperialism* (Vintage, London, 1994).
Scott, Sir Walter. *Waverley* (Penguin, London, 1994).
Selenić, Slobodan. *Prijatelji sa Kosančićevog venca 7* (Svjetlost, Sarajevo, 1990).
Selenić, Slobodan. *Očevi i oci* (Prosveta, Beograd, 1985).
Selenić, Slobodan. 'Two Excerpts from *Fathers and Forefathers*', translated by Ellen Elias-Bursać, *North Dakota Quarterly*, 61/1 (1993), pp. 157–70.
Selenić, Slobodan. *Ubistvo s predumišljajem* (Prosveta, Beograd, 1993).
Selenić, Slobodan. *Premeditated Murder*, translated by Jelena Petrović (Harvill Press, London, 1996).
Selimović, Meša. *Derviš i smrt* (Sloboda, Beograd, 1976).
Selimović, Meša. *Death and the Derviš*, translated by Bogdan Rakić and Stephen M. Dickey (Northwestern University Press, Evanston, Ill., 1996).
Shakespeare, William. *Twelfth Night*, edited by J. N. Lothian and T. W. Craik (Routledge, London and New York, 1994).
Shakespeare, William. *The Winter's Tale*, edited by J. H. P. Pafford (Routledge, London and New York, 1994).
Singleton, Fred. *A Short History of the Yugoslav Peoples* (Cambridge University Press, Cambridge, 1985).
Skerlić, Jovan. *Istorija nove srpske književnosti* (Prosveta, Beograd, 1967).
Smith, Anthony D. *The Ethnic Origins of Nations* (Basil Blackwell, Oxford, 1986).
Šop, Ivan. *Istok u srpskoj književnosti* (Institut za književnost i umetnost, Beograd, 1982).
Stanković, Borisav. *Nečista krv*, Sabrana dela, knj. III (IP "Beograd", Beograd, 1991).
Stanković, Borisav. *Sophka*, translated by Alec Brown (Jonathan Cape, London, 1932).
Stoianovich, Traian. 'The Pattern of Serbian Intellectual Evolution 1830–1880', *Comparative Studies in Society and History*, 1 (1958–9), pp. 242–72.
The Storehouse of General Information, vol. 1 (Cassell, London, 1891).
Taylor, Charles. 'The Politics of Recognition', in Amy Gutman (ed.). *Multiculturalism* (Princeton University Press, Princeton, 1994) pp. 25–73.
Thompson, Mark. 'Interview' (with Cathie Carmichael), *South Slav Journal*, 14/1–2 (1991), pp. 71–6.
Thompson, Mark. *A Paper House: The Ending of Yugoslavia* (Vintage, London, 1992).
Timms, Edward and David Kelley (eds). *Unreal City: Urban Experience in Modern European Literature and Art* (Manchester University Press, Manchester, 1985).
Todorov, Nikolai. *The Balkan City 1400–1900* (University of Washington Press, Seattle, 1983).
Todorova, Maria. 'The Balkans: From Discovery to Invention', *Slavic Review*, 53/2 (1994), pp. 453–82.
Todorova, Maria. *Imagining the Balkans* (Oxford University Press, New York, 1997).

Tsernianski, Milos. *Migrations*, translated by Michael Henry Heim (Harcourt Brace, New York, 1994).

Ugrešić, Dubravka. *Štefica Cvek u raljama života* (Grafički zavod Hrvatske, Zagreb, 1984).

Ugrešić, Dubravka. *Steffie Speck in the Jaws of Life*, translated by Celia Hawkesworth (Virago, London, 1992).

Ugrešić, Dubravka. *Forsiranje romana reke* (August Cesarec, Zagreb, 1988).

Ugrešić, Dubravka. *Fording the Stream of Consciousness*, translated by Michael Henry Heim (Virago, London, 1991).

Ugrešić, Dubravka. *Have a Nice Day: From the Balkan War to the American Dream*, translated by Celia Hawkesworth (Jonathan Cape, London, 1994).

Uskoković, Milutin. *Dela* (Narodno delo, Beograd, 1932).

Velmar-Janković, Svetlana. *Dorćol* (BIGZ, Beograd, 1986).

Velmar-Janković, Svetlana. *Lagum* (BIGZ, Beograd, 1991).

Velmar-Janković, Svetlana. *Dungeon*, translated by Celia Hawkesworth (Dereta, Belgrade, 1996).

Watt, Ian. *The Rise of the Novel: Studies in Defoe, Richardson and Fielding* (Penguin, London, 1972).

West, Rebecca. *Black Lamb and Grey Falcon*, 2 vols (Macmillan, London, 1943).

Wheeler, Harold F. B. (ed.). *The Book of Knowledge: A Pictorial Encyclopaedia for Readers of all Ages*, vol. 5 (Waverley Book Company, London, undated).

White, Hayden. *Tropics of Discourse: Essays in Cultural Criticism* (John Hopkins University Press, Baltimore and London, 1985).

Williams, Raymond. *The Country and the City* (Hogarth Press, London, 1993).

Williams, Henry Smith (ed.). *The Historians' History of the World*, vol. 24 (The Times, London, 1907).

Wilson, Duncan. *The Life and Times of Vuk Stefanović Karadžić 1787–1864* (University of Michigan Press, Ann Arbor, 1986).

Wolff, Larry. *Inventing Eastern Europe: The Map of Civilization on the Mind of the Enlightenment* (Stanford University Press, Stanford, 1994).

Yovitchitch, Lena A. *Pages from Here and There in Serbia* (S. B. Cvijanovich, Belgrad, 1926).

Yovitchitch, Lena A. *Peeps at Many Lands: Yugoslavia* (A. & C. Black, London, 1928).

Other sources have been taken from the daily and weekly press: *The Guardian, The Independent, Politika, Ilustrovana politika*.

Index

182   *Index*